For Charlotte — a lovely person with many wonderful memories of our association over the years.

[signature]

April 2016

FOR THIS YOU WERE CREATED
Memoir of an American Rabbi

SAMUEL E. KARFF

bright sky press
HOUSTON, TEXAS

bright sky press
HOUSTON, TEXAS

2365 Rice Blvd., Suite 202
Houston, Texas 77005

Copyright © 2015 Samuel E. Karff
No part of this book may be reproduced in any form or
by any electronic or mechanical means,
including information storage and retrieval devices
or systems, without prior written permission from the publisher,
except that brief passages may be quoted for reviews.

10   9   8   7   6   5   4   3   2   1

Library of Congress Cataloging-in-Publication Data

Karff, Samuel E., author.
For this you were created / memoir of an American Rabbi / Samuel E. Karff.
pages cm
ISBN 978-1-936474-14-1 (alk. paper)
1. Karff, Samuel E. 2. Rabbis–United States–Biography. I. Title.

BM755.K29315A3 2015
296.8'341092–dc23
[B]   2015015959

Editorial Direction: Lucy Herring Chambers
Managing Editor: Lauren Adams
Designer: Marla Y. Garcia

Printed in Canada through Friesens

*I lovingly dedicate this book to all
who touched my life and
taught me so much during forty years
as a congregational rabbi.*

Rabbi Yochanan ben Zakkai
received [the Torah] from Hillel and Shammai.
He would say: if you have learned much torah,
do not be prideful on that account for it was
for this you were created

– MISHNEH AVOT 2:8

TABLE of CONTENTS

Preface	9
Chapter 1: My Familial Heritage	13
Chapter 2: What Do You Want To Be When You Grow Up?	29
Chapter 3: Why The Rabbinate?	51
Chapter 4: An Unexpected Beginning To My Life As A Rabbi	81
Chapter 5: Actually Experiencing the Congregational Rabbinate	97
Chapter 6: The Chicago Years	113
Chapter 7: The Gift Of Charlevoix	159
Chapter 8: The Years In Houston	189
Chapter 9: Living & Influencing The Change To Post-Modern Reform	227
Chapter 10: Israel & Me	257
Chapter 11: Defending The Faith In A Secular Age	277
Chapter 12: The Rabbi As A Spiritual Guide	293
Chapter 13: Retirement & My Second Vocation	329
Chapter 14: The Three Amigos	367
Chapter 15: Why I Am A Wealthy Man	377
Epilogue	395
Endnotes	397
Acknowledgments	399

PREFACE

AS I APPROACHED MY EIGHTIETH BIRTHday and my next writing project, I quickly decided to work on a life review. At the outset, my more modest hope was that the document might be of some interest to close family and friends. Now that the document is nearing completion, I allow myself the extravagant hope that my life experience may be of some interest and value to more than that close family circle. They say that eighty is the new sixty but my body remains unconvinced. In any case, as this project approached the end of its first draft, I was confronted by a new loss. A number of minor accidents behind the wheel convinced me it was time to take the fateful step and surrender the keys of my car to a grandchild. Those of you who have already confronted this loss or have thus far refused to acknowledge its reality may have a greater understanding of what this milestone represents.

Although I have reached this milestone birthday in generally good health and continue to regard life as a precious gift and dare to hope for more good years of life, I remain firmly convinced that even in this super-technological age the price of being human is and will remain our mortality. Living in its shadow has lent special interest and perhaps even some urgency to this project.

Although the reader will discover that I have not been spared life's darker side and these pages record personal struggle, disappointment, brokenness and some regret—I feel very blessed. If my life were about to end now I would not feel cheated, just sad.

It may be especially difficult for a rabbi to deny that we humans live in the shadow of our mortality because, by virtue of our vocation, we often help others to deal with their dying and seek to console those who have lost loved ones. We conduct many funeral services at which we acknowledge anew that finitude which is the ineluctable fate of each of us, and then attempt to find some goodness and significance in one particular human life.

I write this memoir without consciously attempting to write my own eulogy but in the hope that what I share will provide an honest and interesting glimpse into the life of an American Rabbi in the twentieth century.

You the reader must be the ultimate judge of my effort.

My Father and his Family in Tel Aviv before World War I. Louis is standing on the right behind his older brother Elchanan. My paternal grandmother, Zipporah, is seated at the center. Seated on the left is my Uncle Abe. Centered in the background is a portrait of my then deceased grandfather, Samuel.

My parents, Reba and Louis, are pictured with my maternal grandparents, Yitchak Yoel and Manya Margalit, and their children. The photograph was taken in Jerusalem.

Chapter 1
MY FAMILIAL
HERITAGE

FOR BETTER AND FOR WORSE WE ARE SIGnificantly shaped by the home in which we spend our formative years. At this point, any attempt to understand why I became a rabbi must focus on those primary transmitters of my identity, my parents. My mother, Rifka (Anglicized as Rebecca and shortened to Reba), was born in Jerusalem when Palestine was part of the Ottoman Empire. By her late teens, in the aftermath of World War I, Palestine had become a territory mandated to Great Britain.

Manya, my maternal grandmother, was born in Safed, overlooking the Sea of Galilee which, in the sixteenth century became a great center of Jewish mysticism (Kabbalah). Manya's gravestone in Jerusalem identifies her as a descendent of the Baal Shen Tov (Master of the Good Name), the eighteenth-century founder of the Hasidic movement. My maternal grandfather, Yitzchak Yoel Margalit, was born in the Ukraine, in the town of Oman and migrated to Jerusalem before the First World War. My grandfather directed a home for the aged for much of his working life. Manya and Yitzchak's home was Orthodox. Through his mother, Ytzchak Yoel was a direct descendent of Rabbi Pinchas of Koretz, a leading disciple of Hasidism's Founder.

Although I never knew grandfather Yitzchak, I did visit briefly with grandmother, Manya, during two of my early trips to Israel, shortly before her death. She was quite elderly and frail, but traces of her earlier physical beauty still graced her moon-shaped face. On the first visit in 1954, I was a rabbinic seminary student. While she embraced her oldest grandchild with tears of love, the sight of a non-Orthodox future rabbi dressed in khakis, a polo shirt and sneakers—with an uncovered head—was radically incongruous. Without comment, she filed this scene as just another strange perplexity in her world.

Several years later, in what turned out to be our last visit, Manya gave me a Hebrew Bible that contained this inscription: "To my dear grandson, Rabbi Samuel Karff." I still cherish and use this Bible and consider her words the equivalent of a blessing from my Orthodox grandmother. Yitchak and Manya had six children—five daughters and one son. Virtually all of the girls were blessed, to some degree, with the beauty of their mother, Manya. By general consensus within my family, my mother, the oldest, was the most beautiful of all.

My father, Eliezer (Anglicized as Louis) was born and spent his early childhood in the Russian Ukraine, near the

CHAPTER 1 ❖ MY FAMILIAL HERITAGE

city of Sukurnie. Schmuel (Samuel) Karvasarsky, my paternal grandfather, for whom I was named, was a prosperous grain dealer whose principal customers were the beer manufacturers in Moscow and St. Petersburg. Schmuel and his wife Zipporah had three sons and a daughter. My father was next to the oldest. As my father described it, the family lived on the equivalent of an estate. They had riding horses and servants, but as Jews, their sense of security was threatened by the specter of a deep-rooted Russian anti-Semitism.

Before he had any intentions of leaving Russia, my grandfather was an early Zionist, who believed that, in a world of nation states, Jews could find real security only by recreating a modern Jewish state in the land of their biblical ancestors; where Hebrew would become a spoken language and Jews would no longer be a powerless minority, held hostage to the good will of a periodically hostile Christian or Muslim majority.

Schmuel Karvasarsky was a non-Orthodox Jew who belonged to the Haskalah, a movement that encouraged Jews to get a secular education and dress in modern western style. In his home, they spoke Russian or Hebrew. In the aftermath of the Russo-Japanese War, which Russia lost, anti-Semitic outbursts became rampant and my paternal grandfather decided it was time for his family to leave Russia and become one of the first generation of settlers in the new city of Tel Aviv. Shortly before the First World War, my grandfather succumbed to typhoid fever and left it to his family to help fulfill the Zionist dream.

I cherish an old photograph of my father's family which was taken sometime after his death. In the foreground and centered was my grandmother, Zipporah, who projected a stately elegance. My father appears to be in his twenties.

He is dressed nattily in a tropical suit, which foreshadows his lifelong appreciation of nice clothes. The photograph includes Dad's two brothers, Elchanan and Abraham who, as my Uncle Abe, would become like a second father to me.

Also pictured are my father's sister Sarah and her husband. In the background but dominantly centered is a photograph of my deceased grandfather Schmuel Karvasarsky. His stern image suggests a man of strength. He is formally dressed in a black suit, white shirt and an ascot tie. The photograph's gestalt points to a man who was, and even in death remained, a key presence in his family's life.

I wish I could have questioned him about his internal struggle as he decided between the risks of maintaining his business and his estate in a Russia roiled by the humiliation of defeat or venturing the life of a pioneer in a relatively undeveloped, swamp-infested Tel Aviv. This choice between betting on the future in one's present land versus venturing into a new land of potential peril and promise is a choice as old as our patriarch Abraham and as recent as the pre-Holocaust years in Germany.

A "Mixed Marriage" and Resettlement in the United States

My parents' marriage brought together Orthodox piety and non-Orthodox Haskalah. In 1922, while the United States was experiencing "the roaring twenties", the Middle East was mired in an economic depression. My mother and father, young newlyweds, eyed "the States" as a new world of opportunity where they might live for a few years, find gainful employment, save some money and return home at a time when the middle east depression had ended. When my

CHAPTER 1 · MY FAMILIAL HERITAGE

paternal grandfather left Russia for Tel Aviv, his brother, Tsvi Karvasarsky emigrated to Philadelphia. By then my great uncle had Anglicized his name to Harry Karff. Uncle Harry welcomed my parents to his adopted city and helped them feel at home.

What was to have been a brief interlude in America became a lifetime. Every few years my mother and father would revisit the family in Palestine, but I was born and would grow up in Philadelphia. With the passing years my parents became firmly rooted in the American Jewish community. Drawing on their fluency in the Hebrew language and their understanding of Jewish culture and tradition, they became teachers and later my father became the principal of a Talmud Torah—an afternoon Hebrew school where the student body consisted of elementary- and middle-school-age children.

My parents' vocational task might reasonably be described as "mission impossible" for they were expected to take children who came to their school already wearied from a full day in "regular school" and not only instruct them in the rudiments of Jewish knowledge, but instill pride in a heritage which was often not diligently observed in the home. Virtually all of the parents had some synagogue affiliation. Still, as I learned early in life, there is no better way to feel positive about a subject than to bond with the teacher. By that standard, both my parents were at least partially effective. Over the years when my sister or I met strangers, if they associated our family name with their former Hebrew teachers—my parents—we would hear words of deep appreciation and fond memories from their students.

In our home, Judaism was deeply entrenched. Because Hebrew was a living language for my parents, I had to learn it to participate in family conversations. Both my parents had learned some English already in the Holy Land—my father in Tel Aviv and my mother in Jerusalem. They could hardly expect to be effective teachers to American Jewish children unless they were fluent, but they wanted Hebrew to be our second language. When the children's comprehension of Hebrew prevented our parents from using it for confidential exchanges, they turned to Yiddish and so in time my sister and I not only learned Hebrew, but some Yiddish as well. Can you think of a more powerful motivation to learn another language than to crack the secret code of your parents?

Reared in Orthodox piety, my mother kept a kosher home with two sets of dishes (one for dairy, the other for meat). Fully observant Orthodox Jews will not mix meat and dairy food. My mother had decided, however, that God forbid her son should be deprived of butter on his baked potato. So it was not unusual for me to eat a kosher rib steak on a meat dish and for a buttered potato to be placed next to it on a dairy dish. No Orthodox rabbi would sanction such an arrangement.

From Monday through Thursday we did not eat dinner as a family. Mother's teaching did not end until 6:00 p.m. Sometimes she would be detained by speaking with a parent or child, and returning home required two bus rides. As a principal, my father had both teaching and administrative responsibilities and his school was situated in a neighborhood much farther from our home. In addition to caring for my younger sister, Elana, each weekday afternoon, I was expected to heat the meal Mother had prepared before she went to work and which she sometimes partially shared with us. My dad often did not get home until 8:00 p.m. and he ate while we were doing homework nearby.

CHAPTER 1 ◆ MY FAMILIAL HERITAGE

The Friday evening Shabbat meal was very special. The menu had the standards: chicken soup with noodles or matzo balls and challah bread, etc. Mother would kindle and bless the Sabbath candles. Dad would lead us in the traditional blessings over the cup of wine. Mother would always see that the house was especially tidy in honor of the Sabbath. We were not regular synagogue-goers, but all the major Jewish holidays were observed in our home. We always did attend synagogue on the High Holy Days. On Passover, we observed the prohibition of eating leavened substances, generally, but not punctiliously. Each school day, I brought enough matzo not only for my own lunch, but to feed my curious non-Jewish friends.

My Parents Deepen My Jewish Education

Determined that my Jewish education be much deeper than was attainable in the normal religious school, my parents entrusted me to a private tutor. Every Saturday afternoon during my preteen years I took the subway and the trolley to the other end of town where I studied for an hour or more with Dr. Bethlachmy. He was a warm, charming, and elegant man. My love affair with Agada, the stories embedded in biblical and rabbinic texts, was surely mediated by those Sabbath afternoons studying in Hebrew from a collection of traditional narratives. The book was called, *Sepher Agada* (*The Book of Stories*). Much later I would come to appreciate Agada as more than charming or interesting diversion, but as vessels that may connect us to deep religious truths.

That initiation in Agada would lead in time to my first book as a rabbi, which would be titled *Agada: The Language of Jewish Faith*. Those tutorial sessions with Dr. Bethlachmy were the most delightful part of my Sabbath observance. That my mother allowed me to travel in violation of traditional Sabbath restrictions reflected her deviation from strict Orthodoxy. Moreover, if my Jewish study program had been Orthodox, I would have focused with my tutor on the Halacha—the legal prescriptive literature of the Talmud rather than on the classic Jewish narratives of Agada.

Camp Massad

As if this immersion were not sufficient, my parents introduced me to a Jewish summer camp nestled in the Pocono Mountains, about an hour and a half bus ride from Philadelphia. An unsolicited gift from my Uncle Abe enabled my parents to send me there for the entire summer from age ten to fourteen and my sister for as much time as she desired. Over the years I progressed from camper to senior counselor. Massad, as it was called, was a camp in which Hebrew was the official language. We even had Hebrew words for strikes and balls called by umpires at home plate when we played baseball. Most of the campers came from New York, and most attended modern Orthodox day schools.

The daily program included most sports as well as discussions to deepen our Jewish self-understanding. Evening programs might consist of songs around a campfire, folk dancing, plays and pageants, which would consist of vignettes from past and current Jewish life.

We observed the traditional camp color war. Once I had progressed from being a camper to a counselor, I was recruited to lead one of the two teams into which the camp was divided. I regularly culled the current news events during the camp season by listening to broadcasts on my little radio

CHAPTER 1 ⁂ MY FAMILIAL HERITAGE

and then I would regularly "broadcast" the news in Hebrew on the camp's loudspeaker, which was the equivalent of our radio station.

Camp is not for everyone, but it was an important formative part of my youth. Leaving the humidity of a Philadelphia summer (before air conditioning), surrounded by mountains, swimming in a natural lake, discovering in close quarters the kindness and cruelty which is part of the human condition in all ages, I found camp a very precious experience; and at least one of the friendships would withstand the test of time. At my current age of eighty, I still engage in regular transatlantic phone conversations with Israel Charny, whom I first met at Camp Massad when we were ten years old.

At camp I was able to hone my leadership skills and experience a strong adolescent romance. Camp Massad also helped me realize that I would not find my most compatible Jewish identity living as an observant Orthodox Jew. I did not feel completely at home within the constraints of Orthodox belief and practice. I will return to this issue later, but for now let me say that by temperament, if nothing else, I was not prepared to have any rabbi or any codes of Jewish law deprive me of a certain level of personal autonomy.

As long as I can remember, I believed and intermittently felt that I was living in the presence of God, a mysterious other, a loving, guiding, comforting and empowering spirit. Over the years, my concept of God would develop into a less narcissistic more universal conception. As a child, I found it difficult to imagine that the God who was so personal to me and so concerned with my life was equally concerned with the wellbeing of all God's children. It took years for me to embrace this notion viscerally.

Reba and Louis successfully implanted in me a comfortable strong sense of connection to the Jewish story. In my house, I naturally came to feel connected to the Jewish people, the land of Israel and the Zionist dream. Yet, before the end of my first year in college, if I were asked what do you want to be when you grow up, being a rabbi would not have been on my list.

The Pleasant Memories of Home

I have many pleasant memories of deep paternal and maternal love for us, of being generously validated by proud parents when we made a speech or excelled in an exam.

Many of these nourishing times as a family involved purchasing and consuming food. Each Sunday night was kosher deli time. Weather permitting; we would walk the half a mile to the local deli. The aroma from the pickle barrel, the kosher hotdogs, the corned beef and pastrami, the vegetarian baked beans all activated my salivary glands. It seemed that we quickened our pace on the way home from the deli and immediately sat around the table to devour what was, and would remain for me in later life, the equivalent of a gourmet feast.

Accompanying my father to the grocery store and watching him carefully inspect and select the fruits and vegetables resulted in my life long romance with celery, tomatoes, radishes, turnips, cucumbers, cabbage and raw onions. Many years later, after I was already in seminary, I remember a promotional pamphlet designed to entice Jewish college seniors to consider the Rabbinate. The title on the cover was intended to be *So You Want to Be a Rabbi*. The page proofs returned for final approval mistakenly read, *So You Want to Be a Rabbit*. Recalling that typo always amused me because I

CHAPTER 1 — MY FAMILIAL HERITAGE

became a rabbi whose notion of treats seemed to many of my family and friends more rabbit-like than human.

One of my precious childhood memories was spending some vacation time with our parents in Atlantic City. We would rent a room for a week near the water. Dad rented a bike and I recall with special fondness riding on the back seat of his two-wheeler, holding on to his back as he rode happily along the Boardwalk.

Then there was the mystique of Thanksgiving Day. The Philadelphia weather would be unfailingly chilly as I watched the football game across the street. By the end of the game it was time to sit around the table. I sprinted home to my favorite holiday foods: the turkey drumstick, mother's incomparable stuffing and the pumpkin pie. Throughout the year I enjoyed mother's homemade vegetable soup, her eggplant salad and her trademark chocolate/vanilla cookies.

I much admired my mother's vital energy and her social skills. She could wholeheartedly interact with and charm virtually all the persons I introduced to her, young and old. She was a great teacher and would have actually missed the classroom if an unexpected nest egg had freed her from the need to teach. When mother was in her early eighties she volunteered to teach Hebrew to the residents in the Jewish Home for the Aged, whom she called "those old folks"—as if she were not one of them.

Mother was constantly learning new ways to remain healthy. Late in life, she began to exercise regularly. Once when she was in her early eighties, I observed her on the floor of her apartment doing lots of sit-ups and stretches. Every Saturday afternoon Mother would lie on the couch in the living room and listen to the Metropolitan Opera concerts, and she especially loved Milton Cross's elegant commentaries. Once retired from teaching, she took regular classes and endeared herself to the rabbis who taught them.

Mother had an insatiable curiosity. After I left home for college and seminary, hardly a week passed when she did not send me a clipping from the newspaper or a magazine. My parents had a lovely group of loyal friends, persons who were there for each other to celebrate the joys and cushion the wounds of living. They had a Hebrew culture group that conversed in Hebrew. Each time one member of the group would volunteer to lead the discussion with a brief introduction.

Dad loved to tell jokes. They were of varying quality, but Dad broke into robust laughter even when a particular joke did not evoke a comparable response from his listeners. One joke I still remember was "Did you ever stand in front of a synagogue, squeeze a lemon and watch the Jews come out?" Dad loved to read to me the stories of an Eastern European humorist whose pen name was Shalom Aleichem. He was regarded as the Jewish Mark Twain. Embedded in his humor was a strong, but loving critique of life in the Jewish villages (*shtetl*) of Eastern Europe during the nineteenth century. Like Twain, Shalom Aleichem satirized the darker side of the human condition. His character, Tevye, the dairyman, was the basis for a long running Broadway musical, *Fiddler on the Roof.*

In addition to being our official grocery shopper, Dad also loved to shop for nice clothes. We bought our mens' suits straight from the factory because a family friend owned the business. As a growing child, my clothes were always a little bigger than my actual measurements because "I would soon grow into them." I inherited Dad's love of good clothes. Fortunately, as an adult I could afford to go straight to the retail store and walk out with a suit that actually fit me perfectly.

What must have been a source of anxiety as well as pleasure was Dad's purchase of our family's first automobile. I was already away at school. Dad was in his late fifties when he took the exam and learned to drive and park a car. As I think of it, he displayed much courage driving that car all the way to Boston for a Passover Seder at my Uncle Abe's home. People who knew my father would speak of him as a sweet and gentle man. A psychiatrist and friend who knew me as a client and knew my story once suggested that I was actually blessed by both my parents. My mother endowed me with high energy, intellectual curiosity and social skills; my father modeled for me his gentleness and kindness.

My Parents' Relationship with Each Other

My parents were strong shapers of my Jewish identity, but what did I learn from observing my parents' relationship to each other? We must all come to terms with the home environment created by our parents. Their relation with Elana and me casts a warm glow on our childhood, while their own relationship creates a dark shadow. My childhood home experience was alternately pleasant and disheartening. I felt consistently and deeply loved, even doted upon. From an early age I did internalize the pressure to excel, but although they never articulated it, I felt my parents were living vicariously through me. They expected me to be more successful in American terms than they were able to be, judged by their limited income and lack of advanced educational attainment.

By far the greatest source of my pain as a child was my parent's unhappy, often destructive relationship with each other. Much of the time they seemed held together only by their love for me and Elana. Later, with a higher level of psychological sophistication I realized they remained with each other, not only because of the terrible stigma of divorce in those days, but because of their powerful co-dependency. As an adult, I also realized that I was not able to give mother the unqualified affection she wanted, because of the way she treated my father.

My mother felt that her physical beauty, high energy, resourcefulness and intellectual curiosity entitled her to a more fitting life companion. She did not truly respect my father and resented his heavy dependence on her. In her generous moments she felt patronizingly supportive of him. Periodically, when she felt bitterly unhappy with her lot, Mother would vent her frustration with hurtful words, labeling my father a "failure" and lamenting her need to work while so many of her friends were women of leisure. Not infrequently her speech erupted into a barrage of Hebrew curses. Occasionally, Dad countered with his own hostile comments, but usually he simply cringed painfully and left the battlefield.

At the first opportunity Dad would beseech me to intervene and prevail upon mother to desist. That mediating role was already thrust upon me at age eleven or twelve. Then and later I never thought to decline the role and send them to a therapist. I guess our family had not yet discovered the "age of the therapeutic"—or the age when divorce was devoid of stigma.

I was, of course, deeply saddened for them and for my sister and me. Such episodes left me emotionally conflicted. I understood the reasons for mother's unhappiness. In my attempts to mediate, I would concede that she did not have an easy life, reaffirm my love for her and plead with her to control such hurtful outbursts, because they caused great pain—not only to Dad, but to us, her children. Moreover, in later adolescence, I would tell Mom that such scenes would only inevitably distance my sister and me from our family. Mother would always promise to try, but the efficacy of my remonstrations was at best short-lived. When I began to spend summers in camp, I recall hoping—even praying—that when I returned home things might be different this time, only to discover that some of the darker givens in our lives often remain the same.

The sweet and bitter parts of my home life shaped me in two significant ways. I remain forever grateful for my parents' deep unconditional love for my sister and me, and, in any consideration of a future mate, I would always keep in mind my deeply rooted need to find a mate who would help me create a home for myself and my family that was a secure refuge from life's storms—a home filled with mutual respect and tranquility.

Standing with my younger sister Elana, for whom I was a frequent sitter. We have remained close throughout our lives.

Chapter 2
WHAT DO YOU WANT TO BE WHEN YOU GROW UP?

FROM EARLY CHILDHOOD TO MY SECond year in college, becoming a rabbi was not on my radar. We lived across the street from a park and a baseball diamond. Many spring and summer evenings my father and I watched sandlot teams, whose uniforms advertised their business sponsor. Arbitrarily choosing a team to root for made watching more exciting, but for me playing was always preferable to observing. At summer camp I honed my skills as a slugging, left-handed, first baseman. To be sure, more than occasionally those home runs over the right field fence were more fantasized than slugged. Still, I was obsessed with the game and, like so many others, I dared to dream of a future in baseball. We had no little league teams in those days. We just chose sides for each game. I was good enough to be among the first group chosen by the team captains. Although I was a good student, hitting a home run and winning on the baseball field were as important to me as getting an A on an exam.

When my family acquired a piano, I did not resist taking lessons; but when it was time to practice my scales, piano proved no match for baseball. Irresistibly, my hands left the keyboard as I fetched my left-hander's glove and darted across the street. Prior to my piano lesson, I fervently prayed that God would empower me to perform well for my teacher. I learned relatively early the limitations of petitionary prayer.

Engagement with the piano keyboard was short-lived and even by middle school it became evident my baseball skills were not keeping pace with my physical maturation. As long as weather permitted, fall was a time for football. Since we played on a concrete alley, flanked by car garages, we played touch football, which meant we needed only to touch rather than tackle our opponent to end a play. Each day after school I would play for about forty-five minutes with guys around the neighborhood before dashing home to care for my younger sister while both parents were at work. With my lanky height, large hands and reasonable speed I was adept at catching the passes thrown by our "quarterback" and dashing past the garbage can that marked the goal line.

My sister Elana must have amused herself, because during most of those afternoons, after a fleeting game of football, I was able to fulfill my sitting responsibilities while listening to such radio serials as *Young Widow Brown*, *Terry and the Pirates*, *Jack Armstrong* and *When a Girl Marries*. In the early evening, I listened daily to Lowell Thomas broadcast the news. Artfully, he leavened the hard news with human-interest stories—all delivered with a resonant, velvety voice and perfect cadence. In time I found myself imitating Lowell Thomas' "news cast" which began with "Good evening everybody" and ended with "and now so long until tomorrow." Sometimes I enacted this routine in the solitude of my room, more often in the presence of my obliging sister. Was this the origin of the speaking voice that became my much-admired trademark among my high school peers—and throughout my adult life? Lowell Thomas also taught me the power of a well-told story that illuminated the vagaries of the human condition.

Coming to Terms with Limitations

Relatively early I discovered both my strengths and my limitations. Professional baseball was not in my future. In middle school, a course in "Shop" tested our spatial relations and required that we do mechanical drawing. This assignment proved beyond my capacities. I actually flunked the course. All of which convinced me that I was not destined to be an engineer. Looking back on my life, I remember being taught how to change a tire, but fortunately I have managed to get through life without actually doing it. Joan, my life mate for more than half a century, knows that for better or worse, being mechanically challenged is part of my DNA. At one point, after she used an expandable broom handle with a grasping mechanical hand to change a light bulb embedded in a high ceiling, Joan proclaimed wryly, "How nice it is to have a man around the house."

I confess that whenever my car requires the kind of simple maintenance that many men and some women handle by themselves, I open the hood and rely on the kindness of strangers. Over the years, this ineptness has been revealed to my children and grandchildren. There was that most painful moment when my children, then ages eight and ten, discovered their Dad was an inadequate protector. We were on a brief canoe trip down a segment of northern Michigan's Jordan River (which, like its name sake is also narrow, but more pristine and lush). We rented two canoes. Joan captained one with her one passenger, Amy, and I steered and was accompanied by Rachel and Liz. Our canoe also contained the festive lunch we had bought for a grand picnic once we reached our destination downstream. Neither Joan nor I got more than the most rudimentary instructions shortly before boarding the canoe, but we were assured it was very much like rowing.

Joan's canoe was in the lead. At certain points the current was swift and some menacing branches jutted out from the lush foliage on each bank. Miraculously, Joan's canoe arrived at its destination without incident. Our canoe tipped over. While the water was not over my head, and the girls had life jackets, I swooped them into my arms and deposited them on the bank. Though their fear of harm was momentary, their wet, chilled bodies, and their arched brows registered deep disappointment. Fortunately, two elderly ladies came by in a larger canoe. They helped me right ours, but my two daughters insisted on traveling the rest of the way with those strangers, rather than reenter their father's canoe.

Some Counterbalancing Gifts
As my limitations became starkly evident, my favorable endowments also appeared. By adolescence, thanks in part to high school debating, I had become an articulate and persuasive

speaker. Although somewhat nervous before a talk, once I began to speak, I found myself in comfortable space and even relished the opportunity. When I felt deeply about an issue, my voice and body language conveyed this to my listeners. I felt more effective in oral than written communication and was at ease addressing large and small groups.

Early on, I displayed significant interpersonal skills. Even as a teenager, I found that peers and older adults felt comfortable unburdening themselves to me. I was able to help persons my age and older navigate relationally troubled waters. A good listener, I could suspend judgment until I understood the other person's situation. At times, I saw in other persons more positive qualities than they felt in themselves. By nature, I was more validating than critical, more reconciling than confrontational.

When the differences between me and another were irreconcilable, I honored my convictions, but wherever possible, attributed some legitimacy to the other's views. When there was little or no common ground, I strove to oppose the other's views without devaluing the person. Sol Linowitz was an American Ambassador-at-Large to the Camp David talks between President Carter, Prime Minister Menachem Begin and Egyptian President, Anwar Sadat. Asked to describe his impression of the difference between Begin and Sadat, Linowitz replied, "Sadat could say no and make it almost sound like yes. Begin could say yes and make it sound like no." I was more like Sadat than Begin.

Cultural and socioeconomic barriers did not prevent me from conversing comfortably and meaningfully with persons whose backgrounds were very different from my own. Beneath and beyond our diverse social, economic and cultural differences I could usually discern and respect a common humanity.

By temperament I was not a great risk-taker. Climbing trees or jumping from great heights or indulging in the kind of physical wrestling and boxing that marked the fooling around of adolescent boys did not appeal to me. I can recall no trips to the ER as the result of such rough-housing. On those few occasions at camp when I was confronted by a bully, I managed to disarm him by verbal engagement. Perhaps I naturally internalized the Talmudic admonition: "Do not venture into a dangerous place and pray for a miraculous deliverance."[1]

Generally, I grew even more comfortable with my mechanical ineptitude as my positive endowments were validated and valued by others. Fast-forwarding for a moment, in later years I would serve as an Air Force chaplain and one of my tasks was to deliver "character guidance lectures." It was not unusual for me to address a group of as many as two hundred officers on the base. After one such lecture an Air Force Captain approached the rostrum and asked: "Chaplain, please tell me how you can stand before our large group and speak with such ease? If I were asked to do that I would have a panic attack." I asked the captain, "What is your role in the Air Force, Captain?" His reply, "I'm a fighter pilot." I responded, "Captain, I shudder at the thought of piloting an F16, not to mention engaging in aerial combat." He smiled and said simply, "Thanks sir."

The Years at Central High
Our modest row house was situated in North Philadelphia, about a mile away from Central High School. CHS was a

rigorously academic public high school. It was founded in 1836 and now has a predominantly African American and Hispanic student body. To this day, Central remains rigourously academic and admission is contingent on passing an entrance exam. I began high school in the fall of 1945, shortly after the end of World War II. Our campus was separated from a National Guard armory by a barbed wire fence. During the war, the building housed German prisoners of war. During part of my freshman year, they were still not repatriated. I vividly recall one afternoon when a group of us encountered the "enemy" POWs lounging around their courtyard. Somehow we found ourselves throwing firm snowballs across the barbed wire fence. They countered with their own missiles and a playful but earnest snowball fight ensued. Perhaps, we thought, this battle was our symbolic contribution to the Allied victory in the war.

During my years at Central, I had already forsaken any hope of ever being a varsity high school baseball player, but I remained a serious student. More than a few of our faculty members had earned a Ph.D. in their field, and some were excellent teachers. I maintained an A average, but was still outranked by a few in my class.

Apart from some dating (and a few young women who were featured in my romantic/sexual fantasies) my major extracurricular activity was the Central debating team and our school radio station. Those were the years when "current events" turned me into a news junkie. I began to read *The New York Times* regularly and loved to spend hours in Philadelphia's main public library researching the assigned debate topic. With no access to the Internet, my debate partner and I relied on the volumes of the Reader's Guide, which indexed periodicals by topic. The only debate topic I still remember was "Resolved that Hong Kong be returned to the Chinese government."

The exercise of preparing to debate both sides of a given issue may well have helped shape my tendency to appreciate that there are two sides to many questions. For better or worse, I have a tolerance for ambiguity which leads me to be a political independent rather than inclined to pull a party lever without examining the merits of each candidate on the list.

During those years, I developed a fascination with words. Four years of Latin helped me immensely to discern the meaning of new words. I not only looked up words I couldn't decipher, but would at times open a dictionary randomly and study new words. During my teenage years friends of our family and other adults were impressed by the richness of language in my speeches or even conversation. It took some years for me to fully appreciate that words were intended to communicate thoughts and ideas rather than to flaunt the speaker's extensive vocabulary. Particularly in oral communication, the use of unfamiliar words leads the listener not to consult a dictionary, but to tune the speaker out.

In high school, the assigned readings exposed me to great writing, supple thinking and the power of metaphor. Some of my favorite works were Thomas Wolfe's *You Can't Go Home Again,* Theodor Dreiser's *An American Tragedy,* Dostoevsky's *Crime and Punishment* and *The Brothers Karamazov.* By then I had long graduated from Lamb's *Tales of Shakespeare* to the Bard's originals. My favorites were *Macbeth, Hamlet, Othello* and *King Lear.*

During my high school years, I also attended and graduated from Gratz College, which provided evening classes for college and some high school students who wanted to deepen their Jewish education beyond the elementary level. More than a few graduates used their degree as certification to teach in Conservative and Reform congregational schools. While I enjoyed the opportunity to study Jewish texts during those two weekday evenings, my regular attendance after spending much of the day in an all-male classroom was driven more by the proximity of some attractive women than by my love of those Jewish texts. I had a crush on a somewhat older, beautiful blond student who was the daughter of one of the faculty members.

At Central, my most influential mentor was a crusty, tough-minded English teacher and debate coach. Mr. Pennypacker, himself a proud alumnus of Harvard College, was the one who encouraged me to apply. When he first broached the subject I hastened to inform him that I was not ranked academically at the top of the class and, with my limited finances, I would probably go to an in-town college, like the University of Pennsylvania. Mr. Pennypacker countered that if I tested well on the college exams and was accepted for admission, scholarship and financial aid would materialize. Since I greatly admired him and he was generally very sparing in his praise, I was quite moved when he looked me in the eyes and said, "Trust me Sam Karff, you belong at Harvard." That alone made me an instant convert to his suggestion.

My senior year included an unexpected confrontation with Dr. Farbish, the assistant principal. I had been asked to be one of the three commencement speakers. Since that year, 1949, was a short time after the birth of the new State of Israel—and I was a staunch believer in the importance of its establishment—I used my talk to explain why Israel's rebirth was of such significance. Dr. Farbish scanned the first draft and insisted that I choose another topic. It turned out that he was himself Jewish, but belonged to an organization that had fiercely opposed Israel's creation. I found myself responding to his request by saying that if changing the subject were a precondition for being a speaker, I must withdraw. Although very unnerved by my response, Dr. Farbish must have considered it was more prudent for him to allow me free expression than to be accused of censorship. Moreover, the fact that he belonged to an anti-Zionist organization did not make him an impartial arbiter.

When the graduating class yearbook appeared I learned that I had been voted "Most Likely to Succeed." That news, however welcome, was eclipsed by the arrival of a letter from the Harvard Dean of Admission which stated I was eligible to be a member of the class of 1953.

The Harvard Years

Mr. Pennypacker was only partially right. I did receive a full tuition scholarship, but room and board was not included, which precluded my living on campus. Fortunately, when my Aunt Scotta and Uncle Abe learned of my acceptance, they, who lived in the Boston suburb, only a bus and trolley car ride away from Cambridge, called to congratulate me and offered the vacant bedroom on the third floor of their large suburban home as my residence. I gratefully accepted.

From early childhood, Uncle Abe, my father's younger brother was an important presence. He became like a second father to my sister and me. He provided the funds that enabled us to attend summer camp in the Pocono Mountains and was generally solicitous of our welfare. When Uncle Abe came to this country from Tel Aviv, Palestine in the 1920s, he financed his study of law by teaching Hebrew school. Abe's first marriage was to his first cousin, but she had no interest in homemaking or motherhood, and they were amicably divorced. (Years later May Karff became "America's Women's Chess Champion").

Abe and his partner, Ben, established a small but thriving law firm in downtown Boston. Upon graduation from Portia Law School, and after passing the Massachusetts bar exam, outranking many Harvard law graduates, Scotta Weymouth applied for a position at Karff and Goldberg. Scotta was both bright and beautiful. In time, Abe overcame his social diffidence and asked her to have dinner with him. Their courtship was so subtle and brief that when Scotta announced to Ben Goldberg that she would be absent for the next week because she was getting married, Ben first congratulated her and then asked whom she was marrying. "Your partner," she replied. Ben was both stunned and delighted.

Scotta's father was the descendent of an old Protestant Yankee family (for which the town of Weymouth, Massachusetts was named). Scotta studied and embraced Judaism and they were married in a ceremony conducted by a rabbi.

I felt very much at home living with Scotta, Abe and their two little girls, Carmie and Debbie. During each weekday, I commuted between Newton and Cambridge. Before focusing on the Harvard experience itself, I have reason to be grateful not only for their welcoming me into their home, but for expanding my horizons. Scotta and Abe introduced me to my first Reform worship service. Until then

I had experienced only Orthodox and Conservative worship. They included me in their literary guild subscription. Many Broadway plays were previewed in Boston, and I instantly developed a love for the theater. I was blown away by Robert Anderson's *Tea and Sympathy*, Eugene O'Neal's *Long Day's Journey Into Night*, Tennessee Williams' *A Streetcar Named Desire* and Arthur Miller's *Death of a Salesman*.

The years at Harvard were the most intellectually challenging and exciting years of my life. Harvard provided the environment for study, mind-expanding dialogues with students and faculty and much disciplined reading and reflection. In those days, even the giants in the academy taught courses to undergraduates.

Among the most memorable of my courses was Arthur Schlesinger Jr.'s *Year Long Exploration of the Intellectual History of the United States from Colonial Times to the Present*. Professor Schlesinger was able to integrate the literary, political, economic and religious trends of each period in coherent, captivating lectures. I still have my class notes from that course.

I also relished William Yandell Elliot's *Introduction to Political Theory from Plato's Republic to the Federalist Papers to Marx's Das Kapital*. Professor Elliott had been a mentor to Henry Kissinger during his student days. Although a dull lecturer, Talcott Parsons introduced me to sociology through our study of his classic, *The Social System*. His theoretical framework for understanding human relationships in society would have a far-reaching effect on my later understanding of Judaism. I was also intrigued by Harry Wolfson, one of the very few Jewish tenured professors in those days. His impassioned teaching of the thought of Baruch Spinoza was a great intellectual treat.

Choosing a field of concentration at Harvard in those days was not so monumental a decision. To major in a field did not preclude a student from taking a generous number of courses outside it. The Department of Social Relations attempted to provide a holistic, interdisciplinary understanding of human behavior. This major embodied the insights of clinical and social psychology, sociology, anthropology, social pathology and abnormal psychology. Among the professors who taught in the department were Gordon Allport, Clyde Kluckhohn, Pitirim Sorokin, Henry Murray and Talcott Parsons.

This department's disciplined effort to understand the vagaries of human behavior may have drawn me, perhaps unconsciously, because of my personal history in a family where parents were united in their love for their children but acted so unlovingly and even destructively toward each other.

A Traumatic Debate

My major competitive college sport became the Harvard Debating Team. We won the Harvard/Princeton/Yale Debate Tournament, but by far the most memorable debate of all pitted us against the team representing Norfolk State Prison. I don't recall the debate topics for the Ivy League tournament, but I vividly recall that evening at the prison, which must be recorded as one of the most exciting and frightening moments in my life. Our team was searched and then admitted to the prison grounds. The assistant warden escorted us to the main auditorium where hundreds of inmates were applauding and stomping their feet appreciatively as a jam session featuring a visiting band was coming to an end. That was the first part of the evening's entertainment.

We were scheduled as the next event. The chairman of the evening introduced the debate topic: "Resolved that able-bodied college students be deferred from the draft." (This was the military draft during the Korean War.) The irony was not lost on anyone that we, the students were arguing that college students should not be deferred. The prison team was assigned to argue that college students, like us, should be deferred.

The only part of the debate I still recall were my remarks during rebuttal. In an effort to clinch our case, I took notice of the affirmative's contention that since college students were engaged in disciplined study of issues that would prepare them to occupy important positions in our American society, they could be properly exempt. In response, I said something to this effect: "You gentlemen think that we spend all our time studying, even on weekends. But, if you visited our living quarters on a typical Saturday night you would not find diligent students hitting the books, but raucous revelers guzzling beer. Should college students be deferred so they can have wild orgies in their dormitories?"

"Orgies" was the fateful word. At its mention the prisoners stood and thunderously clapped and shouted. The assistant warden rushed to the stage and whispered in my ear, "We will have no more such talk, son. Are you trying to start a riot?" Meanwhile the guards dispersed through the hall and the inmates were seated. My extemporaneous rebuttal was abruptly ended. During those few minutes, which seemed like hours, my blood pressure must have gone through the roof. I had learned the worst-case scenario for an extemporaneous speech. Now at a safe distance, I can laugh at my folly. At the time I was terrified. Although we had lost the debate, there was some consolation in hearing that some weeks earlier the Oxford University Team visited the prison, and they too lost their debate.

Living on Campus

After two years of commuting I hungered for a taste of living on campus. Since my tuition scholarship was fungible, I decided to contract the four years of study to three plus two summers at the Harvard Summer School. The math worked and I could still graduate without debt. For all its pleasantness, living at my aunt and uncle's home deprived me of a fuller and richer college experience. During one year and two summers I would be able to fill that vacuum.

Harvard was organized into separate houses for upper classmen. I chose Eliot House, which was situated along the banks of the Charles River, because Henry Sosland already occupied a suite there and was looking for someone to share it. Henry and I had gotten to know each other through our activity with Hillel, the Jewish campus fellowship. We shared a love and respect for our Jewish heritage but while he had already committed himself to enter the Jewish Theological Seminary upon graduation, and I had begun to seriously consider the Rabbinate, my vocational goals were still in flux. I allowed myself to consider such options as teaching on a college level, joining the diplomatic service, becoming a news broadcaster, a psychotherapist and an attorney. Although that was the reality, I believe Henry's parents blamed my influence on his choice of the Rabbinate rather than the family business!

Each Harvard house had a distinctive identity. Over the years, Eliot seemed to attract a disproportional number of students from high profile families. During my tenure at Eliot, the house was home to Paul Matisse (the artist's grandson); James Joyce's grandson; Sadri Khan, whose family traced its ancestry back to the prophet Mohammed and whose older brother, Aly, was then married to the Hollywood actress, Rita Hayworth.

In my years, Harvard was purportedly still under a 6% Jewish quota. During his tenure as president of the university, James Conant sought to make each house more representative of the total student body. As a result, Jewish students were strongly encouraged to choose Eliot in order to make it more integrated. The Eliot elite could still find periodic refuge from too much egalitarianism in private clubs, like The Hasty Pudding or the Porcellian. The new mix at Eliot House was not without its ironies. The House Master's receptions, which offered a choice between sherry and tomato juice, were conspicuously boycotted by many of the elite residents and over-patronized by us, who were not welcome at those private clubs. Here's the irony: John Finley, our house master, and a distinguished scholar of Greek classics, hosted the reception when he might well have preferred joining the other residents at their private clubs. At one reception, I overheard Professor Finley referring to someone as "a fine fellow, but impecunious." His comment, though not directed at me, could well have been! On the basis of that declaration, I may be forgiven the conclusion that Professor Finley, for all his other merits, was a snob.

I once asked a son of a high-profile wealthy Jewish family why he made no effort to participate in the group activity of Jewish students. He responded that his parents never made much of their Jewishness and it had no meaning for him. Then he added that he thought all religious and social particularities were needlessly divisive. To which I could not resist responding, "Tell me, if the Porcellian Club were to open its doors to Jews, would you refuse to join?" He smiled, and, in effect conceded my point, only to revert to his initial declaration that Judaism just had never been a meaningful part of his life. The fact remained that, so far in his life, he had only known Jewishness or Judaism as a burden and a barrier, rather than a deep source of spiritual nourishment and meaning.

My most significant Jewish experience during my college years was a discussion group led by Maurice Zigmond, the director of the Harvard Hillel Foundation. Rabbi Zigmond (we students affectionately called him Ziggie) was ordained as a Reform rabbi. He pursued graduate studies in anthropology, and twice weekly he would commute to Yale to teach in the Anthropology Department.

His discussion group at Hillel House drew Jewish undergraduates and graduate students from the greater Boston college community, including Radcliffe, Boston University, MIT, Wellesley, Brandeis and Tufts. Since, in those days, there were no departments of Jewish studies on virtually all those campuses, Ziggie's group provided an informal opportunity for us to engage contemporary Jewish thinkers, like Martin Buber, Franz Rosenzweig, Mordecai Kaplan and Abraham Heschel. We were expected to do the reading in advance of each focused discussion. Rabbi Zigmond was a very loose moderator. He would raise questions and enable us to do most of the talking. Those of us who chose to participate in the group were no doubt seeking to find greater meaning in our Judaism at that stage of our lives. Doubtless, those discussions subliminally led me to consider ever more seriously the possibility of becoming a rabbi. They deepened my appreciation of Judaism as a three dimensional relationship: to the Jewish people (Israel), the Jewish way of life (Torah) and to the God to whom we were covenanted. The respect for different points of view within the group provided enough space for me to find a Jewish way that was most consistent with my beliefs and temperament.

Revisiting Harvard for the 350th Anniversary

Of course my characterization of Jewish life at Harvard during the 1950s must be considered in the context of the discriminatory residential, occupational and social barriers still in place during the fifties. Decades later, much had changed at Harvard and in the United States. Our country had become one of the most open societies for Jews and other minorities in our history. Thirty-seven years after my graduation I would be given an opportunity to revisit the campus and reflect on those changes. In 1986, I was invited to participate in the celebration of Harvard's 350th anniversary. I was given the privilege of speaking at one of three convocations held over the course of the celebration at Memorial Church. The Catholic speaker was Bernard Law, a classmate who was then a cardinal and head of the Catholic Archdiocese of Boston. The Protestant speaker was the senior pastor of Old South Church in Boston, and I was the Jewish speaker.

Although I had passed by Memorial Church many, many times, I never entered it during my years at the college. It seemed like strange, foreign space to me. Speaking from its pulpit as a rabbi in 1986 symbolized how different the interreligious scene had become in our nation.

CHAPTER 2 ⋄ WHAT DO YOU WANT TO BE WHEN YOU GROW UP?

That morning I declared my intention to relate 350 years of Harvard's existence to the 3500 years of a Jewish presence on this Earth.

> I shall speak of the relation between Harvard, prime gateway to the treasures and privileges of a secular American culture and Judaism, the millennial heritage that would shape me and others like me, long before I came to this campus thirty-seven years ago.

An American Jew's encounter with Harvard is, in some respects, the retelling of an old Jewish story. It is the story of our tradition's encounter with a threatening, challenging and seductive world.

> In coming to Cambridge I didn't have to decide, like Sandy Koufax, whether to pitch in the Harvard-Yale game on Yom Kippur. That remained fantasy. I did have to decide whether I would eat pork served in the Eliot House dining hall or whether I would get so involved in campus that I would totally ignore the Jewish Sabbath.[2]

I suggested that Harvard stood for all that was rational, intellectual, liberating and empowering—which made it all the more seductive. During my years, Harvard was a place to keep a low profile regardless of one's particular religious heritage because, at that time, the term "religious intellectual" was for many an oxymoron. I noted,

> Beyond the divinity school, religious narratives were regarded at best sentimentally and religious symbols were

appreciated aesthetically, but neither religious story nor symbol was to be taken too seriously by one who revered the rigorous life of the mind.

In those days at Harvard, it was not uncommon for Jewish students to seal "their assimilation into a privileged secular mainstream. Here they thought as little of their Jewishness and Judaism as the environment would allow and many thought very little indeed." Sometimes however, that environment reminded its Jewish students that being Jewish was still a barrier to total acceptance. Jewish enrollment was carefully restricted by "quota," tenured Jewish faculty members were rare and there were private clubs from which Jews and other minorities were excluded. It also remained true that "the course offerings in western civilization signaled by their silence that no noteworthy Jewish thought had taken place since the dawn of the Christian era."

But I also reminded my listeners that across the centuries many of my people had learned to be enriched by interacting with the larger world without losing their Jewish integrity. I believe that was my experience at Harvard. By way of illustration I chose a biblical text from Deuteronomy (16:20) in which the Israelites were instructed, "Justice, justice shall you pursue." God enters into a covenant with Israel that seems to be a rational conditional agreement in which Israel remains chosen only as long as it observes the terms of the covenant. But as the biblical reader probes further it is evident that the God of Deuteronomy is not only a judge giving each his due, God is also bound to Israel by a covenant of unconditional love. I would come to understand that God's covenant with Israel contains an abiding tension between conditionality and unconditionality which though logically contradictory was resolved in rabbinic narrative and in the concreteness of Jewish life.

That morning in Memorial Church, I briefly related this concept to my studies at Harvard.

> More than 30 years ago in Emerson Hall, not far from where we are, I took a class with Talcott Parsons, a great professor of sociology. He taught me to appreciate the distinction between a social relationship that is impersonal, rational, contractual (which Parsons called 'instrumental adaptive') and a relationship grounded in kinship, inherited privilege, and love (which Parsons called 'expressive').

I never forgot that conceptual tool. In fact, a few years later at rabbinic seminary it helped me understand the narrative theology embedded in the Bible and the Talmud. Much of my approach to rabbinic theology, including my doctoral dissertation, was based on the application of a Harvard professor's theoretical framework to the study of the Covenant relationship between God and Israel. I suggested that morning at Memorial Church that many of us found in this highly charged intellectual environment an opportunity to "enrich our minds without compromising our cherished fidelities."

To be sure, I also suggested that in my time there were some subtle pressures to diminish one's particular loyalties, unless you happened to be white Anglo-Saxon Protestant. What made the 350th celebration even more sanguine for me is the fact that Harvard had significantly mellowed and ripened. I was now experiencing a Harvard that to an unprecedented degree celebrates religious and cultural diversity.

As a token thereof, I referenced a procession that took place some years earlier across Harvard yard. Henry Rosovsky, then Dean of Arts and Sciences, and a committed Jew, held a Torah scroll in his arms and participated in a procession of students and faculty and alumni across the yard to a new, more centrally located Jewish student center. In my time that procession would never have taken place.

These were my concluding words in Memorial Church, "So, an academy with Puritan roots that once taught Hebrew because it was the language of Christianity's Old Testament heritage, now proclaims unambiguously that there are many paths to religious truth." In that context, Harvard had given an additional meaning to an ancient imperative: "Justice, justice shall you pursue."

Chapter 3
WHY THE RABBINATE?

Now that I have considered the familial context that made it natural for me at least to consider the rabbinate the question remains: what prompted me to cast aside the other vocational paths that piqued my interest and matched my skill set? From time to time, especially in the period closer to the fateful decision to enter the seminary, persons asked me, "Why did you decide to become a rabbi?" The subtext of their inquiry seemed to be: given the broad range of options before me, why didn't I choose a vocational path more attuned to those like themselves and many of their peers who did not take religion very seriously? My pat answer: "The choice represented a convergence of my skills, interests and values. I like to do the kinds of things a rabbi does, and Judaism and my religious faith are an important part of who I am."

In retrospect, that answer always seemed inadequate. Michael Polanyi introduced the concept of "tacit knowledge" which is more visceral than normal cognition and below the threshold of consciousness. Tacit knowledge is what enables anyone to transition from studying the grammar of a language to fluently speaking it.

Looking back, choosing the rabbinate was partly based on tacit knowledge. So much was at play, some of it no doubt below the threshold of consciousness. Surely my parents had seen that I learned Judaism on a deeper level than many of my peers and were themselves teachers of Judaism. Studying Agada with Dr. Bet Halachmy as an eleven-year-old, imbibing a love of Judaism through observance of sacred times: Sabbaths, Passover Seders, High Holidays, learning to speak Hebrew as a living language, listening to the inspiring sermons of Rabbi Mortimer J. Cohen when we went to the synagogue where my mother taught and those stimulating "bull sessions" with Rabbi Zigmond at Harvard—all these experiences and more provided a context for choosing the rabbinate as a vocation.

Once the die was cast and I became a rabbi, over the years I could consciously identify what most drew me to the rabbinic vocation. What began as a convergence of skills, interest and values, became in time consciously something much deeper. An ancient rabbi, Rabbi Yochanan ben Zakkai, taught that there are certain moments when what you are doing makes you feel "for this you were created." So many times, as I ministered to a couple who lost a child in a freak accident or sat at the bedside of a man who knew he was dying, I realized I was where I was intended to be.

CHAPTER 3 ⬥ WHY THE RABBINATE?

An Address Confirming My Vocation

In 1984, twenty-eight years after my ordination, I was invited to give a major address at the annual convention of the Central Conference of American Rabbis. I had addressed my peers on more than a few occasions before then and in subsequent years, but in preparation of that address, my conscious self-understanding of why I became a rabbi reached its peak.

Actually, six months earlier, the person invited to address our convention was Elie Wiesel, a justly revered, iconic figure within and beyond the Jewish world. Elie accepted the invitation, and as requested, submitted the title of his talk a month before the actual program. Three weeks before the conference, Wiesel called the vice-president in charge of that year's program to express deep regrets that a suddenly convened conference in Europe required his attendance and that therefore he could not be with us as planned.

Immediately after the program chairman hung up, he called me, explained why he was in a cold sweat and recruited me to pinch-hit. The chairman was also a dear personal friend who imploringly declared, "From you, I will only take yes for an answer." When I accepted, my heart raced and I broke into a cold sweat. As I would discover many times, there is nothing more agonizingly nervewracking or potentially more satisfying than being tested and validated by one's peers. In the three remaining weeks, I labored to compose a talk appropriate to the title Elie had sent: "The Soul of the Rav."

That morning I began by affirming that when we speak of the soul of the rabbi,

We penetrate to the core of what we are and what is entrusted to our care. The rabbi is essentially a teacher; the schoolhouse in which we teach is portable, "Have Torah, will travel." We teach in the classroom and in the sanctuary, in our study and in the intensive care unit and the family waiting room at the local hospital; sometimes even in the whirlpool of the JCC (the Jewish equivalent of the YMCA), when a Jew probes, "Say, Rabbi, I've been meaning to ask you…" I teach when I tell a story to children about a king's perfect diamond which, much to his horror, had a scratch…None could remove the scratch, but one craftsman etched a beautiful rose on that diamond's surface and he used the scratch to make the stem. I teach at a Torah seminar when, after reading of Moses' death before reaching the Promised Land an elderly congregant poignantly observes that all of our lives are incomplete…

The high points of our rabbinic vocation are when we feel we must—we are defined by what we do. At such moments we cannot conceive of ourselves not telling stories to children, not speaking a word of comfort to the bereaved, not addressing a congregation on Kol Nidre night (Yom Kippur).

The rabbi must also study…if we are fortunate, we have all savored those moments of discovery and insight… the sensuous excitement that comes from being gripped by a text that comes from our past and addresses our present. We must be connected not only to the text but also to our students…Given the pastoral pressures imposed by needy congregants…would most of us be content to be left alone to study without interruptions? "You know," said the teacher, "My whole life I have been complaining that my work was interrupted until I discovered that my interruptions were my work." How sad when they no longer interrupt with the words, "Rabbi, I've been meaning to ask you…"

[W]e not only teach Torah, we must strive to be a Torah. The Rav confronts the burden of bearing witness…the burden is greater if we are rooted in the community; if we teach in the midst of a single congregation day after day, week after week, year after year, they will come to know us as well as our teaching. A few will remember if we gave the same sermon every other Rosh Hashanah. More will know if we betray our marriage vows, or if we decry materialism from the pulpit and then stridently press each item in contract negotiations. The Rav who teaches must be nourished by what she imparts. The teaching we embody must appear to make some difference in the quality of our lives. We cannot only model our human frailty. Torah must help us tame our own *yetzer harah* (evil impulse).

We are called to model not only our *menschlichkeit* (human decency) but our faith…the Rav is cast as defender of the faith. Our people need reassurance that in spite of everything, life is not absurd, that beyond the mystery, there is meaning. Do we live the faith we proclaim? As rabbis we also model our struggle for faith, confess our moments of doubt and keep company with Abraham, the Psalmist and Levi Yitzhak of Berditchev, all of whom had their lover's quarrels with God. So we stand at the grave of a young child whose life was snuffed out shortly after dawn and we echo the bitter plaint of her loved ones: "Why, why? Life is so unfair." But we also guide the family to the declaration, "Praised be thou, oh Lord, Judge of

Truth," and we lead the mourners in the recitation of the Kaddish (memorial prayer) which Elie Wiesel calls that "solemn affirmation filled with grandeur and serenity by which man returns to God his crown and his scepter."

Let us confess, stationed in the battlefield as God's defenders, as comforters of life's wounded, we may rise to religious affirmations we may not always feel in our souls. Are we then hypocrites? No, we are modeling that very amalgam of doubt and faith that is the price of living with a God who is both hidden and revealed. Yet our own spiritual nurture and our power to nurture others is enhanced…by those moments when we too have experienced the nearness of the Holy One. For…to us is entrusted the story that life is a covenant. While that covenant may have hidden clauses, beyond the mystery there is meaning.

By virtue of who we are, we enter a very special academy where vulnerability, deep need, and trust engender a sharing of the unvarnished meditations of the heart. Larry was a man in his late sixties. He came to our city to be near his children and grandchildren. Suddenly, a malignant tumor assaulted him and despite initial surgery, the destructive process became irreversible. Larry was dying and he knew he was dying. The body was progressively consumed. The mind was still intact. Larry asked me, "Rabbi, how do you prepare?" I found myself thinking of the rabbinic dictum that we ought to live each day as if it were our last. "Larry," I said, "We prepare all our lives, and you prepared well. You've shown you love and care. You have a proper sense of right and wrong. You've made your share of mistakes like the rest of us but you've earned a good name and you'll be missed. And maybe this is your finest hour and your greatest gift to your family: you've accepted your dying without bitterness, with great consideration for them and an appreciation for every kindness. Larry, I pray when my time comes, I have half your courage and dignity. It is a privilege to know you."

Tears streamed from his eyes as he clasped my hands to his lips and kissed me. I recited the Y'varech'a (the priestly benediction) and the Sh'ma (the affirmation of God's unity and sole claim on our worship) which Larry repeated after me. I felt faint as I left the room. Had I encountered my own mortality?...To be a Rav is to offer some assurance to the dying and their survivors that a human life has not been lived in vain:...To be a Rav to Larry is the burden and privilege of our vocation. Our souls are nourished by our study and our teaching and our learning from those we have come to teach...

When all is said and done...there is one final paradox:... there is a holy insecurity in what we do and who we are... no matter how many great sermons we preach, or good classes we teach, or fine counseling sessions we offer, the troubling questions do not disappear. We continue to have moments of nagging uncertainty as well as those moments of blessed confirmation: *l'chach notzarta* (for such a moment you were created)...But when we think of all the ways of spending that brief interlude from birth to the grave, when we think of what is given to us to be and to do, we have reason to declare...Praised be Thou, O Lord, who has made me a rabbi to your people, Israel.[3]

The Human Quest for Meaning

That talk to my colleagues marked the clearest articulation of my rabbinate as a sacred vocation. The choice now seemed much more than a convergence of my skillsets, interests and values. In retrospect, the fateful decision to enroll in seminary was less a careful, rationally calculated choice and more an acceptance of my destiny, less my choosing and more my being chosen.

Yet in the same "Soul of the Rav" talk, I confessed to my colleagues that "there are more than a few moments when I feel otherwise—when I feel what keeps me a rabbi is my unpreparedness for anything else…" I went on to say that,

> So many of our forebears also were not spared such agonizing self-doubt, including that ancient Rabbinic sage who said, "Don't lust for the table of kings for your table of Torah is greater than theirs and the master will reward you for your labors."

Still, with each passing year as a rabbi, I came closer to not being able to imagine myself in any other life's work.

We human creatures are not only mortal; we know we are mortal. We are also meaning-seeking creatures. Of all living creatures, we alone ask the question: what should I do with my life? The inspired writers of our sacred texts gave us the language to reflect upon the challenge before us. In Psalm 90:

> We bring our years to an end as a tale that is told/The days of our years are threescore years and ten, or even by reason of strength fourscore years/Yet is their pride but travail and vanity/For it is speedily gone, and we fly away…so teach us to number our days that we may get us a heart of wisdom/…let thy work appear unto thy

servants and thy glory upon their children/Establish thou also the work of our hands/Yea the work of our hands establish thou it.

Whether we are religious or not, we believe that some life stories are more filled with meaning than others—that there is a standard by which we must judge our lives. Unless we are sociopaths, we know that we are here on Earth to love, to create, to be a blessing, a healing presence in the lives we touch. The validity of what I have suggested above was brought home to me whenever there was a death in the congregation and I met with the family. In the interval between their kin's death and the actual funeral and burial, I asked them to tell me what they wanted to remember about this person's life. Some would be totally silent in a way that spoke volumes; some would not hesitate to share their regrets: "I wish he had allowed me to get closer to him."

As I presided and gave the eulogy, at virtually every funeral service, I felt an awesome responsibility. Family and friends were not only concerned about the meaning, or relative meaninglessness, of their deceased's life on this earth. The occasion compelled them to assess their own life's meaning. Nothing concentrates the mind more than our encounter with the reality of death.

Wherever possible, my sacred task was to validate a person's life with truth and kindness. A rabbi's abiding nightmare, when we must rely in part or sometimes entirely on the testimony of others, is that we will attribute virtues to the deceased that evoke snickers of disbelief from persons who knew him. Those in the family or congregation who experienced and perhaps suffered from some of the darker side of a person's character ought to be respected in the eulogy that is given.

Thus, in one particular assessment of a person's life, I spoke of a man who was one of the acknowledged leaders in the Jewish community.

> He was exceedingly generous, always seeking to help persons in need, whether by offering employment to a prisoner who had completed his sentence or by offering to help reconcile two estranged members of another family. As an incurable optimist, he took on difficult projects, which, once completed successfully, were of great social value to the community. Many less daring spirits would have shied away from these undertakings. However, this same quality led him to take financial risks and persuade others to follow him where cautious restraint would have been proper and wise.

Those assembled for that funeral service knew that this person had engaged in the unlawful practice of check kiting, was heavily fined and barely averted prison. They also knew that this person had earned the love and respect of his family and many in that room that day for the good in his life. While I said that, "Like all of us mortals, he needed his share of forgiveness," what emerged in balance was the affirmation of a flawed but worthy human life.

What a great source of personal meaning it was for me that day, and many others, to speak the truth, validate the goodness in a particular life on this earth, and thereby bring a measure of closure and comfort to his family and friends.

The One who is the ultimate source of the way we are intended to live makes known to us the kinds of deeds that constitute a meaningful life. Martin Buber, from whom I have learned so much, reminds us that God does not speak to us in a deep baritone voice from Heaven, but through the events in our lives. Those events reveal our task if we are attentive. Emanuel Levinas, another Jewish thinker of the twentieth century, said that the closest we come to experiencing God's presence and call is in the needy human face that confronts us and becomes the medium through which we are summoned to our life tasks.

In his *Autobiographical Fragments*, Buber describes a transformative moment in his life that has had a decisive impact on my own personal counseling. A young man came to see him shortly after Buber had spent a morning of what he describes as "religious enthusiasm." Apparently, Buber was still in that higher spiritual realm and was not fully present to his visitor.

> I conversed openly with him, only I omitted to guess the questions he did not put. Later, not long after, I learned from one of the young man's friends…the essential content of those questions. I learned that he had come to me not casually, but bourn by destiny, not for a chat, but for a decision…What do we expect when we are in despair and yet go to a man, surely a presence by means of which we are told that nevertheless, there is meaning.[4]

Buber learned that the young man took his own life. For Buber this was life transforming: "Since then," he writes, "I possess nothing but the everyday from which I am never taken. The mystery is no longer disclosed, it has escaped or it has made its dwelling here where everything happens as it happens. I know no fullness but each mortal hour's fullness of claim and responsibility."[5]

I read those words while still in seminary and tried to restore them to mind and heart whenever I was asked to counsel with a person in need. So often, I have found myself looking at the face and listening for the real, at times unasked, question. The key is to realize that I may be dealing with a crisis of meaning, and in some instances, a human life may be at stake.

Perhaps, I am now closer to an answer for "Why the Rabbinate?" In a sense, I did not really choose; I was called. It was my destiny. That is why, from this vantage point, I cannot even imagine myself not being a rabbi. But I believe I know why I have found fulfillment in this calling. After forty years, I understand that the search for meaning amidst the frailty and uncertainty is what I am called to help people with, and in striving to do so I have discovered the deepest meaning in my life.

Why Reform Judaism?

Once I was committed to entering seminary, the question remained: Which one? The Orthodox seminary was never an option. My pattern of ritual observance was far removed from Orthodoxy. Moreover, for all its wonderful programs and the persons of quality I came to know and admire there, Camp Massad's modern Orthodoxy did not resonate with me.

From my earliest encounter with biblical and rabbinic texts, I was more drawn to its narratives (Agada) than to its formulation of Jewish law (Halacha). I realized the importance of formulating the ritual norms of behavior that were intended to govern the life of a faithful Jew, but I was always more inclined to probe questions of ethical responsibility than ritual propriety. I was always more interested in the narratives that dealt with the nature of the human creature (are we inherently good or evil) or that probe the mystery of undeserved suffering, than with those which defined in detail what behaviors violated the commandment to rest on the Sabbath. By the time I was to choose a seminary, I realized that my pattern of ritual observance was not likely to change radically.

By temperament and belief, I would find a seminary that did not expect me to conform to dietary and Sabbath restrictions that were not part of my current observance more compatible. More important, I was not prepared to cede to any group of rabbis, past or present, the absolute authority to define in detail my religious obligations. I needed more personal autonomy. I needed my rabbinic mentors to be more "guide than governor" of my Jewish life.

Also by temperament and belief, I would find a seminary that viewed sacred texts as human responses to God's presence in the prophet or sage's life, rather than a literal transcription of divine dictation, more compatible. In other words, there is a human element not only in the rabbi's interpretation of the text but also in the text itself.

Still another factor that impelled me to choose a Reform seminary was its attitude toward change in religious life. Classic Judaism at its best asked and addressed this question: How can we fulfill our people's covenant with God under the conditions of this time and place? When the Jerusalem Temple was destroyed by the Romans in the year 70 CE, Jews could no longer worship by bringing animals for sacrifice to the Temple. In a bold rabbinic response, the people were informed that, henceforth, offering prayers in synagogues wherever Jews lived was the equivalent of the sacrificial cult in the Temple. Indeed, many scholars regard this development as the time when the institution of the synagogue came into its own.

This was a radical rabbinic response to a very different set of circumstances in Jewish life. Unfortunately, such capacity for change was not present in the established Orthodox rabbinate in the nineteenth century when Reform Judaism was born. When Western European Jews experienced new opportunities to participate in the world outside the ghetto, Jews could now observe an aesthetic of worship that differed from their own. Jewish communities had always been influenced by the world around them and not always in a negative way. Thus, as historian Michael Meyer notes,

> Some Jews visited churches and found the service with its aesthetically pleasing music and edifying sermon to be more uplifting than the singsong of the traditional synagogue cantor and his two musical assistants.
>
> They were especially impressed by the decorum and apparent rapt attention of the congregation, while in the synagogues, by contrast, discussion of business matters often provided release from the tedious liturgy understood in its totality by few of the worshipers.[6]

These visitors noticed that men and women worshipped together and that many of the prayers were translated into the German vernacular.

The established rabbinate felt that Judaism was threatened by such exposure to a new, altered manner of worship.

Those rabbis responded by interpreting Jewish law even more restrictively and declaring any change in worship or dress as a forbidden imitation of the Christian world. This defensiveness only accelerated the emergence and growth of Reform Judaism. In this sense, the Reform movement actually reaffirmed the classic notion that new conditions may require changes in Jewish life.

Clearly, for the above reasons, I did not choose an Orthodox seminary, but why did I not attend the seminary which trained rabbis for the Conservative movement? This movement arose first in Europe and then in the United States as a reaction to what was regarded as Reform's overly extreme posture. Actually, I became familiar with Conservative congregations both in Philadelphia and during my years in Boston when I taught in the religious school of a Conservative synagogue. I did consider this option; so why the Hebrew Union College? The Conservative seminary was more concerned with maintaining and enforcing a certain standard of observance, dietary laws and Sabbath observance, etc., among its students. I needed a freer opportunity to form, or reform, my own patterns of observance.

Then too, I had the impression that while the average Conservative Jew did not differ considerably from the average Reform Jew in his or her level of personal ritual observance, there was more of an expectation in the Conservative movement that the rabbi be a surrogate observant Jew. The people might criticize the rabbi's level of dietary observance or Sabbath restrictions without feeling it incumbent on them to adopt that stricter level of observance. I was not willing to be my people's surrogate ritually observant Jew.

Choosing the Hebrew Union College

In any case, those considerations drew me to the Hebrew Union College (HUC), the Reform seminary in Cincinnati, Ohio. I remember the late August day in 1952 when I boarded a Pullman train (for the first time) to make the overnight trip to the "Queen City." I remember being impressed with the architectural splendor of the city's main railroad terminal and the splendid murals that adorned its walls. The cab driver explained that Cincinnati was built on seven hills, and the bridge over the Ohio River separated the city from the Kentucky border. From virtually the first hour I spent in the lounge of the dormitory and met some of my classmates, some senior students and a number of faculty members, I felt at home.

Our living conditions then were quite different from the prevailing situation today. Then, virtually all students lived in the dormitory. Most were unmarried. Lunch and dinner were served by uniformed waiters. We had daily room service to make the beds, clean the rooms and an in-house laundry. Today virtually all students are married or must make their own housing arrangements. Only a lunch buffet is provided on campus.

There is much to be said for the absence of a dormitory in the present paradigm of seminary life. Living in a dormitory for postgraduate study is not conducive to nourishing relationships, especially if one has lived in a dormitory during one's college days. To be sure, there were more close friendships and group study for exams in those days, but there are also more cliques and a display of the darker side of our human nature when we live in close quarters. Daily and Sabbath chapel services were not obligatory and generally they were not well attended. The conduct of the service rotated among the students. I tried to attend those services regularly in the hope of nourishing my own spirit, but also keeping in mind that someday I would encourage a high level of attendance among my congregants. It struck me as inauthentic for future rabbis who had signed on to organized Jewish life to be daily—and sometimes even Sabbath—absentists, or to attend services only when they were on the *bimah* (pulpit) leading them.

Some of our professors were both learned and persons of faith; others taught Judaism as objects of scholarly study without any personal commitment to Judaism as a way of life. The most egregious instance of scholarship removed from such commitments was a class in the Book of Job taught by a Semitics scholar who focused exclusively on the Book's linguistic parallels with other ancient Semitic texts!

My more memorable teachers at our seminary were those whose depth of knowledge was matched by a passionate love of our heritage. Dr. Sheldon Blank taught the Hebrew prophets. Ordinarily a soft spoken, mild mannered man, Dr. Blank was transformed by his teaching of Jeremiah's confessions. He seemed, then, to reincarnate the prophet's anger and self-pity.

Jeremiah accuses God of being "like waters that cannot be relied on" (Jeremiah 15:18). For speaking God's truth to the people, Jeremiah is reviled and persecuted. Through his anguished inner prayer life, the prophet discovers that suffering may also be the price of speaking and doing the right thing! In the depths of his soul, Jeremiah received God's response to his protest: "Let them come to you, not you to them." (Jeremiah 15:19) The prophet is told not to surrender his mission and join his detractors, but to live in the hope that ultimately his detractors will come to acknowledge the truth of his words and his cause. He is told to live in the hope that God will ultimately vindicate the cause to which he has dedicated his life. I can still see and almost hear Dr. Blank embodying the words and the life of Jeremiah.

From immersing myself in the world of the prophets, I realized that they were, for the most part, absolutists and loners. We were blessed by the legacy of the prophets but we also needed priests—and rabbis—who, at their best, incorporate some prophetic qualities. The rabbi needs to be in touch with his own darker side and to have a greater tolerance for ambiguity than the prophet. A rabbi must strive to demonstrate that his teaching is reflected in his way of living, but the rabbi is also best when perceiving himself as a fellow struggler and lover of the people whom he encourages to enhance the quality of their lives. While I greatly admired the prophets and felt privileged to study their legacy, I felt more at home in the world of the rabbis.

To be sure, the early Reformers placed front and center the impassioned social justice message of the prophets, and reacted against the Orthodox rabbinate's rigid preoccupation with ritual propriety. However, their Reform heirs would, in time, discover that the challenge of building a structure of Jewish loyalty across the generations would require some discipline of ritual acts. This was part of the enduring contribution of rabbinic Judaism. The rabbis, deeply imbedded in their communities, also spoke to the Jewish soul struggling to make sacred choices amidst the demands and moral ambiguities of daily life.

Rabbi Eugene Mihaly was probably my most memorable teacher of rabbinic literature and of classic Jewish liturgy, which was essentially composed by the rabbis. Mihaly's introductory course to Talmud was an inspired portrayal of the tension between Agada and Halacha. Reared as an Orthodox Jew, after some years, as a practicing Orthodox rabbi, Eugene Mihaly decided to attend our seminary and become part of our Reform movement. He combined the knowledge garnered after many hours rigorously going over texts with a liberal understanding and interpretation of those texts.

I remember most vividly Mihaly's response to the question: Why does the central prayer (the Amida) during the week, contain so many more petitionary prayers than the Sabbath Amida? Because on the Sabbath we are invited to experience a foretaste of the Messianic Age. Petitionary prayer reminds us of our neediness and all that we lack. Prayers of praise and thanksgiving express appreciation for what we have. Thus, the classic Sabbath liturgy is an intimation of the plenitude, tranquility and fulfillment of Messianic time.

Studying Jewish history with Professor Ellis Rivkin was another richly stimulating intellectual experience. He focused on the challenges that each particular Jewish community needed to address, and he perceptively analyzed the struggle for power between groups in each historical era. Far from constructing an idealized portrait of the Jewish experience, he placed our history in the context of the human capacity for both nobility and brutishness.

I particularly appreciated his insightful discussion of the struggle between the Saducees who championed the biblical text as a validation of their priestly prerogative, and the Pharisees, who championed the concept of a two-fold Torah, a written and an oral revelation that served to justify the leadership claims and teaching of this emerging rabbi class. Rivkin also helped me appreciate the Pharisees' emphasis on personal piety and inwardness rather than total preoccupation with the sacrificial cult. In these terms, Dr. Rivkin explained the great influence of the Pharisees on the emerging Christian community.

As one who stressed the economic determinants of history, Rivkin told us that host societies were friendly to their Jewish inhabitants while they were in a state of economic expansion. When the economic stability of a society was endangered, anti-Jewish scapegoating was much more likely. That theoretical framework could be applied to ancient and very modern societies as well.

Professor Jacob Marcus was known affectionately by many students as "Jake." He began as an historian of the European Jewish experience. In a post-holocaust world, he turned his focus on American Jewish history and became the dean of this relatively young scholarly field. Though not oblivious to the presence of anti-Semitism in America, Dr. Marcus stressed American exceptionalism and saw this country as potentially friendlier to Jewish flourishing than any in history.

Rabbi Leo Baeck spent a few years residing in an apartment on the first floor of our dormitory. Long before, he had become a Jewish person of international renown, widely acclaimed not only for his writings on Judaism but also for his heroic life. Rabbi Baeck was the leader of the Jewish community in Germany before and during the Hitler era. Although presented with ample invitations to leave Germany, he spurned all such offers in order to remain with his people, a decision that led to his internment in the Theresienstadt concentration camp. There, he continued to give lectures on

Judaism and encouraged his kinsmen to find strength and purpose even in their present circumstances. During those years he wrote notes on scraps of paper, which, after the war, became the basis for his book titled, *This People Israel*. After the war, Rabbi Baeck, the Holocaust survivor, lived in London until President Glueck induced him to become a scholar in residence at our Reform seminary's Cincinnati campus.

Virtually every morning, this tall, stooped, figure could be seen walking up and down Clifton Avenue for his daily exercise. I chose to take the one seminar he led in Rabbinic Interpretations of Scripture (Midrash). There were only five in his class. His English was so heavily filtered through his German accent that he was intelligible only intermittently. Whatever benefit I derived from the sessions, and there was much, came not from their content, but from the essence of the man.

I felt the sad irony in this heroic and distinguished rabbi teaching such an undersubscribed class, especially since the seminar was held during what were the last years of Baeck's life. In retrospect, I believe the sparse attendance was attributable to more than Rabbi Baeck's very thick German accent. In the 1950s, the Holocaust was still too fresh and overwhelming to be directly and fully confronted. History reveals that only in the sixties with the Eichmann trial and the publication of Elie Wiesel's poignant, semi-autographical novels, did the American Jewish community begin to come to grips with the Holocaust and its deniers.

Teaching in Local Religious Schools
We received practical experience as future rabbis by teaching in the local Reform religious schools. A Sunday school

curriculum in the 1950s was also excessively sparing in its treatment of the Nazi effort to destroy our people. Once, in response to a question from a member of my eighth-grade class, I spoke of the estimated six million Jews who were killed by the Nazis because they were Jews. At least one student mentioned my extended remarks to her parents.

The child's mother called the director of the religious school to complain: "We want our children to be proud and happy as Jews. Such emphasis on the suffering of our people and the death of millions because they were Jewish will not inspire them to cherish their Jewish identity." In reporting the conversation to me, the director sided with the mother. I was counseled to be more circumspect in the future.

Teaching a group of eighth graders on Sunday morning was, to say the least, a challenging experience. I don't recall the curriculum assigned for that year, but I got the impression that the students found little connection between the questions addressed and those that mattered to them as budding adolescents.

Maintaining discipline was a continuing hassle. The situation reached crisis proportions one Sunday. After treating myself to a quick lunch of lethally caloric but delicious hamburger and french fries at the Big Boy restaurant, I returned to my room on the fourth floor of the dormitory and prepared for a much needed nap.

In those days we had one public phone for each floor. Somehow my students had gotten the number to the phone on our floor. No sooner had I fallen asleep, when a fellow student from down the hall shouted that there was a call for me. When I picked up the phone I heard giggling and a quick click of the receiver to end the call. This was repeated once, giving me just enough time to return to bed and again to be summoned from it. I was both furious and a little amused. Rage trumped my capacity for amusement.

The next Sunday I mentioned that a practical joke had kept me from some much needed rest that previous Sunday afternoon. I acknowledged that I, too, might have found it humorous if it were not at my expense. I didn't ask for the guilty ones to reveal their identity, but calmly declared that any repetition of such actions would result in serious consequences.

Fortunately, I was not tested the next or subsequent Sundays. More fortunate still, this painful experience triggered reappraisal of the curriculum. I realized that the discipline problem was not only a function of my failure to establish clear boundaries at the first session, but the consequence of teaching a curriculum that did not address issues to which the students could easily relate.

After acknowledging that the eighth grade was the most difficult age group, the principal empowered me to pilot a new curriculum on Jewish ethics. Each week, we discussed a different issue. I vividly recall the first week we considered, "Is it ever right not to tell the truth?" Students were presented with cases they could recognize and relate to and they were given some texts from the Bible and Talmudic literature that dealt with the issue of truth.

As I recall, one case involved a teenager who was going to a big school dance. This girl was very unsure of herself. She had a weight problem and lacked self-confidence. The case was addressed to the students. You are standing with her at the refreshment counter and she asks you what you think of her dress. As it happens, you don't think the dress is pretty or stylish, especially for her. How then, should you answer?

The rabbinic text that we included affirmed the importance of telling the truth, but one of the rabbis actually deals with a similar question and asks: "Can you declare a bride to be beautiful if you don't really think she is?" The traditional answer by the school of Rabbi Shammai was, "You tell it like it is." However, the answer of the school of Rabbi Hillel was that, "You don't tell her that, because there is a principle of not telling the whole truth for the sake of peace or kindness." In any case, that was the way the course went, with a combination of rabbinic texts and contemporary cases. Eventually, this pilot led to a text co-authored with a classmate that dealt with ethical issues for the intermediate grades. The level of animated discussion in my class increased considerably henceforth and discipline issues virtually disappeared.

Serving Small Congregations

A more extensive opportunity to practice the rabbinic role was provided by small congregations that could not afford to support a full-time rabbi. These congregations depended on student rabbis from our seminary. My assignment was in Jackson, Tennessee.

Every other week, on a Friday morning, I drove from Cincinnati to the airport in Kentucky (then an hour and a half drive). I then flew to Memphis, took a cab to the downtown bus terminal, and waited for a bus to Jackson, which took close to two hours and seemed to stop at every farmhouse.

I would arrive late in the afternoon, just in time to shower and dress for Sabbath dinner at one of the congregants' homes. I was fatigued before I even got started with my responsibilities. After dinner, we would drive to a small but charming synagogue where I conducted the service, gave the sermon, mingled with the congregation at the reception (Oneg Shabbat) and then collapsed in exhaustion as soon as I returned to my hotel. The next morning I visited my congregants in their shops or offices, socialized with a particular family on Saturday night, conducted a religious school class on Sunday morning, and took a bus and a plane back to Cincinnati that Sunday afternoon.

Those biweekly trips would not have been tolerable or sustainable without the magic pill called Dramamine®. Early on I began taking two Dramamine® pills about twenty minutes before boarding the bus from Memphis to Jackson. After a sound sleep along the way, I arrived in Jackson refreshed, hungry and energized for my Sabbath Eve duties.

During that year, I bonded with many of my congregants and gained much valuable testing of my capacity to be an effective and happy rabbi. Among the congregants were two families who owned small department stores downtown, the Kisbers and the Rosenblooms. Competing in business led these families to develop a classic and robust family feud. Speaking with one of the Kisbers, by then a young man who could laugh at all that competitiveness, I was told of an experience at a football game. Apparently one of the Christian boys felt he was tackled too roughly by the Kisber boy. Spontaneously, the Christian lad shouted, "You're a Christ killer!" Without missing a beat, the Kisber boy remembered responding, "It wasn't us, it was the Rosenblooms!" Though humorous in the telling at that time, it was, of course, fraught with solemn reminders of anti-Semitism.

Not yet ordained, I would not be asked to officiate at a wedding, but I did teach and preside at a number of bar mitzvahs and I was called upon to officiate at my first funeral. A family who lived about fifty miles outside of Jackson was driving their child and two others to Sunday school, when somehow a car door opened and one of the children hurtled to his death. I felt so inadequate and sought counsel from a number of rabbis who taught at our seminary. What I learned from them was that the tragic dimension of a life imposes an insuperable challenge to any rabbi seeking to be a defender of the faith. I also learned that at the very time faith was most difficult to affirm, it was also most desperately needed. I learned that in the freshness of such tragedy, families aren't in need of our theology as much as they need our caring presence, our listening ear and our responsive heart.

During the one High Holiday service I conducted, the Rosenblooms had a cousin who was working as a reporter for *The Nashville Tennessean.* He came to spend the holiday with his family. We met and were drawn into some meaningful conversations. His name was David Halberstam. David was destined to be a star foreign correspondent for the New York Times. He covered the war in Vietnam, wrote a Pulitzer Prize book titled, *The Best and the Brightest* and went on to sustain a reputation as one of our country's finest pundits.

David acknowledged that his Judaism was woefully underdeveloped and added that if I were his rabbi, he would be inclined to consider Judaism more seriously. He meant it as a compliment, but while we exchanged a few notes in subsequent years and he visited us during one of his assignments in Chicago, our acquaintance never ripened into a sustained friendship.

CHAPTER 3 ❖ WHY THE RABBINATE?

A Commitment to Further Study

The years at Hebrew Union College confirmed my decision to become a Reform rabbi. Some friendships with students and faculty were deepened over the years. Over those years, I had also significantly increased my understanding and appreciation of the heritage I would be privileged to teach. Those years at seminary also made me painfully aware of all those texts I had not studied. In that sense, my years at Hebrew Union College were both empowering and humbling.

At the beginning of my senior year at seminary, the provost called me into his office and encouraged me to apply for a Ph.D. program at any academic center. Hebrew Union College would grant me a fellowship that would cover my tuition and expenses with the condition that after I received my Ph.D. degree, I would return to teach at the seminary. The response was easy. Having made the decision to become a rabbi, I knew that I wanted to be primarily a congregational rabbi; but if possible, I would do some college teaching. After all those years in a formal school setting, I needed a change. As it turned out, my next two years as a chaplain at Maxwell Air Force Base would offer a very special kind of change.

While I had no intention of becoming a scholar in the full sense of that word, I did intend to be a learned rabbi. Therefore, I pledged to myself that I would continue to engage in the discipline of Jewish study. Years later, on that day when I offered the address titled "The Soul of the Rav," I made reference to the importance of studying in order to fulfill the meaning of the term "Rav."

> There are moments of study when thoughts leaping into
> my mind, thoughts filtered through the Torah text, the

rabbinic commentaries, and my own sensibilities, have the feel of God's revealing presence. Those are the most authentic moments of study. We are neither prophets nor the daughters or sons of prophets, but we are rabbis and the daughters and sons of rabbis and there are moments when our study casts us as instruments, as messengers of the One whose teaching is revealed to us and through us…I am drawn more to the study of Agada than Halacha, but I can fully ignore neither. If I am away from the texts too long, I am assaulted by pangs of inauthenticity. I feel some withdrawal symptoms. A return to primary and secondary texts is like a fix. It is therapeutic. One must fight for those quiet times, early in the morning before the phone rings, or late at night. Without such extended periods for study I would feel drained, empty. The soul of the Rav is nurtured by study. If we are fortunate, we have all savored those moments of discovery and insight, the joy of deriving a new thought, the sensuous excitement of feeling gripped by a truth that comes from our past and addresses our present. The Rav must study.[7]

Wisely, our seminary provided an alternate earned doctoral degree, DHL (Doctor of Hebrew Letters), that did not include an extended residence requirement. As a chaplain at Maxwell, my work load was so light that I could put in the requisite hours at the office and still devote at least two or three hours each day to study as part of the program leading to a DHL. I borrowed the Jewish texts I needed from the HUC library. They were sent to me promptly from Cincinnati, and I ended my tour of duty with much progress toward that degree.

The requirements included reading and being tested on a significant body of work by two thinkers—writers in different fields. For one of my bodies of text, I chose the field of Modern Hebrew Literature with Professor Ezra Spicehandler as my advisor. He encouraged me to focus on the short stories and novellas of Scholem Abramovich (1836-1917) who wrote satirical pieces about life in the Jewish shtetls in Czarist Russia. He wrote under the pen name, Mendele Mocher S'Forim (Mendele, the Book Seller). I found this literature very accessible. Like my father and grandfather, Mendele was a Haskalah Jew who rejected orthodoxy and at first the Yiddish language for Hebrew. Beneath his trenchant satire there remained a strong love and compassion for his characters.

Although I focused on Mendele's Hebrew writings, he later re-embraced Yiddish as the language in which he could reach the vast majority of his eager readers. Mendele laid the ground work for the master of that literary genre who wrote under the pen name, Scholem Aleichem (Peace Be Unto You), whose mythical town of Kasrilevke and Tevya, the dairy man, would eventually reach millions as the Broadway smash musical, *Fiddler On The Roof*. Both authors had been favorites of my father, so this choice for study enabled me to retrace some of the stories my father told me.

My second field of study brought me to the writings of Martin Buber, many of whose books in German were already translated into English. I had been introduced to Buber's classic, *I-Thou* during those bull sessions at Harvard with the Hillel rabbi, Morris Zigmond. By immersing myself so deeply in Buber's thought, Buber became a formative influence on my personal religious thinking. My advisor was Professor

Eugene Mihaly, who later would become a friend and a neighbor across the lake during our summers in Charlevoix.

My major was rabbinic theology and my focus was on the relationship between God and the Jewish people. Specifically, this was the question I probed: Was the covenant between God and Israel essentially a limited contractual relationship which depended for its initiation solely on Israel's merit, and for its sustainability on the people's fulfillment of God's commandments? Or was this divine-human relationship initiated and sustained essentially by God's unconditional love?

My formulation of the questions was based on Harvard sociologist Talcott Parson's distinction between a more limited relationship sustained by each party's rigorous adherence to mutually agreed upon conditions and a more full bodied, organic relationship grounded in kinship and unconditional love.

In my dissertation, I argued that while some narratives emphasize the strict conditionality of the covenant between God and Israel, and others stress its unconditionality, the overall thrust of rabbinic literature reveals an abiding and creative tension between conditionality and unconditionality. The divine parent, not unlike the effective human parent, exhibits the abiding tension between setting boundaries and unconditional acceptance or between "tough love" and unconditional love.

My study claims that this abiding tension is exquisitely reflected in Talmudic narratives. Moreover, the rabbinic understanding of God's relationship with Israel is my paradigm for understanding God's relationship to humanity.

Chapter 4
AN UNEXPECTED BEGINNING TO MY LIFE AS A RABBI

THE YEAR OF ORDINATION, 1956, WAS six years after the Korean War and in the midst of the Cold War. While clergy were not subject to the draft, the leaders of the Reform movement instituted a "voluntary draft," self-imposed to fill the gap between those rabbis who chose to enter the military chaplaincy as a career and the Armed Forces' need for more of us.

All newly ordained rabbis were thus subject to a lottery. Those who picked a "losing number" were required to spend the next two years in the Army, Navy or Air Force chaplaincy. At first I was disappointed to learn that my civilian rabbinate would be deferred. I quickly recovered, however, from considering myself a loser, to seeing my fate as a potentially valuable opportunity to serve.

I entered the Air Force as a commissioned officer (First Lieutenant) and discovered the State of Texas for the first time. We did our basic training as Air Force chaplains at Lackland Air Force Base in San Antonio. There were twenty-nine clergy in our class. We were Orthodox, Conservative or reform Rabbis, Roman Catholic priests, Greek Orthodox, Episcopalians, Lutherans, Baptists and even Christian Scientist practitioners.

Living with anybody in unairconditioned quarters in August, in Texas, surely tested our tolerance. I would wake up at 4:00 a.m. in a tremendous sweat. Keeping our uniforms in proper military shape was virtually impossible. Fortunately, our shared discomfort resulted, not in testiness toward each other, but in good-humored jesting about our fate. One of our greatest distractions was the TV set in our lounge. Our favorite show was a series called *Sergeant Bilko*.

We may have held diverse views of the messiah, but we all agreed that the air-conditioned lecture room we met in each day was a redemptive experience. Training in military discipline included marching in formation to and from class, led by one of our own. The Catholic priest who led us one day mistakenly yelled, "Left turn," and we walked right into a group of officer candidates who tried valiantly to salute us, even as they struggled, unsuccessfully, to contain their laughter. Generally, our basic training was physically much less rigorous than the non-clergy trainees, except for the day we were required to walk up a seemingly endless outdoor staircase to a ledge shaped like a diving board. In turn, each of us was harnessed to a parachute and commanded to walk to the edge of the ledge and jump. After a brief sense of free fall, the parachute would automatically connect us to a rope that we used to chin ourselves over a shallow ravine.

The chaplain who preceded me made the mistake of looking down and hesitating as he yelled, "I can't do it, Captain." With ill-concealed scorn Captain Secor removed his harness and motioned him to climb down the other staircase. I was next. As the Captain harnessed me, I thought, "They wouldn't subject a bunch of clergy to this exercise unless they regarded it as pretty safe." With that bracing thought, I didn't look down or hesitate, but just jumped. Much to my satisfaction, I had no trouble chinning over the ravine and landing safely.

Each of us shared a room in our quarters with another member of the chaplaincy class. My roommate was a Christian Science practitioner. I cannot say we got to really know each other. Our conversation was limited to the kind of small talk designed to sustain civility. When we were sent to the base hospital to receive our required vaccinations and shots, my roommate took them, not because he believed in their efficacy, but because they were required. The tetanus shot left me with a sore arm. Seeing that my roommate was totally unaffected, I reserved my arm rubbing for the privacy of the bathroom. Damned if I would concede Christian Science's superiority in natural pain control!

The Visit of the Luftwaffe Pilots

The 1950s were part of an era when interfaith relations among clergy were limited to an exchange of civilities. That would change in subsequent decades (which I will discuss later), but in retrospect, this experience of marching to and from class, laughing at *Sergeant Bilko* episodes and living this basic training together did virtually compel us to regard each other in human terms that transcended our normal religious differences.

One of the most memorable experiences during those months in chaplaincy school was the day in class when Captain Secor introduced to us a visiting delegation of German Luftwaffe pilots. Their visit to American air bases was sponsored by the State Department. The visit took place just a decade after the end of World War II.

I don't recall the remarks that one of the Luftwaffe officers was invited to make, but I vividly recall a coffee break after they had left. We were socializing and snacking in an area adjacent to our classroom. Suddenly Captain Secor approached me and asked, "Well Chaplain, what did you think of our visitors?" I replied, "Captain I couldn't help wondering where they were and what they were doing during the war, what they knew about the death camps and Hitler's plans to kill all the Jews in Europe." Captain Secor interjected, "Oh, Karff, I can understand that, being Jewish, you would think that way, but for me they were flying their planes, doing their thing, and we were flying our planes, doing ours." It was as simple as that! Captain Secor's response left me sullen and speechless. I retreated silently from the scene.

When I pondered that conversation and referred to it even years later, I would not convict Captain Secor of anti-Semitism. As members of a particular religious or ethnic group we each have certain events that are part of our "inner history." For us Jews the exodus from Egypt has that status. Each Passover we are called to imagine that it is we who are enslaved and it is we whom God freed from Egyptian bondage. Now, we were not slaves in Egypt, but as long as our peoples' oppression in Egypt remains part of our inner history—as long as we recall it as if this drama were happening to us personally, we may find it more possible to empathize with those who are currently not yet free. So, we read in the Torah more than a few times, "You shall not oppress the stranger. You know the heart of the stranger for you were strangers in the land of Egypt." (Exodus 23:9)

For many Jews, to this day the Holocaust remains part of our inner history—even as it was not part of Captain Secor's inner history. A sobering question which should not be glibly dismissed: for those of us who were alive in those days, even if we were not directly affected, the Holocaust remains part of our inner history. But will the next generation in America today be able to regard it as such?

Even more sobering is the need to recognize the limits of our capacity to experience the trials of another group as part of our inner history. Ten years after that experience with the Luftwaffe pilots and Captain Secor's response, I attended a meeting of local clergy in Chicago, who identified with the goals of the Civil Rights movement.

At one point in our meeting the one black man in our local clergy group asked to be recognized. He went to the blackboard and wrote a particular date. He asked us if we knew what happened on that date. None of us could respond affirmatively. With passionate intensity our black colleague explained, "That was the date those five little black girls were killed when their church was bombed in Birmingham—and the world went on as if nothing had happened." I recalled the event and remembered being horrified by its senseless cruelty, but that event was not really part of my inner history. I did not experience it and respond to it as if it had happened to me and my people.

I would re-encounter my Holocaust inner history in 1970. By then I was in the Air Force chaplain reserves. As such, I received an invitation from the Chief of Chaplain's Office to conduct a religious retreat for American Jewish personnel in the U.S. Armed Forces stationed in Germany.

During that first trip to Germany, we met in the Bavarian Alps at Berchtesgarden, a scene as beautiful as it is depicted in the movie *The Sound of Music*. Berchtesgarden had once been the site of Adolph Hitler's summer retreat, atop what was called the Eagle's Nest. Our group met on the plain below in reconditioned quarters that were now under the control of the United States Armed Forces, but within the lodge that housed Hitler's general staff when they visited him. In this absolutely beautiful natural setting Hitler and his henchmen plotted "the Final Solution" to the Jewish problem.

You can imagine the feelings of our group of Jewish soldiers and their dependents stationed in Germany. One morning we gathered for a brief outdoor service. We made a large circle. At one point, I held the small Torah scroll provided me by the United States government and passed the scroll around so each person could hold it and pass it on. When the Torah was returned to me, I held it high and led the group first in the classic Shma prayer, the Jewish watch word of our faith: "Hear Oh Israel, Adonai is our

God, Adonai alone," which is responded to with the words, "Praised be Adonai's name whose glorious kingdom is for ever and ever." Realizing where we stood, I looked around and saw not a single dry eye among the members of our group. What a very sacred moment for all of us. We concluded our little service by singing the old Jewish folk song, "Am Yisrael Chai, The People Israel Still Lives!"

Over the years, periodically I would be asked to explain the meaning of the "Hear O Israel" prayer and the prescribed response that always followed its recitation. A compelling answer is embodied in this Talmudic narrative: when the patriarch Jacob, his name now Israel, was an old man who knew his remaining days were few, he assembled his children and spoke these words:

> Many years ago my grandfather, Abraham, pledged his faithfulness to God. Before he died, my grandfather passed the covenant to my father, Isaac, who passed it to me. Now, I want to pass the covenant to you, and so, I ask, "After I die, will you remain faithful to it?" The sons replied, "Shma Yisrael—Hear o Israel, Adonai is our God, Adonai alone!" Whereupon Jacob-Israel replied, "If you will remain faithful, then, 'Praised be the name of God whose glorious kingdom is forever and ever.'"[8]

When we recite these pages, we may remember our sacred roots and reaffirm our loyalty to God's covenant with Israel. The recitation of that prayer at the site where Hitler planned the total destruction of our people was very poignant for all of us survivors.

Life After Chaplaincy School

My first assignment as chaplain brought me to Maxwell Air Force Base in Montgomery, Alabama. I had a small apartment in the Bachelor Officer's Quarters, situated across the street from a rather lavish Officer's Club. Maxwell also boasted two eighteen-hole golf courses. Because it was the site of Air University, and some sixty full colonels were enrolled in the Air War College, Maxwell also contained the staff and command school for captains and majors, which further swelled our officer contingent. My principal duties consisted of keeping regular office hours at the base chapel together with Catholic, Baptist and Episcopal chaplains. On Friday nights, I would hold regular Sabbath services followed by an Oneg Shabbat reception with goodies provided by the local office of the Jewish Welfare Board.

Prior to my assignment there, the Reform rabbi in Montgomery served as auxiliary Jewish chaplain. Rabbi Eugene Blachshleger was determined to hate me before we ever met, and for good reason. Thanks to me, he lost a nice stipend from the U.S. government which supplemented the meager salary at his small congregation. When I had been in Montgomery for a month and a half and had still not met Rabbi Blachshleger, I called and asked if I could drop by. The voice on the other end of the line was curt and cold, but being a gentleman, he could not easily refuse to see me.

We met and before the end of that first encounter, Gene regarded me no longer as a supplanter, but as a potential soul mate; and, in time, he embraced me as the son he and wife, Bernice, never had. Rabbi Blachshleger invited me to preach at his synagogue during the High Holy Days and introduced me to congregants closer to my own age.

CHAPTER 4 ❖ AN UNEXPECTED BEGINNING TO MY LIFE AS A RABBI

Throughout his ministry Gene wrestled with the thin line that separated his desire to be one of the guys—an off-color-joke-telling friend to his congregants—from his desire to be respected as their spiritual leader. I periodically helped him accept himself as he was, not only because I could discern in him neither the will nor the desire to change, but because he was genuinely loved by his people for being present in their times of need and sharing their pain.

We all need some external validation from those whom we respect. Although I was very different from Gene in temperament and aspiration, I could give Gene that validation. I admired his honesty, his humility, his steadfast love and respect for Bernice and his desire to serve his people and uphold the good name of the Jewish community in his town of Montgomery.

Over the years, my friendship with Gene and Bernice was sustained and deepened. When his congregation dedicated a new sanctuary, Rabbi Blachshleger invited me to participate in the dedication. At my wedding, Gene Blachshleger co-officiated with Joan's rabbi. When Gene died, Bernice invited me to preside at Gene's funeral.

My year and a half in Montgomery coincided with the Civil Rights struggle. By the fall of 1957 when I arrived at Maxwell Air Force Base, Rosa Parks' refusal to go to the back of the bus, the ensuing bus boycott by the black community and the Supreme Court's ruling that outlawed bus segregation had all taken place. The remaining milestones in the South's part of the struggle would take place after I had left Montgomery.

My experiences in the heart of the American South led me to modify my stereotypical view of the region. I came to know persons who harbored the same negative view of enforced segregation as I, who read the same books and journals and who knew the country was living through a major social change that was needed and inevitable.

I was wrong in dismissing Southern Jewry as a bunch of rednecks. To be sure, some accepted segregated public restrooms, drinking fountains and restaurants as part of the natural order of things. More than a few were sympathetic to the Civil Rights cause but felt especially vulnerable to anti-Semitism and feared public words or acts which would result in reprisals against them and their families.

I have been spared such dilemmas. In my post-Montgomery years, I supported controversial issues both in Chicago and Houston, but I would never be exposed to the potential consequences for myself or for my family that faced Montgomery's Jews and all Civil Rights activists in Alabama in those days.

My year and a half as chaplain were the most undemanding and least strenuous in my working life. I kept regular hours at the chapel, but the Jewish population on base was very small. Those personnel who lived off base, tended to affiliate with the local congregations in town. In truth, Rabbi Blachshleger's contention that Maxwell didn't need a full time Jewish chaplain was absolutely correct.

Early on at Maxwell Air Force base I learned that rank has its privileges. Each morning, when I retrieved my car from the garage behind our building, I could leave by driving through either end of our garage alley and end up at the chapel. One morning I noticed workmen building a wall on one end of the alley. When I asked the workmen what this was all about, I was told that many officers use that alleyway as a shortcut to the golf course and the base commander decided to put an end to that thru traffic. I gave the matter no further thought, but much to my surprise, a week later I saw the same workmen tearing down the wall. Again, I asked for the reason and one replied: "The base commander didn't want this alley used as a shortcut to the golf course, but the commanding General uses it as a shortcut to the golf course." Yes, rank has its privileges. Was this what critics have meant when they complain that there is much waste in the defense budget?

I did experience the sense of being needed on those occasions when I was on night duty and responded to emergencies for all my colleagues. This provided more opportunity for meaningful counseling as a chaplain, rather than as a Jewish chaplain. Perhaps my most meaningful chaplaincy experience on the base was during a visit to the hospital one night. I was summoned by a physician to visit a Jewish airman in the psychiatric section. I was given no extensive background. The physician himself had not had an opportunity to do full testing and make a diagnosis. The airman seemed terribly troubled and restless, but did not communicate with anyone. He just stared into space, his body rigid, his facial affect troubling.

I visited with him that night, but might just as well have not been in the room. I was totally ignored. Any gesture and attempt to hold his hand was rejected. I left feeling very impotent—a total failure. The next day I felt compelled to return that evening on my own. For some reason, I decided to take along the little Torah scroll that is provided to each Jewish chaplain by the Jewish Welfare Board.

After encountering the same seemingly catatonic unresponsiveness, I placed the Torah scroll on the airman's chest, let go and recited the Sh'ma Israel prayer in Hebrew and English again and again. "*Sh'ma Yis'ra'eil Adonai Eloheinu Adonai echad.* Hear O'Israel, the Lord is our God, the Lord Alone."

At first no response, but by the fifteenth repetition, he held the Torah tightly to his chest, he sobbed aloud, and then silence, his hands now removed from the scroll. I could not bring him to talk or even to recite the Sh'ma with me. This occurred shortly before I was scheduled to leave the camp and the Air Force for civilian life. So I never saw him again, but his response to the Torah scroll and the Sh'ma prayer remained with me. It taught me that religious symbols may have some powerful effect on those who have at some time responded to them. I would live to experience much more moving demonstrations of that power in many of my future encounters with Jews in need.

Some months before that vignette at the hospital, I received what would be my most meaningful assignment during those years in active service as a chaplain. I was called to temporary duty (TDY) and given orders to conduct a Passover Seder in Goosebay, Labrador. In preparation for this experience I quickly looked up Labrador in an encyclopedia and recalled the following reference: "The coast of Labrador is bleak enough to blight any man's soul." During the winter months, the unprotected exposure of any portion of the human body to the elements for more than a few minutes could be hazardous to one's health—even one's life. For much of the year Goosebay is inaccessible, except by air. I hitched a ride on a B29 to an Air Force base in New Jersey and from there got a flight to Goosebay.

During my years in the Air Force, I often flew on B29s. We had jump seats and were equipped with parachutes. Why were those flights more unnerving to me than civilian flights

CHAPTER 4 · AN UNEXPECTED BEGINNING TO MY LIFE AS A RABBI

I undertook before and after my years as chaplain? While these planes were of World War II vintage, this was the 1950s; by aircraft standards, these planes were regarded neither as too old nor as unserviceable. Moreover, by purely rational standards, I was more protected against the contingencies of flight in a B29 than in a commercial aircraft. After all, I was armed with a parachute, and, if necessary, could exit the plane and drift toward the ground.

This conundrum was easily solved: in a Boeing commercial pane I am totally dependent on the pilot to get me to my destination safely. Here I have some personal responsibilities (which, with my extremely limited technical ability, could subject me to errors that were self-destructive). After all, I did have to properly pull the rip cord and glide to Earth. On those occasions when there is nothing really I can do to determine my safe flight, I am prepared to assume that the pilot would not be in that position if he were not competent and the plane not airworthy. At least that's the assumption I make, so I am more relaxed on the average commercial aircraft than I ever was on those B29s.

Incidentally, upon reaching the tarmac, after a safe landing, I am generally prone to recite part of the traditional Hebrew blessing for arriving safely at one's destination: "Praised be thou, oh Lord, who bestows kindnesses beyond our merits."

Now back to my mission in Goosebay. I learned some time later that my assignment was triggered by a call from a Colonel Abrams to the Chief of Air Force Chaplains in Washington, in which he insisted that there is no place on this Earth more in need of a Jewish chaplain at Passover than the remote and isolated Goosebay Air Base under his command. This base was part of General Curtis Lemay's

Strategic Air Command and, I learned, Colonel Abrams was one of "Lemay's Favorite Boys."

I stayed during much of Passover. Not only did I conduct one of the most personally meaningful Seders in my life, but also I was able to visit with each of the Jewish airmen and tutor the base commander's son for his upcoming bar mitzvah.

We received a shipment of matzo, gefilte fish, horseradish, and kosher almond and chocolate flavored macaroons, all flown in from New York, compliments of the Jewish Welfare Board. In addition, we were indebted to the mess sergeant on base whose roast lamb and chicken soup with matzo balls were outstanding. We also managed to assemble a lamb bone, some greens and horseradish for the traditional Seder plate.

In addition to the small number of Jewish officers and airmen, the base commander and his family attended the Seder. Most significant; however, was the welcome extended to a group of Jewish airmen who were stationed at the remote radar sites that ringed the Arctic Circle, which were situated not too far from the Soviet Union with which we were then engaged in a "Cold War." Those airmen who arrived on helicopters truly felt as if they were experiencing their own (temporary) deliverance from Egypt.

During that week, I felt deeply needed, useful and appreciated. Incidentally, our on-base congregants eagerly consumed all of the leftovers during the remaining days of the festival. Some of their opened containers needed to be refrigerated. No problem. We just placed all that needed refrigeration in a make-shift cabinet outdoors. I was glad to be in Labrador and not unhappy to return to a more friendly environment. As I recall, tours of duty for enlisted personnel lasted only a year before they were rotated out because of problems with alcohol addiction and depression that abounded when deployments were extended.

I cannot leave that chaplaincy period without some comment on our formal curriculum with our prime instructor. Much of what we learned had little relevance for a life outside the military world. At first I struggled to be attentive, but soon gave up the struggle.

The transition from struggling to be there to what Albert Camus calls being "absent even when I took up the most space," occurred after one particular session. One morning, our instructor was giving us a crash course on Marxist ideology in which he spoke of the conflict between "the protariot and the boorgazee (sic)." From that point on my spirit was elsewhere. As a consequence, I who had usually been a high academic achiever, graduated from Chaplaincy School ranking twenty-seventh out of twenty-nine in my class.

Rabbi Louis Mann, my predecessor at Chicago Sinai Congregation. The picture was taken in front of a bronze plaque/bust hung in honor of his distinguished ministry, on the day he installed me as Senior Rabbi of Sinai Congregation.

Chapter 5
ACTUALLY EXPERIENCING THE CONGREGATIONAL RABBINATE

DURING MY LAST FEW MONTHS AS A CHAPlain, the interviews began which would determine where I would spend my first years in the congregational rabbinate. I was invited to interview for the position of assistant rabbi at a number of congregations. In each of those visits I had the opportunity to meet and be considered by the senior rabbi and a group of lay leaders.

My goals were to be mentored by a seasoned, senior colleague, who loved his vocation, had much to teach me and could inspire my respect. I chose and was chosen by Rabbi Abraham J. Feldman and by the lay leaders of Congregation Beth Israel in West Hartford, Connecticut. Returning to New England, to an old established congregation with a senior rabbi who had earned the respect and admiration not only of its own members but also of the community at large was a pleasant prospect.

Rabbi Feldman or "AJ," as he was affectionately called by his close friends, possessed a natural dignity without being pompous. He had revitalized his congregation and successfully cultivated a large Sabbath Eve attendance. He and his wife, Helen, embraced me warmly. She not only helped me find a suitable apartment, but assisted me in choosing practical furnishings. I was invited to be a regular guest at their Shabbat eve table. Their daughter, Ella, and her husband, Chuck Norwood, were very solicitous of AJ's welfare; they made sure to vet me as loyal associate rather than potential supplanter before allowing themselves to become my close personal friends. I admired their loyalty and would not disappoint them. I preached every fifth Friday night and alternated with AJ in giving the homily (D'var Torah) on Sabbath morning.

As I got to know Rabbi Feldman, there was much to admire and emulate. As the child of an orthodox upbringing, AJ had a deep love for the Jewish tradition even as he was grateful that the Reform option was available to him. Like me, he was not born into Reform, but embraced it as an adult. Although he was committed to the survival and the flourishing of Judaism, he felt great respect for the best in other great religious traditions and was actively engaged to promote the welfare of the larger community.

AJ believed strongly that the Jew who respects himself is more likely to be respected by his Christian neighbors. I found in him an authentic, forthright, caring and admirable champion of our heritage.

CHAPTER 5 ❖ ACTUALLY EXPERIENCING THE CONGREGATIONAL RABBINATE

Early on, however, I discovered several dispositions that were antithetical to my own personality. AJ seemed impervious to self-doubt, and there was a simple decisiveness in his declarations. Already in Hartford, but also through the years of my rabbinate, my sermons wrestled with the opposing perspectives and showed a greater tolerance for ambiguity.

When I came to Hartford, Rabbi Feldman was a seasoned rabbi in his sixties. This may account, in part, for our different style of sermon preparation. On the Friday nights he preached, AJ would isolate himself in the Temple library for an hour on Friday afternoon before emerging with a handwritten outline from which he preached that evening's sermon. By contrast, I spent five or more hours earlier in the week in sermon preparation. I might revise and prepare the delivery on Friday mornings, but I never began working on the sermon that close to the actual presentation. In fairness, I must add that many of AJ's sermons were well-received by the congregation, and by me. Over the years, my sermon preparation time diminished, but I never felt confident enough to adopt Rabbi Feldman's Friday afternoon preparation.

Even if Rabbi Feldman had not been a worthy teacher, my two years in Hartford would still have been glorious, for in this venue I had the blessing of meeting my life companion, Joan Gabriel Mag. Joan grew up at Beth Israel, and after graduating with honors from Mount Holyoke, she took a job teaching modern dance at Hofstra College in New York.

The relaxed, tranquil pace of my life as a chaplain at Air University was abruptly followed in Hartford by an incredibly full round of activities as teacher, preacher, visitor of congregants in the hospitals, youth group advisor, teller of children's stories, presider at weddings, baby namings and funerals—and counselor to persons much older and more experienced in life than I.

Given this demanding list of duties, and the fact that Joan was living and working in New York, it is not surprising that we had only four dates before we announced our engagement. We did not date until December, were engaged the following April, and married in June. As you can imagine, our three daughters would never be told until they were married, we had only four dates before our wedding. They do know that our marriage has so far lasted fifty-five years.

With no adequate lead time, we found that all the weekend time slots for a temple wedding were already taken. So, our marriage took place on a Monday, at noon on June 29th. AJ and Eugene Blachshleger co-officiated. The night before the wedding Joan stayed at her parents' home, and I was invited to spend that night at the home of my good friends, Charles and Ella Norwood (AJ's daughter and son-in-law).

In the middle of the wedding ceremony, a sudden electrical blackout darkened the sanctuary and incapacitated the organ. There was an anxious stir in the pews, but AJ continued the ceremony with such poise and finesse that some of the guests actually felt the extinguishing of the lights was planned for dramatic effect. Fortunately, power was restored before the scheduled lunch and reception in the next room—so we were spared from eating partially baked food and from feeling the sweltering heat of late-June in the Connecticut valley.

Marriage as a Liminal Event

Each of life's transitions or liminal moments may bring a mixture of joy and anxiety. This is certainly the case with weddings when either or both parents are saddled with responsibility for making wedding preparations in consultation with their son or daughter. On the surface the tension and irritability that sometimes appears at such times may seem to be triggered by the potential mistakes of the florist or the caterer, but it seems that at times the underlying cause of this "craziness" stems from the imminent change in their daughter or son's center of gravity. The father and mother must come to terms with their child's transfer of primary loyalty from parent to spouse. A certain emotional as well as physical separation from the family of origin must occur if this couple is to feel free to love each other and build a new home together. But such reconfiguring may induce anxiety for all the stakeholders.

If my memory serves me correctly, there was relatively little premarital tension or craziness in either of our families of origin. Both sets of parents felt exceedingly grateful that Joan and I had found each other. Both had already grown accustomed to our living independently and yet sensed our strong emotional ties to our families of origin.

Joan does recall that her mother, Fannie, was very anxious while making arrangements for fear that something might not be right at a wedding reception to which 150 guests were invited. Let me just conclude that, as far as we know, the anxiety of Joan's mother was strictly related to her perfectionism. We can only imagine the high anxiety she felt during that electrical blackout! At their best, traditional wedding rituals both mark the change in the lives of the principals and help all of us, including the wedding guests, to navigate through an event which brings to mind our own level of marital happiness or regret.

In its classic phase the Reform movement followed the western custom in which the father of the bride escorts her down the aisle and then both sets of parents sit together in the front row of the sanctuary. That was the practice Rabbi Feldman followed at our wedding. However, since my father was my best man, he stood with me just beyond the wedding canopy. My own preference in later years was the more traditional Jewish custom where both parents accompany their son or daughter down the aisle, and then bride and groom ascend together and stand under the *chuppah* (wedding canopy) as both sets of parents stand beside them.

Rabbi Feldman forbade me to break the traditional glass at the end of the ceremony. He reasoned that its origin was superstitious, a way of chasing evil spirits on such a joyous occasion. Later, the breaking of the glass was interpreted as a way of recognizing the tragic dimension of our people's life—specifically the destruction of the second temple by the Romans. I have yet to meet a bride and groom who, at their wedding, are inclined to think and mourn the destruction of the Jerusalem temple!

During the first years of my congregational rabbinate, I followed Rabbi Feldman's practice, but I came to feel strongly that the association of the breaking of the glass with the wedding ceremony was so intense that it needed to be reinstated, and reinterpreted. By juxtaposing bride and groom sharing a glass of sweet wine with the breaking of the glass, the officiating rabbi may suggest that the commitment of bride and groom to share the all of their life means they are willing to share the sweet joy as well as the brokenness.

These comments stem from recalling memories of my own wedding fifty-five years ago. In the course of my rabbinate I would witness and be part of leading and supporting a trend from classical reform to postmodern reform, based on the fundamental question each generation of Jewish leaders must ask: "How can we best fulfill our covenant with God under the conditions of this time and place?" But, I am getting ahead of our story.

The Strains and Stresses of Married Life

Our first year of marriage was not without its strains and stresses. I was trying to be both a young rabbi, who was deeply responsive to the needs of the congregation, and upon whom AJ understandably bestowed a whole bevy of duties (including youth group adviser) that he felt disinclined or ill equipped to perform.

My young bride was discovering how she could be a successful rabbi's wife. I remember two very stressful occasions that first year. One had actually occurred when we were engaged but not yet married. One of the four dates I mentioned previously had involved asking Joan to accompany me to a dinner dance sponsored by the temple men's group. From Joan's perspective, I was so involved in meeting and socializing with my congregants that she felt she was amidst many strangers without sufficient attention or nourishing gestures or even acknowledgement from her future life partner. That night there had been tears and even some honest misgivings about the life to which she had perhaps mistakenly committed herself.

Another critical point was that the bar mitzvah service luncheons at the synagogue, virtually every Sabbath morning, could last for several hours, and AJ and Helen stayed virtually to the end. I took my cue from my senior rabbi. When we got home, Joan made unmistakably clear that, even prior to our having children, she could not endure this weekly routine for the foreseeable future. She would not mind sharing lunch with a family to whom we were personally close, but she was particularly bothered by the extended time before and after the actual meal was being served.

Fortunately, I took Joan's concerns seriously and assured her that we would be leaving those luncheons much earlier than AJ. I also assured her that whenever we were in a public setting, whether it was strange or familiar, I would do much better in acknowledging and nourishing her. Both incidents were emblematic of the persistent need to find that middle ground which would enable me to be successful both as a rabbi and as husband—and eventually as a father. This art of balancing the roles would challenge me throughout my congregational rabbinate. Sometimes I did better than other times. With greater personal security and the wisdom of experience, I came to recognize that there is a vast difference between attending to a person who needed counseling and being present socially at events where I was not actually needed.

During those two good years in Hartford, I had the privilege to learn the fundamentals of the rabbinate by shadowing and assisting a respected and admired older colleague. Deferring to a senior colleague had the benefit of sheltering me from sole responsibility. The disadvantage also was being spared from sole responsibility. There is no substitute for

CHAPTER 5 ⁕ ACTUALLY EXPERIENCING THE CONGREGATIONAL RABBINATE

growing by assuming the perils and the joy of being the rabbi of the congregation. That sheltering was soon to change.

Toward the middle of my second year in Hartford, I began to explore opportunities to be the rabbi of a congregation that had its name on the list seeking rabbinic leadership. The president of Temple Beth El in Flint, Michigan called and invited me to interview with their search committee. After that visit, I concluded that this congregation would be a good place to serve at this point in my life. The opportunity to exercise full pastoral and preaching responsibilities, to manage more of my own daily schedule and to have major opportunity to affect the program and tone of a congregation was an exciting prospect. Fortunately, after receiving a briefing from me, Joan was looking forward to the move as well.

Shortly before we became formally engaged, I explained to Joan that we might be serving in a remote community. I asked her if she would be comfortable joining me even in a place like Oshkosh? Now, I have never been to Oshkosh, and I intended no slur to the folks in that town, but Joan knew the thrust of my question, and her answer was warmly reassuring.

We were planning to arrive in Flint several months before Rosh Hashanah and the High Holy Day season. By the time we made travel arrangements, Joan was eight months pregnant with our first child. In those days, the obstetrician advised against flying. Joan, accompanied by her mother, Fannie, took an overnight train with Pullman car accommodations to Flint.

The congregation welcomed us with genuine graciousness and warmth. They had a home, which they owned, and called a "rabbinage" (a Jewish counterpart to the parsonage). The home was located in a pleasant neighborhood. It was near the campus of the Mott Foundation. C. S. Mott was the largest individual holder of General Motors stock. His philanthropy enabled the establishment of a small, but fine, cultural and arts center. In addition to being virtually adjacent to that center, our home was only fifteen minutes away from the temple.

From the moment of our arrival the congregation seemed to understand the difficulty of moving a family to another city. Some came to help move the furniture, which the van had deposited a few days earlier, to its proper place. We were bombarded with home prepared goodies and made to feel exceedingly welcome. A month later, Joan went into labor at McClaren Hospital. The day she entered the hospital coincided with the death of Ellis Warren, the congregation's much respected patriarch, past president and generous donor. Early in my new life as the rabbi of a congregation I was again confronted with the need to balance my rabbinic vocation against the personal concerns of our family. In those days, budding fathers were not permitted into the labor and delivery area. From early evening to 3:00 a.m. the next morning, I was secluded in the waiting area, anxiously anticipating the announcement of our baby's birth. Periodically a nurse would come to give me progress reports, and she finally came with the news that I was the father of a healthy baby girl.

In the meantime, I realized the Warren funeral was scheduled for 10:00 a.m. that very morning. What a struggle to concentrate on writing words that would appropriately give comfort to the family and affirm the significance of a very

CHAPTER 5 ⋄ ACTUALLY EXPERIENCING THE CONGREGATIONAL RABBINATE

productive and meaningful human life when all I had in my mind was the imminent birth of our first child. Fortunately, Ellis Warren died at a ripe old age. Therefore, I did not have to face that even starker conflict between marking a tragic death and anticipating the arrival of new life. At about 3:30 that morning I could enter the sacred space and hold my new daughter—Rachel Lee Karff. After I kissed Joan and recited the appropriate prayer of thanksgiving for the gift of new life, I rushed home to finish the eulogy, allow myself a few hours' sleep, and with the help of two alarm clocks awake in time to drink some strong coffee and drive to the temple for the massive funeral service. The temple was then situated on the Ballenger highway, right across the road from the McClaren Hospital where Rachel was born. To add still more significance to that day, it was my twenty-eighth birthday.

The service fulfilled its purpose. The family was pleased and the congregation had vetted the new rabbi as presider and eulogizer on such occasions. Then, to quote Job, "I girded up my loins" and prayed for the additional strength to accompany the family in a limo to the burial site in Detroit, then about an hour and a half away. Late afternoon when I returned to the temple and drove my car back across the highway to the hospital, Joan took one look at me and said, "My God, you need this bed more than I!"

My Personal Crisis

One of my favorite Talmudic stories tells of Rabbi Jochanan falling ill. Rabbi Hanina visited him, asked his colleague and friend to "give me your hand," which he did. And, according to the Talmud, Rabbi Jochanan experienced a genuine healing. We do not know if this was a healing of the body or of the spirit or both, for the two are generally so intertwined. When Rabbi Jochanan's disciples asked: "Our rabbi has healed so many others, why couldn't he heal himself?" The Talmud simply replies, "The prisoner cannot free himself from the prison."[9] We, who in various professions are called to be healers of others, may at times delude ourselves into thinking we should be able to heal ourselves. For a rabbi or therapist to go to another therapist may be perceived by the person seeking help, and perhaps by others, as a sign of weakness. Yet, every wise healer will heed that Talmudic dictum. Little did I realize when we arrived in Flint that before long I would be faced with that need.

I was married only a year when Joan became pregnant with Rachel, and fourteen months after Rachel's birth our daughter, Amy was born (I would later brag about my productive rabbinate in Flint). I had so much to be thankful for. Things in Flint seemed to be going well. Young couples were drawn into the congregation. My adult education classes, life cycle observances and sermons were generally well received. I had become active in the larger community and my representations seemed to evoke pride in the members of our congregation. In fact, congregants paid me the strange compliment of saying, "Rabbi you will not be here long; you're too good."

But, internally, I was plagued by much anxiety and soon realized I was battling depression. I perceived anything less than total involvement in the temple by my contemporaries as a sign of personal failure. I felt more fear of failure than excitement or the joy of creativity when I prepared or delivered my sermons. I found any social gathering with friends more a threatening chore than a pleasure.

CHAPTER 5 ⬥ ACTUALLY EXPERIENCING THE CONGREGATIONAL RABBINATE

I still recall sitting at the table and nibbling at food that I once savored and devoured. I had lost my appetite, was drained of any desire for sexual intimacy with my wife and could not really enjoy playing with my daughters. I responded to the crisis in two ways. After some toughing it out and fervent praying that my depression would end, I finally overcame my reluctance and acknowledged that sometimes prayer is not enough and that "the prisoner cannot free himself from the prison."

Fortunately, I found a wonderful psychotherapist. He was a warm, discerning healer who validated my competencies and virtues at a time when my self-worth needed bolstering from a credible, external human source. Essentially, he helped me see that I was my father's son without necessarily having inherited those limitations of my father that were so threatening to me.

The healing I received in those many hours exploring my childhood experiences in relationship to my parents, though not without pain, came to be regarded as providential, as an instance of God's redeeming love. And, yes, my therapist became for me, an angel, a messenger of the Holy One at a crucial time in my life.

Simultaneously I struggled to listen—to really listen to those religious stories in the Agada that infused my preaching and teaching. In other words, I tried to practice what I preached. Under the best circumstances I would have combined my psychotherapy with a visit to a rabbi for this kind of spiritual counsel. Unfortunately, there was no rabbi in this small community with whom I felt comfortable sharing my inner anguish.

At one point when I was well into my therapy, the validity of those stories from my religious life attained the clarity of a fresh revelation. I remember scribbling on a scrap of paper the words that leaped to my mind faster than I could write them, "I am of worth even though sometimes I mess up or fail, because of God's unconditional love and because I am created in the image of the divine. I have tasks to do. I should focus, not on whether I will succeed or fail, but on doing the task I am intended to do with all my heart, as an offering to my creator. I must believe that if I do all that I can, God, the redeemer and helper will somehow sustain me." In that crisis, and in subsequent years, I had reason to believe that the wisdom of my faith and its stories was healing and at least as important as my psychotherapy. Those notes I scribbled many years ago became too tattered to preserve in my wallet, but the message has remained indelibly with me.

An Auspicious Phone Call

After putting aside my doctoral study during those two years in Hartford, the Flint congregation enabled me to budget some time for study. Periodically, I found the best place for a quiet environment and freedom from interruptions was the Flint Public Library. I would instruct my secretary to hold phone messages for me, "unless it was an emergency." Thus, I made considerable progress toward the fulfillment of the requirements for my doctorate.

One afternoon, deeply immersed in my study project, the librarian came over to my seat and said I had a long distance phone call. Thinking it was an emergency, I feared it must be bad news from my family. Much to my surprise and relief, the call was from Rabbi Louis Mann, the senior rabbi of

CHAPTER 5 ⬥ ACTUALLY EXPERIENCING THE CONGREGATIONAL RABBINATE

the historic Sinai Congregation, the oldest reform synagogue in Illinois.

I had never met Rabbi Mann personally, but knew of him by reputation—and from the comments made by the HUC seminary students who grew up in his congregation. I was a little taken aback by the fact that the rabbi pursued me to the library even though his call could hardly be considered an emergency. In time I would learn that whenever Louis Mann wanted a prompt response to his agenda, he considered the matter an emergency!

He introduced himself on the phone and told me he was planning to retire that year, had done his research, and decided that I just might be his worthy successor. He had passed on the information to the lay leadership, but before contacting me, they wanted Rabbi Mann to ascertain if I was interested in being considered.

Actually, while I did not plan to spend my entire rabbinate in Flint, I hardly planned to leave after only two years. In any event, that call was fateful, for it set in motion a clandestine scouting trip by two venerable leaders of Sinai Congregation, one the current president and the other his immediate predecessor. Their mission was to observe me at a Sabbath Eve service while remaining anonymous, and then to meet with Joan and me at their hotel. They may have intended this to be a low profile excursion, but in such a small congregation as ours with only seventy worshipers at a normal Sabbath Eve service, those two elegantly dressed men sitting in the last pew of the sanctuary aroused both attention and suspicion.

That visit led to an invitation to fly to Chicago, preach a sermon, tell a story to the children in the religious school, meet more extensively with Rabbi Mann and then visit with the other trustees. Following my visitors' departure, I called the president of my congregation, a man who had become a dear friend, and told him I was being considered for a pulpit in Chicago and wanted him to be the first to know. He expressed a mixture of happiness for me and personal sadness that our family might be leaving Flint even earlier than the congregation expected.

It turned out that the trip to Chicago evoked a very positive emotional response in me, and it soon became clear the feeling was mutual. This visit would in turn lead to thirteen wonderful years in Chicago for my family. The truth was not lost on me that without that timely healing relationship with my wonderful psychotherapist I could not have even considered such a move.

Chapter 6
THE CHICAGO YEARS

SURELY OUR THIRTEEN YEARS IN CHICAGO were of critical importance in shaping the contours of my rabbinate. Those happen to have been turbulent years for Chicago and for our nation. Just listing some of the events that coincided with our tenure in the Windy City would justify that judgment: the assassination of President Kennedy, Martin Luther King's crusade for open housing in the segregated white neighborhood of Cicero. To this, add the student protests of the Vietnam War, which at the University of Chicago neighborhood culminated in the seizure, occupation and trashing of the administration building. Somewhat later, the assassination of Dr. King was followed by riots in many American cities, including Chicago. Then there were the riots in Grant Park during the 1968 Democratic National Convention.

During our Chicago years, daughter Elizabeth would be born. With three daughters, I felt triply blessed. We all adjusted to highrise and midrise apartment living. Most of our Chicago years were spent in a high first floor of a twelve-story apartment building with two apartments to a floor. The children in the building could easily access each other by stairway or elevator. Joan called the building a "vertical kibbutz." The apartment building faced Lake Michigan and was a few blocks away from the temple.

My Rabbinic Predecessors at Chicago Sinai Congregation

Historically, Sinai was the oldest Reform congregation in Illinois and one of the older such congregations in the country. Its distinction for many years was linked to the rabbinic leadership of Emil G. Hirsch, who came to be regarded as the titan of classical Reform Judaism in America. Dr. Hirsch had emigrated from Germany. He was a respected scholar who contributed articles to the Jewish encyclopedia, Judaism's equivalent of the old *Encyclopedia Britannica*. Hirsch taught at the University of Chicago and was the founder and editor of *The Reform Advocate*, a national publication dedicated to the basic tenets of the Reform movement.

In those years—before movies or television or the Internet and when many of our people did not go to college—Hirsch's hour-and-a-half lecture sermons drew many non-Jews as well to hear him speak. Dr. Hirsch, as he was generally called, was also engaged in some of the burning social issues of his day, including the rise of the trade union movement. It took some courage for him to champion the right of workers to organize in a congregation that included such business leaders as Julius Rosenwald of Sears and Roebuck.

Hirsch was known for his sardonic wit. When the *Chicago Tribune*, which ardently opposed the trade union movement, published a cartoon that caricatured Rabbi Hirsch's "Jewish nose," Hirsch had an opportunity to get the last word. He happened to meet the cartoonist at a social gathering and confronted him with the words "so you are the snot that ran down my nose."

In the 1920s, the Christian Science movement was making more than a few converts within the Reform Jewish community. Hirsch seized every opportunity to critique this development. During a large gathering where he was a guest on the dais, Rabbi Hirsch approached the rostrum and bellowed in his strong stentorian voice, "Attention please, is there a Christian Scientist in the house?" Pausing for a moment, he continued, "Because I am sitting in a draft, and I'd like to change places with him."

In 1962 when Hirsch's successor Louis Mann retired, I became Mann's successor. Dr. Mann was a native of Louisville, Kentucky. He was ordained at the Hebrew Union College at about the same time as Rabbi Feldman. Mann did his graduate work at Yale. He cherished his friendship with and support for Margaret Sanger, who championed the birth control movement. He liked to quip, "Margaret went to jail, and I went to Yale." Louis Mann had studied psychology and used his sermons to popularize his practical insights. He loved to adorn his sermons with catchy aphorisms that encapsulated practical wisdom.

Dr. Mann and I developed a very cordial relationship. He did not personally agree with everything I came to stand for, either on or off the pulpit, but he respected my autonomy. In those years, Dr. Mann suffered from a progressive neurological condition that was painful enough to cause him to wince periodically. Although I had welcomed him to sit on the bimah, he came to me one day and explained that he was choosing to sit in the pew with his wife, Ruth, because he feared that his periodic wincing might be interpreted by observant congregants as disapproval of my sermon, when it was actually only a way of responding to his physical pain.

When I became Sinai's senior rabbi, the congregation had about 1,200 families, but there were only 350 children in the religious school. By then the membership was heavily skewed toward the middle and upper age brackets, as many young couples had moved to the suburbs in quest of a house with a garden and a finer public school system.

This demographic trend drew the cadre of young families who stayed in the city even closer together. During that period, Joan and I and our children forged some friendships that would last a lifetime. Couples like ourselves, who remained urban dwellers, found it desirable during middle and high school to enroll our children in the University of Chicago Laboratory School or, if we lived on the north side of Chicago, some comparable private school.

My Defense of Classical Reform

My forty-year span as a reform rabbi would enable me to witness and, as a leader of the Central Conference of American Rabbis, to help shape the different phases of our movement in twentieth century America. During our Chicago years, Sinai was—much more than Beth Israel in Hartford or Beth El in Flint, a classical reform congregation. This meant that my predecessors de-emphasized ritual propriety and affirmed the centrality of the biblical prophetic heritage of social justice. For them, Judaism was essentially, "ethical monotheism." The Jewish people are intended to bear charter witness to God's demand for justice. God summons us to join with all persons of good will to help build a messianic age of peace and righteousness. Our seminary in Cincinnati taught this kind of classical reform, and I found in its philosophy and practice a compatible gateway into organized religious Jewish life.

As part of my introduction to Chicago Sinai congregation, I found it important to preach a sermon titled "Reform: Betrayer or defender of the faith?" The title signified my concern that Reform was subjected to unkind criticism by those Jews who belonged to Conservative and Orthodox congregations. They dismissed Reform as the pathway toward total assimilation. Moreover, more than a few Reform Jews, having internalized this view, allowed themselves to think the other movements were more authentic.

In that sermon, I reaffirmed the basic principle that enabled Judaism to survive for thousands of years. In each generation we have asked anew, "How can we best serve God and be faithful to our covenant under the conditions of this time and place?" I suggested that authentic Judaism, far from being static and unchangeable, had undergone many changes—from animal sacrifice in the ancient temple to prayer in the synagogue, from the leadership of priests to the emergence of rabbis.

Nothing more dramatically demonstrates the Reform principle than the attitude toward divorce. The Torah never forbade divorce. In fact, in the biblical period a man could sever the marital bond with ease. So, with no adequate provision for a woman in the event that a husband tired of his wife and sent her forth, the early rabbis felt this violated the will of a God who cared for his creatures, male and female, and was especially sensitive to the needs of the most vulnerable in the society.

Equal to the challenge, the rabbis introduced something new—a marriage contract known as a *ketubah*. It legally protected the woman from the capricious whims of the male world. Today the ketubah is a key element in every Orthodox and Conservative wedding ceremony. This innovation placed marriage and divorce in the hands of a rabbinic court. Indeed, a marriage can be legalized or dissolved only by rabbinic decree.

What the rabbis did retain is the biblical principle that the man can divorce his wife, but a woman must gain the consent of her husband before divorcing him. If a woman left her husband without such a divorce decree signed by her husband she is called an *agunah*. She is not free to remarry until the decree has been issued. Much abuse of this male power has resulted from the recalcitrant husband or the husband who disappears out of town without having granted the divorce.

The early reformers reasoned that this procedure may have been suitable in the age of the ghetto, when Jews were not citizens of the land in which they lived. However, in an age when we Jews participate in making and are bound by the laws of the land, and when civil law safeguards and defines the rights of women, the ketubah as a legal document has no place in the wedding ceremony.

We Reform rabbis believe that we should seek to guide a Jewish bride and groom by teaching and moral suasion, but not by legally enforceable sanctions. The rabbi should appeal to the conscience and to Jewish ethical principles, but he (or now she) ought not to possess binding legal power over the lives of our people.

In recent years our movement has reappropriated the ketubah as a beautiful expression of the responsibilities and duties of a couple to each other. In its modified form, the ketubah is still designed ornamentally. It bears the signatures of bride, groom, witnesses and the officiating rabbi or cantor, but all legal stipulations in the marriage are enforceable by civil law.

In its classical phase, Reform also discarded the requirement for males to worship with covered heads. This was justified first by an appeal to history. There is no clear-cut basis for the skullcap in either biblical or Talmudic literature. The studies of the great Talmudist, Jacob Lauterbach, revealed that it was a custom originally adopted from non-Jewish sources in Babylonia where the head covering was regarded as a sign of reverence. As late as the Middle Ages, French Orthodox authorities did not regard the skullcap as mandatory.

In that early sermon at Sinai I concluded, "In our society a man shows reverence by taking off his hat. In worshiping bareheaded we are following the amenities of our age, even as the Babylonian Jews followed the usages of theirs." We maintain our distinctiveness as Jews by worshipping in a synagogue rather than a church, under the sign of the Ark containing the Torah scroll, rather than in a church under the sign of a cross or crucifix.

The service at which I gave that Sinai sermon was our main preaching service and it was held on Sunday mornings. What possible Jewish precedent could be cited in support of such a change? For one thing it is a *mitzvah* (commandment) for Jews to worship every day, not only on the Sabbath. Moreover, from ancient times the Torah scroll was read not only each Sabbath morning but also at every Monday and Thursday morning service. Those were market days, and one could reach many people who might otherwise not hear the Torah read.

At Sinai, initially Rabbi Hirsch conducted a Sabbath and Sunday morning service. When it became obvious that most of the Jewish merchants were at their stores on Saturday morning, when the attendance on Saturday was confined to a small cadre of women, the leaders of the congregation persuaded the rabbi to conserve his energy and discontinue that Sabbath morning service. I heard from reliable sources that, once that liturgical revision was put into effect, Hirsch spent each Sabbath morning worshipping at another synagogue.

Some Changes I Initiated

The absence of a service on the actual Sabbath continued to be the practice at Sinai during Rabbi Mann's rabbinate. Late in his tenure; however, his associate rabbi, Richard Hertz, who by then had married Dr. Mann's daughter, persuaded him to hold an early Sabbath Eve service in the Louis L. Mann Chapel. It included a brief homily (D'Var Torah) based on the week's Torah portion.

During the early days of my rabbinate at Sinai, I asked that at the Sunday morning service we discard the prayer pamphlets then in vogue and use the Union Prayer Book's weekday morning service. My reasons for doing so were to be sure our worship embodied the traditional rubrics of a Jewish service (including some Hebrew texts) and to clearly signify that we regard the Sunday morning service as a weekday liturgical event rather than a substitute for the traditional Sabbath.

I also introduced a weekly Sabbath morning service conducted by members of the Sinai Men's Club. One of the ironies of this development is that in our form our Sabbath morning service resembled the Orthodox men's *minyan* (a meeting of Jews for public worship). Following the service we adjourned to the library for an hour of Torah study. Initially only men showed up, but gradually women began to join us.

Many Reform congregations had abandoned bar mitzvah because it was male oriented and denied an opportunity for a group of adolescent boys and girls to experience a covenant renewal ceremony together. Called "confirmation," the service and ceremony Reform created was held on Shavuot–because it occurs seven weeks after Passover. It commemorates the anniversary of the giving of the Torah at Sinai when the children of Israel proclaimed: "All which the Lord has spoken we will do and harken." To be sure the term "confirmation" was borrowed from the Christian church, but it was not unusual in Jewish history to borrow ceremonies from our neighbors and Judaize them.

Teaching the confirmation class, bonding with them and presiding at their confirmation was a spiritually significant experience for most of them and for me. The congregation was not prepared then to reinstitute bar mitzvah, and, because of its tendency to accentuate the extensive, sometimes lavish social event—with more bar than mitzvah—I was ambivalent about championing its reintroduction.

However, I did create an event that enabled boys and girls to experience the essence of the traditional ceremony. They would choose a portion of the Torah close to their thirteenth birthday, learn to read a portion in Hebrew and prepare a brief homily on its meaning to them personally. This ceremony was held at the regular men's club Sabbath morning service. Reading from the Torah scroll, reciting its blessings, conducting a portion of the Sabbath liturgy and then being blessed by the rabbi—usually in the presence of family and a few close friends—was the essence of what we came to call Bar or Bat Torah. Two of my three daughters experienced this ritual; and, in each case, after the service we took two or three of her closest friends to a restaurant for lunch.

When I came to Sinai, Hebrew instruction was voluntary. We made it an integral part of the religious school experience. Most of our service was in English. The rationale for the use of the vernacular in prayer was justified by the rabbinic dictum that you are permitted to recite even the Shma in the language you understand. When asked what value there is in learning to read certain prayers in Hebrew, even if you aren't able to translate them, I pointed to the fact that we find singing "The Star Spangled Banner" very meaningful, but we are not attentive to the meaning of each word we recite. I would also reference the recitation of the Kaddish memorial prayer in Aramaic (which was already the practice at Sinai before I came). Clearly its sacred power comes not from our understanding of each word, but from its context and cadence. Words have a denotative and connotative dimension. The Hebrew language not only unites us with Jews in every place and every age, but its very allusiveness can point to the ultimate mystery at the heart of the religious experience.

At this stage of my rabbinic life, I was comfortable following the classical Reform Jewish practice, even as I felt compelled to make some modifications in Sinai's specific embodiments thereof. Rabbi Mann's pulpit attire consisted of wearing a formal morning suit with black jacket and striped trousers. Without fuss or fanfare I just appeared one Sunday morning in a plain dark suit with white shirt and conservative tie. Most congregants did not even notice the difference or, if they did, made no comment about it.

I had no difficulty justifying the Sunday service to myself or to external critics as long as we had bona fide regular worship each Sabbath evening and morning, and as long as the service enabled and actually drew many more worshippers than we could hope for on Friday evening or Saturday morning. Preaching was judged an important, even central component of the Reform service.

The Limits of Autonomy

In that initial assessment of classical Reform in the sermon titled, "Betrayer or defender of the faith"—I concluded that "Reform is no betrayer of the faith, but may itself be betrayed by some who claim to be its friends." There are those in our ranks who view Reform as the path of most convenience, who view our movement as a system of negations ("I don't do this, I don't do that, I am Reform."). There are, for example, those who proudly boast that Reform invests the individual's conscience with ultimate authority—that no rabbi or group of rabbis may dictate to me in detail what I must do to be a loyal Jew. I happen to agree and endorse that component, but with some qualifications.

Even if we grant that Reform emphasizes more autonomy for the individual than other streams of Judaism, we must ask: Are there no limits, no boundaries within which we must exercise our freedom to choose? During our years at Sinai I developed a careful and deliberate response to that question. We share with all faithful Jews a commitment to the continuity of a Jewish witness in history. Can we frame a concept of personal autonomy that is compatible with the goal of the survival of the Jewish people and the Jewish message in history?

I wrestled with the issue of autonomy and its limits in a responsible Reform Judaism. I found it useful to distinguish between Orthodoxy and Reform by contrasting two styles of coaching in a football game. One coach will communicate to the quarterback from the bench all the plays he should choose. Another coach's style may train the players and the quarterback in a system of plays, but within that structure of plays, the quarterback could choose the specific play he believes will best advance the cause of the team at that moment. The first system is akin to the Orthodox way of playing the game of Judaism. The second allows each of us more freedom to shape the pattern of our Jewish lives.

To translate this into actual Jewish living, I taught that there are two kinds of *mitzvoth* (commandments): category mitzvot define the boundaries within which we must make our personal choices. For example, the observance of the Sabbath is a category mitzvah that is part of the more general category mitzvah that we are commanded to live by Jewish time. Each of the great festivals in our calendar needs to be observed in some distinctively Jewish way. Shabbat, the Sabbath, needs to be different from the other days of the week. The specific ways to make it so may include that we refrain from much of the work we do on other days, make time to enjoy our families, study the Torah portion of the week individually or in a class, attend Sabbath services, etc.

A second boundary or category mitzvah within which we must exercise our personal choice is to mark each event in the life cycle—birth, coming of age, consecration of love, death—in a recognizably Jewish way.

A third category mitzvah is to find the major source of our ethical judgments, not in *The New York Times* or the *Wall Street Journal* editorial page, but by seeking to root our moral life in the teachings of Torah.

A fourth category mitzvah: a Reform Jew must continue at each stage of life to study his or her heritage—by attending adult education class, or reading Jewish books, or listening to lectures or sermons on Judaism. In other words, a Reform Jew must be an informed Jew.

And, there is a fifth boundary mitzvah: to make one's Judaism a communal experience—to affirm one's membership in the Jewish people by public synagogue worship and by feeling a special kinship with Jews all over the world. Our rabbis expressed it in the commandment "Do not separate yourself from the Jewish community." Being a Jew at heart is not sufficient. Finding our way to identify publically with this community is an essential dimension of living responsibly as a Jew.

Within these boundaries or guidelines, I am very comfortable with the principle of Reform autonomy. You and I may not observe Passover or Sabbath or mourn our dead in an identical way; but, while we may not be on identical paths, if we observe the category mitzvoth, we will be traveling on the same landscape.

The wisdom of allowing this individuation of our Jewish obligations can be illustrated with the obligation to mourn our dead. Traditionally, in Judaism there are different mandatory periods of mourning with the most extensive restrictions applying during the first three days after the funeral and the first week. Still, other restrictions are retained over the period of a month, and the formal period of mourning does not end completely until almost a year has elapsed. What if one has nursed a beloved dying of cancer over many months? In all likelihood that caretaker has done significant mourning before the actual death has taken place. My inclination as a Reform rabbi, would be to take cognizance of this reality in guiding that person to an appropriate period of formal mourning, rather than insisting that she fall into the prescribed pattern of Orthodox Judaism.

Some critics of Reform contend that it offers a short path to assimilation. From my thirteen years as rabbi of Chicago Sinai Congregation, I can attest that the families I knew and the children I taught and confirmed loved their Judaism and were as committed to its preservation in their lives as any other devoted Jew.

I have come to believe that the proclivity toward Reform or Orthodox Jewish practice is not only a matter of what you can believe or how you were raised, but it is also a matter of temperament. By temperament, I need to feel a greater measure of personal autonomy than Orthodoxy allows. Yet, others find a great measure of security in a more structured ritual life, one that is mandated in all its particularities.

The Importance of the Sermon at Sinai

The years in Chicago enabled me to freely exercise and hone my skills as a rabbi. This was certainly true in the area of preaching. In preparation for writing this portion of the memoir, I re-read most of the sermons published in the Sinai pulpit during my thirteen years in Chicago. My supposition was confirmed. In all those years as an expounder of the message of Judaism, I never allowed the congregation to infer that I was calling them to attain that higher standard of Jewish authenticity or probity that I had already attained. No fair observer could discern a "holier than thou" posture in my preaching. Perhaps because I was really struggling as they were. I shared with them our need to reclaim and live in greater fidelity to the spiritual wisdom embodied in Torah.

In my sermons I strove to acknowledge and respect just how difficult virtually all our lives become at one time or another. Not all our suffering is self-inflicted. Life, at best, is both wonderfully awesome and at times just awful. We must never allow the call to accountability and judgment to eclipse our shared need for empathy, understanding and love.

During my second year at Sinai, our nation was forced to come to terms with the assassination of our President. Sunday, November 24th was but two days after that fateful shot in Dallas. That weekend houses of worship all over America were crowded. The attendance at Sinai that Sunday morning resembled the look of the sanctuary at the peak of the High Holy Day season.

At first it was important to place this event above the din of partisan politics. Kennedy was a polarizing figure. Here are excerpts from my memorial sermon:

It would be unseemly at this hour to sit in judgment of his errors, but surely to appreciate his greatness does not require us to shroud him in a pall of perfection. I would hope that at this hour, honorable political loyalties need not obscure the fine mettle of a great American statesman...

He had a keen sense of the balance of terror which separates East and West from cataclysmic clash. His pursuit of peace was based not on maudlin sentimentality but on the hard facts of contemporary life. It was in this spirit that he declared, "Mankind must put an end to war or war will put an end to mankind"... President Kennedy will be remembered as a man who pressed for and vigorously championed the Test Ban Treaty, which he properly regarded as a small but important milestone in the pursuit of peace.

Our late President, despite his youth, was not primarily a dreamer of dreams, but a man schooled in the ambiguities of politics, sobered by the complexity of human problems and deeply aware of the unevenness of human progress... He was an astute politician who could, on occasion, rise to the level of a statesman... In introducing his civil rights bill the President declared, "We are confronted primarily with a moral issue...a moral crisis as a country and a people. It cannot be met by repressive police action. It cannot be left to increased demonstrations on the streets... It is a time to act in the Congress, in your State and local legislative body, and above all, in our daily lives."

Do we wish to resurrect that voice from the stillness inflicted by an assassin? Then let us shatter self-seeking partisanship with the radiant intensity of our moral commitment as a nation. Let us regard the Civil Right Bill as the President's Last Will and Testament. By enacting it into law, let us offer a redemptive act for the soul of our late chief executive!

John F. Kennedy led the land he loved, not infallibly, but with skill, forbearance and courage… In God he has now found his ultimate repose. This week we Jews read of Jacob, the lonely, frightened fugitive, resting his head upon a stone in the wilderness. As he lapses into an uneasy slumber and dreams, he beholds angels ascending and descending a ladder extended to Heaven—silent witnesses to the loving, guiding and sustaining presence of God. Jacob awakes renewed in strength and re-consecrated in purpose. Hopefully, he dares to proclaim, "Surely the Lord is even in this place and I knew it not." Who among us has not yearned desperately for the supporting hand of God?

We may dream no dreams, but we can offer our prayers. Humbly we pray that God may send the healing balm of comfort to the family of him who has departed for his eternal rest. Fervently we ask that God grant strength and wise counsel to him who now must lead us. Trustingly we beseech the Lord to gird our loins for the unfinished tasks which lay ahead. May this Nation under God discover now, as did Jacob of old "that surely the Lord is even in this place and we knew it not."

The multitude who filled our sanctuary that morning, like others in houses of worship around the country, needed to have their sorrow expressed and the significance of our President's all too brief life proclaimed; in the midst of a national tragedy, they needed their clergy to reaffirm God's benevolent presence in our lives as individuals and as a nation, and at a time of high anxiety, they yearned to reaffirm hope for the future. Those who spoke from synagogues and churches all over America that weekend sought, however imperfectly, to address that need.

Saul Bellow, My Preaching and the Quest for Meaning
I have expressed being drawn into the rabbinic vocation by its preoccupation with questions of life's meaning. At its best, the words and thoughts of a sermon respond to that question. For this reason alone, it should not be surprising that my favorite contemporary American writer is Saul Bellow. Occasionally his words found their way to illustrate a theme in my preaching. Before documenting Bellow's passion for meaning let me share a personal connection to the man.

The day Joan and I moved to the apartment building that would be our home for most of our years in Chicago, Saul Bellow was moving into another apartment in our building with his wife, Susan. Out of curiosity, or simply seeking a respite from the burden of helping his wife move in, Mr. Bellow appeared at our backdoor and introduced himself. After a brief acknowledgment of our shared exhaustion, we wished each other well and returned to our tasks.

Over the years, I got to know Saul Bellow much more through his writing than from our occasional meetings in the elevator or our shared discomfort at the annual shareholders meeting. I knew not to expect Saul's presence at any of our services—even when my sermon was based on one of his novels. I knew that "institutional Judaism" was not his thing, though his literary imagination was consumed by a passion for meaning and a hunger for the sacred.

I cannot resist one anecdotal reference to two of our encounters in the elevator. I knew that his cousin was a Semitics scholar who taught at our seminary in Cincinnati. At that time our President was the world-renowned archeologist, Nelson Glueck, best known as the discoverer and excavator of King Solomon's copper mines.

At one of our meetings in the elevator I suggested to Bellow that since his cousin taught at the Hebrew Union College, he might consider spending a few days as a visiting fellow. The students and faculty would surely savor the treat, and he might enjoy it also. Bellow replied, "Let them invite me, and I will consider it." I lost no time in calling Dr. Glueck and relaying the news. He seemed delighted and promised to dictate a letter of invitation that very day.

Weeks passed and I heard nothing from either Saul or Nelson Glueck. I next encountered Saul as we both waited for the elevator. I asked him if he had ever heard from Dr. Glueck. He replied curtly, "Yes, I heard and I'm not going. I can spell his name correctly and have even read one of his books, but he seems to think my name is Bellows and he has obviously not read any of mine!" Someone later explained to me that members of the family from whom Saul Bellow was bitterly estranged spelled the family name with an s. Apparently that is how Dr. Glueck spelled it also!

Let me now explain why, long before Bellow was awarded the Nobel Prize for Literature, his novels provided a fruitful text for my sermons. While he rejected being typed as a Jewish writer, Bellow's work is informed by a Jewish consciousness, and his characters are driven by a spiritual hunger.

Consider with me the novel, *Herzog*. Moses Elkanah Herzog, one of Bellow's most memorable characters, is a middle-aged man, a Jewish intellectual, of brilliant mind and ironic humor, who is at his wit's end and in danger of losing his mind. Herzog is nursing the wounds of a disastrous second marriage. He has lost custody of his children and misses them dearly. He bemoans not having attained his full potential, fully cognizant that his academic status has diminished. His second wife has taken up with his best friend. He has invested his life savings in a home in the Berkshire Mountains, which remains for all intents and purposes an abandoned shack. Herzog is a *schlemiel,* a man who seems particularly adept at bungling his life. He both indulges in self-pity and scorns it. He laughs bitterly at his foibles, but somehow does not surrender his sense of indestructible worth and dignity.

Herzog seems to have much reason to give up, to break down, to brood endlessly and even to take his life. Yet, he does not, and when another Jewish intellectual named Shapiro preaches to him a total pessimism and cynicism about life and its possibilities, Herzog writes Shapiro a letter: "I can't accept this foolish dreariness. We are talking about the whole life of mankind. The subject is too great, too deep for such weakness, cowardice, too deep Shapiro…you are too intelligent for this, you inherited rich blood, your father's peddled apples."[10]

Through Herzog, Bellow argues that the modern Jewish intellectual who is tempted to take a cocktail glass in hand and cynically bemoan the hopelessness of the human situation should remember his ghetto ancestors and the apple peddlers in the old immigrant neighborhoods of Chicago, New York or Montreal—and reclaim that generation's indestructible sense of human dignity and promise. Throughout the centuries the Jewish people had so much cause for despairing, but somehow they didn't. Their descendants should show no less courage and hope. World-weariness is not a permissible Jewish trait.

That brings us to a second theme in Bellow's writing: human accountability. He seems to be saying that we are summoned. We have responsibility to strive to be a *mensch* (a decent person). At one point Herzog says "we owe a human life to this waking spell of existence, regardless of the void. After all we have no positive knowledge of the void..."[11] Even the skeptics should not preclude the possibility that there is a God who calls us to account in some way for the quality of our life.

This theme is even more strongly articulated in a later novel, *Mr. Sammler's Planet*. This novel also found a presence in my preaching. Sammler is a Holocaust survivor, scarred by the memory of climbing out of a mass grave over the dead body of his own wife. Sammler's nephew, Elya Gruner, befriends him and helps him reaffirm life. Sammler is well aware of the darker side of Elya's life. He is a "mixed bag." But as he now stands in the presence of Elya's corpse, prior to the hospital's performance of an autopsy, Sammler prays in a mental whisper:

> Remember, God, the soul of Elya Gruner...At his best, this man was kinder than at my best I have ever been or ever could be. He was aware that he must meet, and did meet—through all the confusion and degraded clowning of this life...he did meet the terms of his contract. The terms which in his inmost heart each man knows. As I know mine. As all know. For that is the truth of it—that we all know God, that we know, that we know, that we know.[12]

When the award of the Nobel Prize was first announced the Academy wrote that "Bellow is a man who keeps on trying to find a foothold in a tottering world, one who can never relinquish his faith that the value of life depends on its dignity, not its success, and that the truth must triumph at the last." The Academy does not mention the source of Bellow's vision, but to paraphrase Mr. Sammler, "We know, we know, we know."[13]

Occasionally, I drew my sermon text not from Saul Bellow's books, but from works by non-Jewish writers. When the musical play, *Man of La Mancha* based on Cervantes' novel, *Don Quixote,* appeared in a Chicago theater, I based a sermon on it. My congregation knew that I would always link the themes of such works of art to our biblical rabbinic heritage.

The book/play tells the story of Alonzo, a retired country squire with much time for brooding. He reads about and observes human cruelty and other evil. Pressed by grim reality to the brink of despair, Alonzo creates a fantasy world and strives to live in it. He fancies himself a noble knight, defender of the right. As Don Quixote, he sees Aldonza, not as a winsome wench who sells affection most casually, but as Dulcinea, a noble and innocent lady whom he will protect, if necessary, with his life.

When a professor at the university confronts Alonzo and says, "There are no giants, no chivalry, no knights. There have been no knights for 300 years, these are the facts." Don Quixote responds, "Facts are the enemy of truth." The theater audience responds to that line with applause. At that point, consciously or unconsciously the audience affirms that we must distinguish between illusion and bold faith. As it happens, Don Quixote treats Aldonza with respect; he convicts her of unsuspected virtue. By the end of the play we realize that Aldonza has become Dulcinea!

CHAPTER 6 ◆ THE CHICAGO YEARS

To the congregation that morning I suggested,

> There is a thin line between naive illusion and bold faith. When the line has been crossed in one direction we mock. When it is crossed in the other, we applaud. The life of faith does not demand that we divide the world into noble knights and monstrous villains. It does call us to acknowledge that while none of us is flawless, some persons are better than others, and most of us can become better than we are.
>
> The Bible (Torah) sees the human creature as an animal with a soul. Aldonza is capable of becoming Dulcinea. Jacob can become Israel. Such faith in the unfulfilled promise of creation is not an illusion.
>
> Who inhabits the world of truth? He who sees a patch of wilderness as an unclaimable wasteland, or he who sees the challenge to create a land flowing with milk and honey? Who inhabits the world of truth? She who recoils from a destructive human relationship to scoff at all notions of love or she who continues to court both the risks and promise of human commitment?
>
> Who inhabits a world of truth? He who declares that life is a 'tale of sound and fury signifying nothing' or he who affirms that we are here for a purpose, that each of us is intended to be God's partner in partially fulfilling the promise of creation? The life of mature faith…calls us to distinguish between the world as it is and the world as it might be, and to believe that by our effort we may in part bridge the gap between them. In this sense "facts may be the enemy of truth." In this spirit a Prophet of truth declared, "Your old men shall dream dreams and your youth shall see visions."

Over the years my preaching has often been more explicitly rooted in a particular Biblical text, and always when I give a Dvar Torah, a message embedded in the Sabbath morning Torah service. While I have drawn heavily from rabbinic commentaries on the text, the most poignant of such textural sermons have been those in which the text starkly illumines and seems to address with healing, our human struggle.

Professor Michael Meyer, a distinguished historian of Reform Judaism, reminds us that the early German Reformers of the nineteenth century spoke repeatedly of the need to integrate Lehre and Leben, Torah and Life. At its best classical rabbinic study, teaching and preaching powerfully linked the text to the lives of those who received the teaching. Occasionally, in an uncanny way, the texts and life were a seamless web.

Many years after we left Chicago, during my service as a rabbi of Congregation Beth Israel in Houston, at a Sabbath morning service, Joshua, the boy celebrating his bar mitzvah, read the Torah portion in Genesis where Joseph is no longer able to conceal his identity or his love for his brothers.

Years earlier, because Father Jacob favored Joseph, his brothers resented him so deeply that they overpowered him and sold him to a caravan of traders traveling to Egypt. They felt they would never see their brother again and told their father a wild beast had devoured him.

Years later, there is a famine in Canaan. Jacob has learned there is an abundance of grain in Egypt and dispatches his sons to go there. Unbeknownst to his brothers, Joseph's fortunes have changed radically. He is now second in command to Pharaoh, and it is he the brothers confront in their quest for grain. Joseph recognizes them, but they did not recognize him.

Wanting to test whether his brothers feel any remorse, Joseph conceals his identity and treats them in a very cold, impersonal way. But at one point, *Lo yuchal l'hitapek*—he could not control himself. Joseph can no longer conceal his feelings of love. He breaks into tears and reveals himself to his brothers. There is a happy ending.

In his bar mitzvah speech, Josh described how close he is to his brother who is eight years older and told the congregation that his brother, who was sitting on the pulpit, had come home for the occasion and how happy he was to see him. At first, Josh treated the bond with a light touch and the congregation responded to his playing it cool. But then, as Josh made an additional reference to his brother, he paused, choked up and sobbed quietly. At first, all felt compassion for a thirteen-year old who stood emotionally over-exposed in the public domain. Josh was able to recover his composure and finish his talk, and each of us knew we had witnessed a singular moment when Torah and life became one. In my personal remarks that day to Josh, before blessing him, I simply took note of this very special instance that deepened the significance of his bar mitzvah for all of us.

There was only one moment I can recall in my own preaching when Torah and life became so starkly one. It was a High Holy Day sermon and I was trying to distinguish between magic and religion. In magic, the performer's tricks are totally in his control. In religion, there is no predictable connection between what we pray for and what actually occurs. When asked to use my presumed closer relationship to God to secure an answer to my prayer, I would remind the petitioner that I am in sales, not administration! We do not control God's will, or as William James put it, God is not a cosmic bellhop.

To dramatize the point, I said that evening, "For example, if I were to say, if you are indeed God and you have the power that we attribute to you, then let there be a sign, a clap of thunder." And just at that moment, there was a loud burst of thunder! A collective gasp was heard in the sanctuary. Thank God, I could not pull that off at the later service! Because of that anomaly, everyone remembers that sermon. Despite such anomalies, the goal of preaching remains to help our people rediscover the relation between the text of Torah and our human life.

Other Programs During the Chicago Years

Although anchored in Hyde Park, we were able to attract members from the metropolitan area. With the involvement of creative congregants, a responsive lay leadership—and a small endowment fund, we were able to bring to the congregation, and the larger community, some enriching programs.

Sparked in part by the publication of Elizabeth Kubler Ross's book, *On Death and Dying* (1969) we were the first congregation in the area to stimulate a broad discussion of a subject that customarily evoked considerable denial in our culture. We had reached a point where we could talk about sex but widely ignored coming to terms with our own mortality.

At that time, more than few resisted actually focusing on this subject. We called the program "On Dying with Dignity." The librarian who assembled books for additional reading insisted on calling it "The Dignity Project." In retrospect, it was a considerable achievement to enlist a critical mass of participants to engage this vital topic.

CHAPTER 6 ◆ THE CHICAGO YEARS

With the advances in medicine, it became possible not only to cure more conditions but also to hold death at bay by the use of ventilators. This added to the physician's job description the challenge of helping families distinguish between what constitutes prolonging a patient's life and what is only prolonging that patient's dying. The emergence of the hospice movement was an attempt to humanize and personalize how we responded to the challenge of our mortality in the age of high tech medicine. This new reality also affected the role of clergy by raising the question: Is it ever right to withdraw mechanical life-sustaining devices?

At first, the task of attracting a sizable community of participants for such discussions seemed daunting, especially among a Jewish constituency so focused on life as the highest value. Nevertheless, we succeeded in attracting a substantial group for a series of discussions that focused on "Dying with Dignity." The discussions included the ethical and spiritual guidance we may derive from our Jewish heritage as well as how to help insure that one's will is honored even in situations where that person is no longer able to articulate it.

One of our most ambitious programs was city-wide Bible study that involved as many as 250 participants from the southern suburbs to the northern suburbs and all points in between. The rabbis trained a cadre of small group discussion leaders who studied the book of Genesis. As I recall, the program lasted from fall through the spring. It resulted in many congregants actually reading the Genesis text for the first time and having the opportunity to discuss what meaning these ancient narratives can have for our personal lives.

In both these projects, my partner was Dr. Howard Sulkin, then associated with the University of Chicago. Howard was an organization theorist who specialized in adult education and in leading effective social change.

Encountering Debbie Friedman

During a week's presence at the Reform movement's youth camp in Oconomowoc, Wisconsin, I encountered a very talented song leader and composer still in her teens. The guitar was her instrument of choice, and adolescents were her favorite cohort. Debbie Friedman was gifted with a soulful voice and tons of charisma. Her favorite musical style was folk rock in the tradition of Peter, Paul and Mary, or Simon and Garfunkel. She was destined to make her mark as composer, song leader and performer of Jewish liturgical texts. She often used a mixture of Hebrew and English in her compositions. Judging from the response of her audience or congregation, she struck a resonant chord not only in the teens but also among their parents.

We were fortunate to bring her to Chicago and our congregation. At religious school services, she led the singing, and I told a combination of original and traditional Jewish stories to the children. Telling stories to children became one of my favorite rabbinic tasks!

Thanks to our Endowment Fund, we were able to commission a number of Debbie's compositions, including a confirmation service anthem in which she used the words of the Prophet Joel: "Your old shall dream dreams and your youth shall see visions" (Joel 3:1). This became the standard processional and recessional for the confirmation service not only at Beth Israel but also at more than a few other congregations.

Undoubtedly, the most ambitious project we commissioned was a Chanukah dance service. Chanukah celebrates the rededication of the Temple in Jerusalem to God after its desecration by the pagan king Antiochus. This project arose in my mind because Chanukah, a relatively minor holiday in the traditional Jewish calendar, occurs during or near the Winter Solstice and is thus inevitably juxtaposed with the Christmas season. Much could be written about the "magnification of Chanukah" because Jewish parents have seen it in invidious comparison to the glory of the Christmas season. In response, some felt the need to give children a gift for each of the eight days of lighting the Chanukah menorah.

In truth, it would be fairer to equate the High Holiday season in Judaism (Rosh Hashanah and Yom Kippur) with the importance of Christmas, even as Passover may be reasonably compared in importance to Easter. Whether we like it or not, in the sociology of American religion, Jewish children do compare Chanukah to Christmas. While both do attach significance to kindling lights, the appeal of Christmas music finds no counterpart in songs such as "I Have a Little Dreidel" or even "Rock of Ages."

The Chanukah dance service, which occurred on the Sabbath Eve in the midst of Chanukah, when the great congregational menorah was lit on a Sabbath/Chanukah Service, became a powerful congregational response to the grandeur and inspiration of the Christmas season.

Debbie Friedman composed Chanukah music in the folk rock idiom, and she and a large children's choir performed it. The music was integrated into the actual service and accompanied by the specially choreographed movement of dancers on the bimah. (Later, when that service was performed a number of times in Houston, the choreography and dancers were provided by my wife, Joan, and her modern dance company.) The sanctuary, during all such enhanced services, was almost as full as during the High Holiday season, and the effect was emotionally and spiritually enchanting.

For a number of reasons, including the monumental effort and considerable expense required, after several annual presentations in Chicago and the subsequent ones in Houston, we reverted to a more low key observance of Chanukah. Apart from one traditional Jew (also a maverick critic by temperament) who blasted the service as a resurgence of paganism, the overwhelming response to the phenomenon of women dancing in front of the sacred ark was positive.

Debbie Friedman was destined to become a nationally prominent figure on the American Jewish scene. Her compositions were used not only in most Reform congregations but also in more than a few that belonged to the Conservative movement. When Debbie died at a relatively young age, the Reform cantorial school was renamed for her. Although she evoked some considerably negative response among a sizable group of cantors, she raised a goodly number of disciples (and wannabe's) among the cantorate.

The Larger Community

In the years of Rabbis Kohler, Hirsch and Mann, the rabbi was perceived by congregants as an important "Ambassador to the Gentiles." At a time when anti-Semitism was not dead, even in America—restrictive housing covenants, exclusion from the corporate executive suite and certain social exclusions—a lingering sense of insecurity remained within the American Jewish community, even in such larger cities as Chicago.

CHAPTER 6 ❖ THE CHICAGO YEARS

The American rabbi was judged in large part by his degree of popularity and acceptance in the non-Jewish community. Even during my tenure, this residual insecurity resulted in the anomaly of congregants proudly attending an adult education event at a church where I was the guest lecturer—who would not have attended the same lecture at our synagogue! These congregants seemed more eager for me to impress the non-Jewish community with the merits of Judaism than to become more educated Jews themselves.

Fortunately, during my latter years in the rabbinate, Jewish acceptance in America had grown so exponentially that this ambassadorial role receded in importance. Consequently, if I were so engaged outside the congregation or outside the city that I was not sufficiently responsive to their pastoral and spiritual needs, my congregants would criticize me for not minding the congregational store!

That said, I would add that the communal/interfaith dimension of my rabbinate has been significant, but not dominant. I enjoyed the opportunity to teach an understanding of Judaism to the women of the First Presbyterian Church a great deal—but not more than I relished the opportunity to teach Torah within my own congregational family.

Judaism is not directly and actively a proselytizing religion. We welcome converts but do not believe one must become Jewish for the salvation of one's soul. Still, there is a very positive (non-defensive) reason for teaching the Jewish heritage to the community at large.

Indeed, the ancient rabbis taught that when we fulfill our covenant with God, we bear witness to the spiritual power of Judaism by living faithfully as Jews. Let our neighbors see that our Judaism drives us to be honest in our commercial relations, to be responsive to the needs of a stranger in our midst and to act as if every human being is created in the divine image and possesses an inalienable dignity—and some at least outside our covenant may be drawn to become part of us.

By the same token, the rabbi, by his teaching and social engagement in sacred causes within the larger community, is also fulfilling his rabbinic function by doing his or her part to repair the brokenness in that tiny corner of God's world entrusted to our care.

New Relations with Our Catholic Neighbors

I grew up in a neighborhood in Philadelphia that was mostly a mixture of Catholics and Jews. The large Catholic Church in our neighborhood was "Holy Name Cathedral." I never thought of entering that church, much less attending a service there. Essentially it was considered part of the "enemy camp." When we did pass the church as pedestrians, my family and I instinctively walked on the opposite side of the street. Of course, my Catholic counterparts were forbidden to enter a synagogue or, for that matter, a Protestant Church.

A seismic change in interfaith relations was brought about by the historic second Vatican Council convened by Pope John the XXIII in 1962. Most notably, the decree that emerged from the counsel on the relation of the Church to the Jews made anti-Semitism a sin, invalidated the role of the Jewish people as Christ killers and encouraged respectful dialogue and fraternal relations between Catholics and Jews.

Shortly after the Council, I extended an invitation to Cardinal John Cody to join us for dinner at our home and then to address the members of our synagogue. He eagerly accepted and the entire event was of symbolic significance.

CHAPTER 6 ❖ THE CHICAGO YEARS

His Eminence was driven to our home and accompanied at our dinner table by a young, handsome and impressive priest, Father Edward Egan. That night, both Joan and I concluded that this young priest was likely to go far in the church.

That statement proved prophetic. Father Egan was destined years later to become the leader of the Catholic Archdiocese of New York. Early in his tenure, Cardinal Egan accepted an invitation to address the National Board meeting of the Anti-Defamation League of B'nai Brith, an organization formed to defend Jews and all other Americans from prejudice and discrimination. By then I was already serving Congregation Beth Israel in Houston. Members of my congregation attended that board meeting in New York City and heard the Cardinal's address.

Given the large Jewish community in his diocese, the Cardinal made an effort to establish his bona fides as someone who had a long history of friendly relations with our people. At one point in the speech, Cardinal Egan said, "When I was a young priest in Chicago, I worked closely with a rabbi named Sam Karff. Does anyone know what has happened to him?" After the Cardinal concluded, several ADL members from Houston came up to Father Egan and told him where I was at that time and what I was doing. He sent warm regards and they reported the incident to me.

In response, I sent the Cardinal a handwritten note addressed to "Cardinal Ed." He sent me a comparable note to "Rabbi Sam" and made me promise that when planning our next visit to New York we let him know, so that we could visit him at his residence near St. Patrick's Cathedral. Unfortunately, that next time coincided with Easter Sunday. Joan and I were walking in Central Park, observing the Easter Parade as it wound its way past the church. The marchers were warmly greeted and at one point blessed by the Cardinal. Trying to visit with him on Easter Sunday would have been equivalent to his attempt to visit with a rabbi on Yom Kippur.

The fruits of the Vatican Council made possible much closer collaboration between priests and rabbis than was possible during Ed Egan's early priesthood in Chicago. That Council portended the best kind of collaboration by interfaith clergy—grounded in the noblest humanistic teachings of our faiths, and targeting such social evils as racial prejudice, poverty and homelessness.

The Hyde Park Neighborhood
Sinai congregation was situated in the Hyde Park neighborhood in which the dominant institution was the University of Chicago. Our neighborhood was an experiment in controlled integration. It was surrounded by a black ghetto to the immediate south, north and west. Its boundary on the east was the great saltless sea called Lake Michigan. The University either controlled or would acquire control of most of the real estate in our neighborhood. It used that power to provide facilities for the University, high quality living accommodations for its faculty and housing affordable for middle and upper middle class blacks and whites. President Obama's large home is among a significant number of elegant old residences in that neighborhood.

Within the neighborhood and the city at large there were opportunities for meaningful interfaith social action. Unfortunately, my very first encounter with Mayor Daley and City Hall was naively ineffectual. It focused not on fostering racial justice but on saving trees. Shortly after I occupied my office at the Temple, the head of the Hyde Park Clergy Council visited with me and invited me to join the organization. He then urged me to be part of a small delegation of local clergy who were planning to petition Mayor Daley in person about saving trees in the park across the street.

Without going into much detail, the president of the Council assured me that this was about the Mayor's desire to eliminate a curve in the outer drive which led to the offices downtown. The Mayor, it seemed, was all too willing to sacrifice leafy trees that beautified our urban setting in order to expedite by a few minutes the car trip of business and professional persons to their offices downtown.

Since I like trees as much as the next person, and my own children, usually accompanied by their mother or me, often played in that park, I readily agreed to join the Hyde Park delegation. A few days later I found myself in the Mayor's conference room as our leader made an eloquent plea to save the trees. Although he frequently fractured the English language, the senior Richard Daley was one of the shrewdest politicians I have ever met. The Mayor listened patiently to our presentation. He then pushed a button that signaled the entry of several senior staff members armed with charts that graphically revealed some vital statistics.

Addressing us as "honorable gentlemen of the clergy" (clergy were then not gender inclusive), the Mayor continued, "If you look at the charts my staff has prepared, you will find a list of children who were killed by motorists speeding around that curve whose view of them was obstructed by trees. In order to straighten the road we need to chop down some of those trees. Now, honorable clergy, I ask you, if you had to choose between those trees and those children's lives, which would you choose?"

At that moment my colleagues and I wished we had a button to push and a trap door that would have given us a hasty exit from the scene. At age thirty, I learned never to sign a petition or join a cause without doing my due diligence.

My Relation to the Civil Rights Movement

We came to Chicago close to the peak of the Civil Rights movement. I concluded an early sermon on the subject with these words,

> The new American revolution is the greatest domestic challenge to our free society since the Civil War. In proper perspective, this is not a revolt of the black man against his white neighbor, but a revolution designed to fulfill the great American dream shared by white man and Negro alike. The road to the fulfillment of this dream is not easy. The stakes are high. Many a white man needs to atone for and combat his pernicious prejudice; many a Negro may need to forgive and forego his anti-White stereotype.
>
> May the time not be distant when Negro and white man are free to like or dislike each other without regard to the color of their skin. The glorious dream of interracial harmony, so eloquently expressed by Martin Luther King in front of the Lincoln Memorial this summer, need not remain a mere fantasy. It must not remain a mere fantasy.

Our early years in Chicago coincided with the formation of the Chicago Conference on Religion and Race. This was a small group of clergy and business leaders, including, most notably Ben Heineman, the chairman of the Chicago and Northwestern Railway. The Episcopal bishop was the chair of the conference. I was its vice-chair. We urged city leaders to recognize that any successful effort to avoid massive violence in our city must include not only a critical mass of law enforcement officers, but vigorous efforts to demand and enforce a code of respect, even for those who are apprehended on suspicion of criminal activity. It must bring more city services to our underserved communities and combat racial discrimination in mortgage lending and unfair employment practice.

To me, the most poignant foundation for our efforts was found in the Prophet Isaiah's understanding of God's response to a rhetorical question: "Do you want rest? Then give rest to the weary" (Isaiah 28:12). We tried to mobilize clergy of all faiths in the Chicago area, not to focus only on racial injustice in the South while ignoring the moral challenges in our own home community.

Experience in the Hyde Park neighborhood and elsewhere demonstrated that integration is most easily achieved when it is based on two principles: economic parity (where both white and black residents are economically equivalent, usually middle or upper middle class) and the principle that a white majority in a neighborhood is not likely to surrender its majority status without exercising the option to move when the "tipping point" has been reached.

Martin Luther King in Chicago

One of the greatest challenges Dr. Martin Luther King faced resulted from the misguided counsel by some black leaders in Chicago that it was time to bring the Civil Rights campaign north. The kind of voting rights and desegregation of public facilities that King's efforts won at great sacrifice in the South were already enjoyed by black Americans in the North. Dr. King's new crusade for integrated or open housing brought him to Chicago in 1966 as he moved his family to a dingy apartment in the black ghetto on the west side of the city.

When his advisors convinced him to stage open housing marches in several all-white areas, there were shouts of hate and some hurling of rocks (one of which struck Dr. King, but caused only minor injury). Raising the ante, some of Dr. King's advisors urged him to conduct a march for open housing in the all-white area of Cicero, a neighborhood consisting of many rows of modest bungalows occupied by a low-income immigrant community of Polish Catholics.

Fearing a blood bath, Mayor Daley convened a summit meeting at The Palmer House, a downtown hotel. Around that long rectangular table were representatives of four groups: the mayor and his aides; the Chicago Realty Board; Dr. King and his aides; and the Chicago Conference on Religion and Race, represented by the Episcopal Bishop, Ben Heineman and me.

That room was charged with a level of tension that defies adequate description. The mayor urged Dr. King to realize that the result of such a march would be a massive riot that would dwarf the disturbances of the two previous marches. From that meeting emerged a joint agreement that resulted in Dr. King's suspending the march in Cicero and the mayor pledging to work for fair housing laws, fair employment practices and mortgage lending that was not racially discriminatory.

That meeting enabled me to observe at close range one of the truly remarkable figures in modern American history.

Most vividly, I recall a telltale sign of Dr. King's emotional state. He, who to my knowledge never publically smoked, kept lighting, smoking and relighting one cigarette after another.

Alas, the pledges made at the meeting by the mayor did not result in any significant change in the situation of black people in Chicago. Only after King's assassination in 1968 and the massive rioting that followed in its wake did those reforms become embodied in local or federal law.

For me this episode also raised a less frequently discussed issue of justice: Is it right to place the heaviest burden of social change on the people in our city whose members are least capable of bearing it? Some of my congregants, who were staunch supporters of desegregated housing and desegregated schools, and who condemned the prejudice of the folks in Cicero, lived in the luxurious high-rises along the northern part of the Chicago lake front and could well afford and did send their children to private schools. Those working class Polish immigrants had far fewer options.

Response to the Vietnam War

Our years in Chicago also coincided with the tragic War in Vietnam. Like too many others, my vocal opposition to the war was late in coming. I bought the government's domino theory that even as we stopped communist expansion into Western Europe, by economic measures and the readiness to use force if necessary, we must also set boundaries to the communist Chinese expansion in Asia.

Only the massacre at My Lai and its absurd defense by U.S. Army Lieutenant Cally ("We had to destroy the village in order to save it"), brought me into more active support of *Clergy and Laymen Concerned about Vietnam.*

Following the revelation of the atrocities our side committed at My Lai, I preached a sermon which included these words,

> It is easy for us with cocktail glass in hand to watch the gore of My Lai on TV and be ashamed of those men who did not act like Americans of whom we could be proud. But, we must not purge ourselves so easily. If we have sanctioned this war, are we fully innocent bystanders in this shameful carnage? At best, war is brutal. The conditions under which wars like this must be fought are particularly dehumanizing to victor and vanquished alike. Therefore, no American president should commit our nation to a conflict which so endangers our soul, unless there is a clear and present danger to our physical survival as a nation. By that standard, who would now say that our engagement in Vietnam is justified?

The war was also fought on American campuses—including the University of Chicago in our neighborhood. Edward Levi, previously Dean of its Law School and who would later distinguish himself as the U.S. Attorney General who restored integrity to the Justice Department after the Watergate scandal, was then serving as the first Jewish President of the University of Chicago.

Levi, a member of my congregation, was the grandson of Rabbi Emil G. Hirsch. As their protest against the Vietnam War, a group of students took over the administration building of the university, occupied it, and thoroughly trashed the president's office, even daubing the walls with human feces.

When he heard the news, President Levi asked his wife, Kate, to call me and see if I might come over to their house. She described her husband as shaken to his very core. When I encountered him, his hands were clammy and he was almost in tears. Ed Levi's enlightened world of reason and civility was destroyed. He who was normally so articulate was virtually speechless. There was little I could say either, and yet my presence, Kate later told me, was deeply appreciated. President Levi obviously recovered his composure sufficiently to respond wisely to the existing situation. He refused the Chicago Police permission to enter the campus. He just waited the students out until exhaustion and hunger caused them to exit the building. All who had participated in this protest were summarily expelled from the university. All urgent appeals for clemency from the shocked parents were firmly resisted. They argued that such severity did not take sufficient account of the students' frustration, and that by expelling them President Levi was jeopardizing their professional future. The president remained adamant and implacable.

That said, the destructive acting out by those students seemed less pure than a nobly driven protest against the Vietnam War. I was no less disgusted by the students daubing the wall with feces and trashing the facilities than President Levi was. It brought to mind the tension between the need to avoid social chaos and the need to speak truth to our national leaders' misguided use of power. Our Rabbinic sages embodied each side of the tension. One sage opined: "Pray for the welfare of the government for were it not for the government people would swallow each other alive,"[14] anticipating by many centuries the sentiments of Thomas Hobbes. The other side of this tension is reflected in the words of a Rabbinic sage who said "the sword comes into the world because of justice delayed or justice denied,"[15] To honor the first, social activists must avoid resorting to violence and pillage. To honor the second principle, political leaders must be responsible to human needs for change to the status quo.

University Teaching as a Form of Community Outreach

At the time in my seminary education, when I knew I wanted to be a congregational rabbi and not a full time academician, I also planned to do some college teaching. The DHL degree enabled me to fulfill that aspiration. In the aftermath of the Vatican Council, I was invited to teach a course in Hebrew Scriptures at Notre Dame University. Since that campus was situated in South Bend, Indiana—about a two-and-a-half-hour ride from the south side of Chicago—I agreed to teach a two-hour course once a week during that academic year.

Because of what was called the "lake snow effect" I could leave Chicago when the air was frigid but dry only to arrive in South Bend and be greeted with eight-to-twelve inches of snow! In spite of that anomaly, I genuinely enjoyed teaching on the campus of the "Fighting Irish." By the end of the year students affectionately called me "Rabbi McKarffy!"

The invitation to teach at Notre Dame could not have been extended before the reforms put into place by the Vatican Council. To my knowledge, I was the first rabbi to teach a course at that Catholic University. These days, I believe Notre Dame has a Chair of Jewish Studies.

Teaching in South Bend was enjoyable, but the University of Chicago Divinity School was just eight minutes from my home. When Dean Joseph Kittagawa invited me to teach a course on the Intellectual History of Modern Judaism, first in Europe and then in the United States, I considered it an offer I could not refuse. For our remaining years at Sinai, the Divinity School of the University was my academic home.

I mean no hyperbole when I say that during those years I received so much more than I gave. Not only did engaging high-caliber students foster my own intellectual growth, but also taking the opportunity to listen to lectures by other faculty and to engage them in conversation provided additional opportunities to hone my own theological reflections. Among the luminaries of that faculty were Mircea Eliade, Paul Ricouer, Martin Marty, Joseph Sittler, Langdon Gilkey and Dean Kittagawa himself.

During those years I cultivated the difficult art of effectively expounding the wisdom of my heritage without even appearing to proselytize. Teaching Torah in the synagogue where I strive unabashed to convey the spiritual truths of my heritage is different from the more detached stance of the academician who analyzes and clarifies but is not in a "selling" mode.

Demographic Challenges

Despite the frigid, turbulent winter weather, we loved our years in Chicago. I loved the congregation, many of its members, the good friends we had made along the way and the rhythm of the city itself. We would have loved to stay as long as the leaders and members of the congregation were pleased to have us stay.

Unfortunately, demographic realities increasingly cast doubt on the wisdom of that option. With each passing year, I had many more funerals than baby-namings. Congregants in ever larger numbers moved to the northern suburbs in search of better schools and psychic safety. (One of our friends actually justified the move by saying that a number of their children's bikes had been stolen by young toughs from the adjacent neighborhood. To keep their children from having instinctive fear of and prejudice against blacks, they said, "we had to move to the northern suburbs!")

We loved Hyde Park, and, if my total commitment had been to university teaching, we could have easily remained. But the writing was on the wall: the number of the children in the religious school dwindled exponentially. The trend was ominous. Some of our leaders thought of a merger with a congregation on the near north side of the city. That congregation also experienced this demographic challenge, but more moderately. Their senior rabbi was about to retire, and leaders from both congregations huddled to explore the possibility and wisdom of a merger.

We wanted so much to remain in Chicago that I "psyched" myself to view it as a plausible option for both congregations and for me. The merger had to be approved by two-thirds of the members present at an annual meeting of each congregation. That summer, I commuted at least once a week from our summer cottage to the city in order to sell the merger. My youngest daughter, Liz, then eight-years-old, was engaged in a theological conversation with Kathy, a Catholic child from the cottage next door. I overheard the exchange of questions: Kathy asked Liz if she believed in Jesus or if she believed in God. Liz had her own questions for Kathy: Do you believe in Jesus? Do you believe in God? And, Kathy, do you believe in mergers" So much of our family conversation had involved the prospect of a merger that Liz elevated the term to an article of religious belief!

Fortunately, a majority approved, but the merger proposal did not receive the required two-thirds vote and was therefore defeated. In retrospect I realize that the outcome was a blessing. For me to carry on the kind of pastoral rabbinate that was integral to my being would have been physically impossible. My health would have been radically compromised.

An alternative proposal was to move our congregation to the Near North Side where most of our members already resided. During our initial explorations of that option, I received an offer to serve Congregation Beth Israel in Houston, the oldest synagogue in Texas, with its own distinctive history in Texas. After a few inquiries, I realized that the potential large givers, who would make such a move to the North Side possible, were not amenable to the proposition. In the meantime, the more I met with the young new leadership group at Beth Israel, the better I felt about such a move to Houston—though there remained some regret that we could not stay in Chicago.

Fortunately, I realized that my considerably younger, but very able associate (who even then was older than I when we came to Sinai), could well rise to the occasion if invited to do so. I then more comfortably accepted the invitation to move to Houston and was able to persuade Joan that this move was appropriate and virtually unavoidable.

Sinai had given us a wonderful thirteen years. Some of the friendships we made there have lasted a lifetime. The congregation continued its demographic descent until some thirty years after we left; Sinai was reduced from 1200 to several hundred members and only a handful of children in the religious school. At that point, there were a few deep pockets in persons who were willing and able to move Sinai to the Near North Side in order to secure its future. Sinai then rose again, phoenix-like, out of the ashes and today constitutes a re-energized, vibrant congregation on the Near North Side of Chicago, with some 900 members and a religious school and preschool, both of which are thriving. On more than several occasions I have been invited to speak at the new Sinai. Each time it has been a sentimental journey.

Chapter 7
THE GIFT OF CHARLEVOIX

Keeping My Life Ledger in Balance

THE JOY AND FRUSTRATION OF A CONgregational rabbinate is its multi-facetedness. In the course of a week you may be called upon to share some Torah thoughts with the congregation's lay leaders, tell a story to children, counsel a person who has sustained a life-transforming injury, preach a Sabbath sermon, give a talk to docents at the Holocaust Museum about the history of anti-Semitism, give a college lecture on a "Jewish view of Jesus" and participate in a meeting of an interfaith clergy coalition for criminal justice.

This multitasking is part of the attractiveness, richness and meaningfulness of being a rabbi. One gentle cynic observed that the contemporary rabbi is actually paid to be a dilettante! That is an ever-lurking danger—that we dabble superficially but generally fail to grapple seriously with a subject and provide a clear, thoughtful and occasionally inspiring presentation of it. Even if one has been blessed with some of the gifts to respond adequately, there must be time for study and research and reflection. Too often we labor under pressing deadlines.

If we are granted a day off each week and several weeks of vacation each year, we would normally use that time for family responsibilities and recreation. Early on in my rabbinic life I realized that by the spring of a synagogue year the barrel was close to empty. My mind needed to be renewed.

During my first summer as a full-time rabbi, I met a veteran rabbi who had grappled with and discovered a solution to this conundrum. In late May of 1956, following my ordination, I had several months of possible leisure before reporting for basic training to Lackland Air Force Base in San Antonio to prepare to serve as a chaplain. As I was contemplating what to do during that interval I received an offer from a somewhat older colleague, then serving as an associate rabbi at Temple Israel in Boston. This colleague needed to spend several months in Nevada in order to qualify for a no-fault divorce. His senior rabbi at the congregation granted him this time away as long as he identified a suitable interim rabbi to serve the congregation during what was normally a period of reduced demand and minimal activity.

Fortunately, he thought of me. Essentially, I was to preside and preach at a weekly Sabbath morning service, visit congregants who were hospitalized and requested a pastoral visit and preside at any funerals. I accepted and while

CHAPTER 7 ❖ THE GIFT OF CHARLEVOIX

I received extraordinarily valuable and practical experience, I did not expect so many funerals. There were thirteen deaths in seven weeks. Anticipating that possibility and realizing my experience conducting funerals was virtually nonexistent, the associate rabbi graciously left me copies of about ten of his own eulogies, which he had used at various services.

Clearly, the high point of that summer in Boston was an invitation I received to visit the senior rabbi of the congregation at his summer cottage in East Jaffrey, New Hampshire. During that two-night stay, I discovered that this quiet cottage in the woods on the shore of a small lake was the place to which Rabbi Roland Gittelson retreated with his wife and children and a carton of books for the months of July and August. Early each morning, he would sit at a small desk and write what became, over many such summers, lectures for adult education, articles for journals, High Holiday sermons and four books. Did he accept no personal requests for his pastoral services during those months? Because Rabbi Gittelson chose able younger colleagues to assist him, there were few such requests. If there were deaths of persons under tragic circumstances or those to whom he was personally very bonded, he would drive back to Boston and perform the ceremony. In the afternoons he would play with his family, row his little boat, or swim in the lake. This was also a time for serious and recreational reading.

I left the Gittelson's cottage with one over-arching thought: that's what I want to do when I grow up! Six years later, after completing my years as a chaplain, and the two terms as assistant rabbi in Hartford, followed by two years as a "solo rabbi" of Temple Beth El in Flint, Michigan, I was invited to become the senior rabbi of Chicago's Sinai

Congregation. Dr. Louis Mann, who was retiring, spent each July and August in Charlevoix in northern Michigan. What made our wonderful years in Chicago even more precious was that it was during those years that we discovered what the town's people had labeled "Charlevoix, The Beautiful."

Lest anyone entertain a smidgen of doubt, the motorists who enter the town or drive through it to their next destination will notice that all of Bridge Street in the summer is framed on both sides by a spectacular ribbon of petunias—all planted and watered by town volunteers! The town population year round is under three thousand. It is situated where Lake Michigan and Lake Charlevoix meet. A channel connects the two bodies of water, and a charming drawbridge right in the middle of downtown opens during the day every half hour so the large yachts and high-masted sailboats can navigate from one waterway to the other.

Generally, the Michigan Northland is marked by green rolling hills, a plethora of blue (sometimes turquoise) lakes and a stunning, unpolluted blue sky. Charlevoix is about fifty-five miles from the straits of Mackinac, where Lake Michigan and Lake Superior meet.

Some years ago, after we returned to Charlevoix from an anniversary cruise that ended in the port of Cork, Ireland, I needed my once-a-summer haircut. Sitting in Daryl's barber chair, I was describing to him how the topography of Cork reminded us so much of the northern Michigan landscape. Daryl looked at me with mild disdain and explained that his Irish ancestors settled here in part because of that similarity! To clinch his point, Daryl declared, "Why do you think we have an area called Boyne City and Antrim County and a ship to Beaver Island named the Emerald Islander?"

CHAPTER 7 — THE GIFT OF CHARLEVOIX

Rediscovering the World of Nature

For three weeks during our first summer in Chicago, we rented a small furnished cottage forty yards from the shore of Lake Charlevoix. Once I engaged my first rabbinic colleague, who was able, recently ordained and a Chicagoan who actually grew up in the congregation, those three weeks at the cottage quickly became eight. The unanimous family response to our summer venue was love at first sight. Our small cottage provided a welcome contrast to highrise apartment living the rest of the year. Our two (soon to be three) little girls loved the freedom to roam and their father's much greater daily presence! Charlevoix was a nourishing place, not only for our children, but also for Joan and me.

However, to reach Charlevoix we drove through the western part of Michigan for seven hours with our little girls, a teenage mother's helper, a cat and our summer clothes. We had to ship our carton of books. By the time our densely packed car stopped for lunch in Kalamazoo, I had what we then called "an Excedrin® headache."

Ours was one of eight cottages nestled between the lake, with its sandy bottom, and a forest of birch trees. Blessedly, my biological clock awakened me by 5:00 a.m. I prayed the morning service facing east as the sun appeared across the lake. How fitting at such a moment to recite the words of Psalm 19: "The heavens declare the glory of God and the sky reveals his handiwork" (Psalms 19:2).

In verse 5, the psalmist describes the sun rising over the horizon: "Like a groom coming forth from the chamber. Like a hero eager to run his course. His rising place is at one end of heaven and his circuit reaches the other; nothing escapes his heat."

I must confess that reciting my morning prayers in a man-made sanctuary has never moved me as much as standing at the shores of our lake at dawn when the sun's orbal appearance is preceded by a sky drenched in variations of spectacular reddish hues. I had never been much of a naturalist in my childhood and for most of the year I am sustained by the clamor, the human density and the vital energy that is part of a large urban scene. I am mostly indoors and even at night am conditioned to accept that we cannot see the stars because of our polluted environment.

By June, I begin to thrill at the prospect of huddling closer to a much more pristine nature. On most Charlevoix nights, with no big city lights and much less carbon emissions, the constellations and planets become clearly etched against the pitch-black sky. In such a tabernacle, the psalmist's words become more starkly evocative. The shrill call of seagulls, the alternately gentle/harsh sound of the water announcing its presence, the dependable disappearance and reappearance of the sun and moon—all give special meaning to "praised be thou oh Lord…who renews daily the work of creation."

In the summer, our family's encounter with nature is much more interactive. We not only behold the wild ducks but also woo them to shore with our surplus bread and crackers. Seeing no sign that we are game hunters, they venture toward us ever more boldly. By the middle of the summer, Joan has them literally eating out of her hand. To this day; however, they resist being picked up and cuddled.

Our dependable response to their quacks of hunger has emboldened them to express impatience and indignation when we do not respond immediately. One morning, we were eating breakfast when a mother duck summoned us by smashing her beak against the screen door. Unwittingly, that mother duck had alerted me to fulfill the rabbinic commandment that you must feed your animals before you feed yourself.

Once, while in the cottage I would hear Joan shouting: "Stop it immediately!" When I explored the cause of this outburst, I discovered Joan was breaking up a fight between two mother ducks. Each with her young behind her was contesting the right of the other's offspring to be there. While Joan assured them there was enough food for all, the fighting ceased only after we separated the groups and fed each separately.

On another occasion, Joan spotted a mother duck and five offspring waddling toward the cottage. Four of the ducklings were of equal size and fleshiness. The fifth was a runt: smaller, scrawnier, and hyper-tense, obviously rejected by mother and siblings—a vivid reenactment of the "Ugly Duckling" story. In this Charlevoix scene, the duckling's sibling pecked meanly at his feathers and chased him away from the food supply. The mother did not rise to the runt's defense. Exhibit A of the survival of the fittest. Apparently, the runt was not fit to survive. The rabbis would understand the survival of the fittest motif as an example of "the world of nature follows its natural course."[16]

At our worst, we humans can be cruel bullies. At our best we are taught not only to celebrate the awesome beauty of nature as God's gift, but also to counter the survival of the fittest mentality with the imperatives of Torah. The ancient Rabbis remind us that all living creatures have a claim on our respect and kindness—including that ugly duckling. This ethos is reflected in the old Walt Disney cartoons, when the cat is chasing the little mouse and we are conditioned to root for the mouse.

In our personal drama (which made its way into a Charlevoix sermon), I diverted the mother duck and her favorite offspring by feeding them while Joan fed the scrawny little one. We knew that the survival power of the runt was doubtful, but somehow what we did was as important for us as for the rejected duckling. It marked the boundary between the law of nature and the law of the Torah. To be fully human is to know that the weak are especially entitled to our care and protection. The commandments of the Torah lead us to resist the world's "natural course." We are taught to recite a blessing that thanks God for the gifts of nature; but when dangerous viruses follow their natural course and do not hear the commandment to heal the sick, we can hear that commandment. And, at our best, we do respond to that commandment. In human life our rabbis teach us that the highest form of assistance to the needy is to provide them with the capacity to help themselves.

With few exceptions, all of our summers were spent in Northern Michigan. When the girls were young, I did my morning studying and writing at a room at the local high school. When the girls grew up and began to make other plans for themselves and their spouses for much of the summer, I turned one room into a study, which I would use for many years.

Virtually all the writing I have done apart from sermons took place in Charlevoix. Quite by accident, one summer I reflected on our summer experiences and was moved to shape them into a "Charlevoix Sermon." The response of the congregation was so appreciative that this one homiletical venture instantly morphed into an annual "Charlevoix Sermon." You might call this my version of Garrison Keillor's

Lake Wobegone, which delights many hundreds of thousands of us on NPR.

In 1970, we learned that our landlord, a retired osteopathic physician from Grand Rapids, would no longer be renting the eight cottages on our part of the lake. Each year he intended to sell one. By selling each on contract, he not only maximized his financial return, but also made them accessible to a young rabbi with limited funds.

Fearing we would lose our claim to future Charlevoix summers in our favorite part of the lake, we purchased the cottage two doors away for $25,000 (sic). Because of its floor to ceiling sliding glass doors, it offered an even more expansive view of the lake's dramas—from sailboat races and water skiers to spectacular sunrises and awesome electrical storms.

Alas, as owners, we were responsible for the cottage's maintenance. When shortly after the actual purchase, a leak from the ceiling near the fireplace required a water bucket brigade to keep the floor from flooding, I asked our former landlord "Whom shall I call?" His gruff reply unnerved me: "What do you mean who do you call? You fix it yourself."

"But I don't have a ladder or the rest of the stuff."

"You can borrow my ladder and buy a caulking gun and some tar at the hardware store."

So I, a technically challenged guy who's never been on a roof and who flunked spatial relations in middle school, was trapped into venturing far beyond my comfort zone or level of competence. Trembling internally, I placed the ladder against the wall and inched my way toward the roof with a caulking gun in one hand and a can of pitch in the other. Front-seat witnesses to this drama were Joan and our three little girls. From the ground, they alternately worried and giggled.

I climbed without losing touch with the sides of the ladder. Once on the roof, the slantiness of it seemed like Mt. Everest as I tentatively crawled up to the area surrounding the chimney. I reached for the caulking gun but couldn't unlatch the trigger. Fortunately, my neighbor Joe had just docked his boat after a successful fishing expedition in Lake Michigan. Obviously amused by my request, Joe rushed to the rescue. He ran up the ladder. He stood erect as he strutted up the slanted roof. With what seemed to me a disdainful look, Joe snatched the caulking gun, unlocked it, tested it, then gave it back to me, walked erect to the ladder, swiftly descended and disappeared into his rental cottage.

Somewhat shamed because my technical disability had been so blatantly exposed, I caulked where there was evidence of previous caulking, then dipped the brush in the can, drenched the chimney area with tar and cautiously, very cautiously, crawled back to the ladder—reaching back after each short stroke to fetch the caulking gun and the can of tar. I was much relieved to descend safely and be greeted by my four women as a returning hero. The bad news is that I had done the work in my tennis whites—now full of tar and unredeemable. The good news is that the leak was gone and that spot on the roof remained leak-free for ten years.

From ascent to descent during this experience, I was in a state of high anxiety. After a Coke® and a bit of lunch I felt exhausted. I know persons who are both well-endowed intellectually and also great at figuring out how to fix mechanical things. To my regret, I am not one of them. Before long, my children stopped asking me to fix things that required some mechanical skill. Subsequently, my grandchildren have discovered their grandfather's technical limitations.

CHAPTER 7 ❖ THE GIFT OF CHARLEVOIX

Pearl Rowe—One of the Great Women of Charlevoix

For twenty-two years my sermons were broadcast on Sunday mornings on a local radio station in Houston. From time to time the listening audience confronted me as I encountered them at various civic venues and asked about the persons I had introduced them to in my annual Charlevoix sermon. Some became even more bonded to my characters than I. Among their all-time favorites were Pearl and John Rowe.

The couple had retired in Charlevoix some twenty years before our first summer there. In this stage of their lives they decided to plant and till a very large flower and vegetable garden. For years, we as a family pedaled our bikes to Rowe's garden and picked fresh dill, carrots, beets or little potatoes and raspberries. We usually left before Rowe's tomatoes and corn were ripe enough for picking.

Pearl's husband John used to call me "Rev'rand." Pearl and John's love for each other was patently evident, and when he died she grieved deeply. Her deepest sources of healing were her life at her church and her beloved garden. After John's death, she confined herself to growing flowers. Each Sunday, most of the churches in town had their altars or pulpits graced with bouquets of flowers painstakingly arranged by Pearl.

Pearl's backyard was a wondrous place where chipmunks, squirrels, robins and rabbits felt very much at home. Pearl talked to the chipmunks and the flowers and the trees and she believed they talked back. In the garden she was most conscious of John's spiritual presence. She communed with him as well. Pearl loved life. She knew well its darker side, which led her to celebrate even more robustly life's beauty and goodness. Tending to her garden was the best antidote to sadness and the best distraction from the pain of her arthritis.

At age seventy-eight, after John's death, Pearl told me that without John to chauffeur her for the first time in her life, she was taking driving lessons. Pearl was both scared and excited and laughed aloud as she described her initial performance behind the wheel.

One summer as we sat in her garden and schmoozed she told us of a man who had a condominium in town. The previous fall, he had come by each day and bought some flowers for his wife. Pearl, who was hardly bashful, asked, "Why don't you bring your wife here?" The man replied, "She won't leave the house ever since our eighteen-year-old daughter died of leukemia a few months ago. My wife is an interior decorator, and she won't work or leave the house whether we're in Detroit or Charlevoix. She just can't get over it."

Pearl responded, "I understand. John and I had a son, who was also eighteen. And he also died of leukemia." The man responded, "So you know. You do understand." And they both dissolved into tears. As he left the man promised to bring his wife to Pearl's garden, and he did. The two mothers had a very poignant conversation with lots of tears. After relating the story, Pearl proudly added, "This woman is now back at work, and we have become good friends." That's Pearl Rowe.

Pearl loved to cook and eat. Even when she was widowed and lived alone, she prepared her favorite foods, heavy on fruits and vegetables, fresh dill, onion and garlic. When I asked Pearl how she managed to keep busy in the long winter months, she rattled off all the household chores and tinkering she caught up on. We suggested that at her age she might want to hire others to do the work. Pearl responded with a twinkle, "I'll do that when I'm old." She did have help each spring to prepare the garden for planting, but it was she alone who tended the garden—and for her this tending was a way of fulfilling the biblical command to be a responsible steward of that tiny portion of God's world entrusted to our care.

Nothing spoke more eloquently to the sterling quality of Pearl's character than her advice to a grown grandchild. She told us how delighted she was when her grandson got a job in a plant thirty miles from Charlevoix and told her he intended to buy a house for sale about a block from her so he could be nearby and take care of her. Hearing this, Pearl instantly asked her grandson if he had checked out the travel conditions in winter. She went on to suggest that given the harshness of Charlevoix winters he should probably buy a house closer to the plant where he worked. Then he could plan his visits to his grandmother according to the weather conditions.

Joan and I were both deeply moved by this sign of Pearl's character. At ninety-two and living alone, Pearl could still focus on more than just her own needs and conveniences. Obviously, it would have been so comforting to have her grandson virtually next door. But even in old age Pearl had not lost the healing grace of selfless love. No wonder from year to year my congregants and radio listeners expected an update on the life of Pearl Rowe.

Our children always regarded it as a special treat to visit Rowe's garden, not only to pick the carrots or raspberries, but to observe Pearl's smile, enjoy her robust hug, her laughter and listen to the life wisdom of a great woman. When she turned a hundred, Pearl agreed to leave her house and garden and enter the local nursing home. Pearl died a few years later. Each time we return to Charlevoix we realize anew how much she gave us and how much we miss her.

Sabbaths in Charlevoix

One of the very many blessings that the time in Charlevoix bestows is true Sabbath rest. Being able to adorn the Sabbath table, recite the prescribed prayers and blessings and enjoy a Sabbath meal with home-baked challah bread and Joan's incomparable chicken soup—and then to attend a Sabbath worship service as a congregant sitting with my family—what a blessing!

Although the northern Michigan Jewish population is miniscule (at last count about thirty families spread over a thirty mile radius), Congregation B'nai Israel has managed to survive for over a hundred years. Fortunately, this small core is bolstered by hundreds more, who, like us, are summer people. They don't all come to synagogue weekly but they pay their annual dues and help support the congregation. The full-time congregational base is sustained by a continuing influx of a few couples, including professionals who are prepared to diminish their potential income in exchange for a great quality of life.

The congregation is housed in a former church that outgrew the space. It is situated in Petoskey, Michigan sixteen miles north of us. Over the years we have become bonded to many and have renewed the bond each summer. Students from our seminary, The Hebrew Union College in Cincinnati, serve the congregation. They are in full residence during July and August and then return every few weekends during the rest of the year. The congregation has honored my desire to be a worshipping congregant, but I have spoken at significant milestones (The Centennial Celebration) and have been able to mentor the student rabbis upon request.

The Beautiful Irene Gordon

Irene Gordon, another congregant, was an elegant woman who grew up in Petoskey. Her parents had a clothing store. Irene must have been a stunning woman. In her late teens she caught the eye of a dashing young man from Chicago, whose parents summered near Petoskey. His name was Ernest Hemingway. One summer, virtually every day, they played tennis together. Irene Goldstein (her maiden name) is listed in the various Hemingway biographies. In the living room of her home she proudly displayed a handwritten "love letter" from Hemingway. She and Ernest were the same age and shared the same birthday.

We were in Charlevoix enough years to observe Irene's graceful aging. Even in her frailest years, when her hearing was radically diminished, she remained a handsome woman with a captivating smile. The year her congregants celebrated her ninety-fifth birthday, she had just recently given up her daily swim in the water of Lake Michigan. But she continued to attend every Sabbath service and, during the winter months in New York City, she was a regular Sabbath worshipper at Temple Emanu El on Fifth Avenue.

During our latter years in Charlevoix, the Reform movement was in a clearly discernible process of change, which I will describe more fully later. This neo or post-modern Reform resulted in more use of Hebrew hymns, more Hebrew prayers; some men and women chose to wear the prayer shawl (*tallit*) and some chose to to wear a *kipah* (head covering). Irene's winter congregation at Temple Emanu El in New York was resistant to this trend, and so was Irene. When she came back to northern Michigan each summer, the student rabbis generally adopted the new mode of dress in their pulpit attire and in their choice of prayers. Irene was not happy with this trend and vocally expressed her displeasure; but, unlike some others in her generation, she did not boycott the temple. Not only was her attendance as regular as ever, but she also graciously welcomed the new generation of students. This capacity to accept the changes brought by a new generation, without allowing that difference in perspective to alienate her from a precious part of her life, was, I think, another mark of this great lady.

On that Sabbath Eve when I asked Irene the proverbial question, "To what do you attribute your longevity?" she replied instantly, "Every day, as long as I can remember, I wake up and recite the words from the Psalm, 'This is the day that the Lord has made, let us rejoice therein.'" By her hundredth birthday the world posthumously celebrated the life of her friend Ernest. Knowing of her relationship to him, the local librarian asked if she would give a talk about Hemingway. The Friday night we celebrated her centennial, I happened to be sitting next to Irene at the service. At its conclusion, I noted that she had agreed to give a talk about Hemingway. She responded, "I don't know what I'm going to talk about. I told him I could never marry out of my faith. Besides, he didn't even kiss me goodnight."

From Irene's comment, the text of the love letter and some knowledge of changing cultural norms, I would add this gloss to Irene's comments that Friday night. In her

Hemingway period, there were "those women who did and those women who didn't" and that was the dividing line for a woman's respectability. Hemingway, who was understandably smitten by her beauty, rightly perceived Irene as a woman on the other side of that dividing line, and when she made clear she could not see herself marrying a person who wasn't Jewish, she became, in Ernest's eyes, a woman on a pedestal to admire but not to touch.

Irene died at age 105. Each year the congregation continues to observe her birthday. On that occasion, the student rabbi takes the old Union Prayer Book, which Irene loved, out of the closet, and the congregation uses it for Worship that night to remember and honor her. Fortunately, that custom began while Irene was still alive to enjoy it.

Our Town Cares for a Special Needs Person

Among those neighbors featured from time to time in my annual Charlevoix sermon was Sybil Lieberman. Sybil was the daughter of a Charlevoix family who ran a clothing store on Bridge Street. By the time we started our Charlevoix summers, Sybil's parents were deceased. Their store was sold and renamed by a different clothier. We knew Sybil in her middle and elderly years. From long-time residents we learned that Sybil had an older brother who had estranged himself from her and moved far away. She lived alone in what had been her parents' house.

From birth, Sybil was what we would call a "special needs child." She was labeled by that generation of doctors as "retarded." Her formal education was severely limited. She could express her desires and feelings cogently but was not capable of such elemental life skills as entering deposits and withdrawals in the checkbook and balancing her account. Before their deaths, mindful of her limitations, Sybil's parents contracted with the local bank to handle her accounts. The bank gave her a monthly allowance and she signed bills, which the merchants around town knew to submit to the bank for reimbursement. I believe Sybil was the only credit customer at McDonald's®.

Child-like even in her adult years, Sybil failed to censor her speech and found deferring immediate gratification extremely difficult. Living alone, she did no cooking but frequently attended church socials around town and the local McDonald's® for her steady diet of junk food. With her mangy dog, Sybil was a very visible fixture around town.

Generally, the townspeople responded to Sybil with kindness. Efforts were even made to grant her some symbols of esteem and recognition that were normally absent in her life. Thus, during the Venetian Festival parade, Sybil was invited to sit in the fire marshal's car. She flashed beaming smiles and waved to the crowd as the marshal drove his siren-equipped car along the path of the parade.

Sybil knew she was Jewish and loved to be taken to our Sabbath Eve service in Petoskey. When we first summered there, our town's largest employer was bringing Sybil. Gordon Friedman manufactured the exhibit cases for greeting cards that appeared all over the country in drug stores and greeting card shops. He was one of the most honorable, decent human beings I have ever met. The concern he showed his workers by granting them the option of a four-day work week (to maximize opportunities for hunting and fishing) he also extended to Sybil and offered to take her to the Sabbath service on Friday nights.

CHAPTER 7 · THE GIFT OF CHARLEVOIX

Tragically, Gordon was battling inner demons that led him to take his own life. He was deeply mourned, not only by his family, but also by the community at large.

No one rushed to replace Gordon as Sybil's driver to Temple. We offered to accompany Sybil, and she quickly became bonded to Joan and our daughters. While Sybil exhibited child-like behavior, (each time we passed a motel she shouted, "Vacancy!" or "No vacancy!") her comments could be insightful but at times inappropriate. Sybil insisted on sitting next to me. On one particular night, during the student rabbi's sermon, Sybil stood up and shouted, "BORING!" I'm sure Sybil's judgment of the student rabbi's sermon was shared by many including me and my family. However, Sybil had no internal censor and the result was not only hurtful to the rabbi but totally discordant with the spirit of the place and the moment. Sybil smiled with obvious self-satisfaction at the attention she had attracted.

People in the community alternately humored, befriended and kept their distance from her. One additional episode really cast serious doubt on our decision to bring Sybil with us. We had out-of-town guests one weekend and had no room in our car for Sybil. When Joan called to say so, Sybil replied with tears and a whining plea for reconsideration. Joan finally had to hang up. That night at services, we looked around and saw Sybil arriving late with a bunch of balloons in her hand, wearing her jangling jewelry and sitting herself directly behind us. I kept trying to wrest the balloons from her as inconspicuously as possible while my family could not successfully contain their giggling. In those years, a public bus ran between Charlevoix and Petoskey and Sybil somehow got the balloons, got the tickets and was determined to have the last word in her conversation with Joan.

A few days later, the president of the congregation called me. In effect he told me that while my intentions were honorable, the result in this case was untenable. I was reminded that in those summer days they only had a student rabbi in residence during the months of July and August through the High Holy Days, which made these summer services especially important. We had to reassess the merit of our intended mitzvah. Understandably, we felt good about taking Sybil, but we agreed that the collateral damage wrought by that deed made its continuation impossible.

We maintained some contact with Sybil and we judged the character of the student rabbis each summer by the way they related to her. Some totally ignored her, a few took her to a fast food restaurant of her choice. On one such occasion, Sybil binged voraciously on junk food and then threw up all over the student rabbi's new car. He later relayed the incident to us with good-natured laughter. He passed the test of character.

As so often in life, needy and lonely persons will not set limits on the claims they make upon you. Instead, you must set limits. But while we could not remove the loneliness or radically change the trajectory of Sybil's life, we could seek some opportunities to provide a pleasant interval—as our best student rabbis did.

Joan, made periodic calls to Sybil and, accompanied by one or another daughter, brought her a gift on her birthday. On another occasion Joan took her out to lunch. When we encountered her on the street in town we exchanged greetings and hugs, but we had no sustained contact with her.

Sybil died in her home. The funeral was well-attended; a student rabbi conducted the service, and the city manager was present. The next day, in addition to listing her name among the recently deceased persons in the community, the Charlevoix Courier devoted an editorial to Sybil. The writer noted that Sybil could not have survived in those big cities, but Charlevoix took care of Sybil and enabled her to find some redeeming moments in her sad life. The editorial concluded, "Sybil needed us for her life, and we needed her for our souls."

"For This You Were Created"

For the last service one summer, Matt and his wife, Monica, were in the congregation. Because of Matt's terminal illness, they had missed many Sabbaths. At the reception following the service, I came up to Matt and said how good it was to see him. He beamed and asked if we would be around for a while because he needed to ask me some questions. I responded that in a few days we would be returning to Houston and would not return to Charlevoix until next summer. Matt's reply: "Then I'll have to just ask you next summer." Although not intended as such, I received his response as a well-deserved rebuke. How dare I expect a man with a terminal illness to defer his questions for a year?

I called Matt the next morning and asked directions to his home. We set a time for the visit. Since he lived about an hour and a half from us, Joan decided to accompany me. While Matt and I talked, she visited with Monica. When I sat with Matt on his porch and listened to his story, I felt I was just where God intended me to be, doing what I was intended to be doing—as the Rabbis say of such moments, "l'chach notzarta"—for such a moment were you created.

We humans are by nature meaning-seeking creatures. Meaning is the sense that we have something to live for—even when we've experienced life's darker side. When our life is ending, meaning is the sense that for all our human frailties, we have a good life résumé. Matt Kline, who was facing the nearness of death at age forty-six, wanted that meeting with me, a rabbi, because he needed some external validation that he had done well. He was not formally a religiously observant man, but he needed some sense that his life was significantly in sync with how our tradition teaches us that God wants us to live. He never asked that question directly but I rightly intuited that this was on his mind: he needed me to help him do a life review.

So I asked Matt to tell me what made him feel good about his life, what was he proud of? He pondered the question then responded that his greatest blessing was Monica's and his love for each other. She was there for him not only in good times but also through the recent illness. He was grateful and proud of the kind of persons his son and daughter were becoming. He told me that moving from his place of birth was a risk that paid great dividends. After working for someone else in the roofing business, he became a successful independent businessman, loved what he did, made many friends and extended himself to help those in need. He was active with groups he felt were trying to improve life for all residents in northern Michigan including his employees, his neighbors and even strangers.

He was grateful to leave his family financially secure. When he shared in confidence some parts of his life that he regretted, I told him we all have some regrets. We're not expected to have a perfect life. We all need forgiveness from our Creator and from each other. But, we need to know that all things considered, we lived our life as a mensch, as a decent human being. "For whatever it's worth, Matt, I think you are a mensch." Judging by his expression, that heartfelt comment meant very much.

In response to his questions, we talked about the mystery of undeserved suffering, the meaning of hope and trust at such times and about Judaism's view of our post-mortal destiny. I told him that my own hope at such times comes from my trust that the God who brought us into the world and has been with us in our journey here will be with us in our post-mortal destiny. I also told Matt that he would continue to live on this Earth in the memory of those who would miss him.

As in similar circumstances during my long rabbinate I felt terribly impotent, but I knew that the time we shared and the words we exchanged were healing to his spirit and a sad but precious privilege for me. Before we parted I bestowed upon him the priestly benediction in Hebrew and English. Matt thanked me for coming. We hugged. He asked for my email address and phone number. Shortly after we returned to Houston, I received an email thanking me for the visit. Some months later, we learned that Matt had died.

In my note to Monica I mentioned how grateful Matt was for her love, and I repeated in essence what I had said to him about our immortality: we live on not only in the hearts of those who loved and cherished us but the God who is with us in this life is with us in the world beyond. That soul which binds us most intimately to God returns to the God who gave it.

A Cup of Joy and the Broken Glass

The lake in front of our cottage with its shimmery blue water beckons us to enter—but it can also be perilously stormy. I remember some twenty-five years ago, when the water level on Lake Charlevoix threatened to overwhelm the cottages on its shore including our neighbor, George Weber, whose cottage was lower than ours. He took his very soggy lawn as an ominous portent and in panic sold the home he had loved for so many years. When in Genesis we read the description of the world's creation, God leaves for last the creation of us human creatures. And then we read, "God saw all that God had made and behold it was good." Surely the Torah does not suggest that our lived life is devoid of evil or suffering. As I have suggested earlier, the Torah means to say that life is a mixed bag—awesomely beautiful and at times, awfully miserable. Hence, at a traditional wedding we invite the groom and bride to drink from a cup of sweet wine and then before the end of the ceremony usually the groom, on behalf of both, stomps on and shatters a glass. Life is both sweet wine and a broken glass. The challenge of lovers and friends is to accept the all of life and affirm that life is worth its price. Fortunate are those who know that darker side of life and seize all the more passionately the opportunities for joy and gratitude.

Certainly part of the magnetic attraction of the Charlevoix sermons has been the stories of persons who both accepted the brokenness they could not fix and strove to repair the brokenness they could repair in their own lives and others. Whether we are formally religious or not, we know that Emile Durkheim was right when he said that religion in its essence has to do with "life in its seriousness." Unless we are sociopaths, we know that we are here on Earth to heal and not to harm, to help and not to be insensitive to the pain of another, to love and not to hate, to build and not destroy, to respect the inalienable dignity of everyone—ours and our neighbor's and the stranger in our midst. Thus, we fulfill God's intention for us and discover the deepest meaning of our lives.

Diving for the Sake of Widows

One day, Joan and I were walking along the shore of our lake when we spotted a small group of men in diving suits. When we asked them what they were doing, they first dismissed the question lightly by saying they were searching for the sunken remains of gangster Al Capone's luxury yacht which sank in Lake Charlevoix many years earlier and had never been found. Then they shared the real reason for their diving.

They told us they were from downstate, the small city of Saginaw. One of them explained that Lake Charlevoix's waters were much colder than the summer waters in the lake near them. They came north to practice their diving skills in preparation for next winter. The members of this little group volunteer each winter to aid the sheriff's office. One of them explained that more than a few men in their community love to ice fish once their lake is frozen. Unfortunately, at least a few are involved each season in fatal accidents because they misjudged the firmness of the ice in that part of the lake.

What was their mission as volunteers? Their spokesman explained that the fishermen's widows could not collect insurance, which many depended on for their livelihood, until the body had been retrieved and certified by the sheriff's office as deceased. These divers' mission was to retrieve the body so that the family could experience closure at the funeral service or at least the widow could have the peace of mind of knowing that the insurance would now be forthcoming.

As I thought about this episode, I was reminded of the various times the Torah commands us to care for the widow; not to ignore her needs but to recognize her vulnerability and help sustain her. Specifically in Exodus 22, we read, "You shall not ill-treat any widow or orphan. If you do mistreat them, I will heed their outcry as soon as they cry out to me…"

The Rosenthal Family: From "See You in Church" to "Shabbat Shalom"

Our Charlevoix summers and the sermons inspired by them also added poignant particularity to the age-old struggle for Jewish survival. Through all these centuries there have been so relatively few of us, and yet somehow we managed to survive. Under the best of circumstances those who are born into and those who choose to embrace the people and the faith of Abraham and Sarah find profound meaning in doing so. The experiences I have had and shared from our summers in Charlevoix illustrate the drama of sustaining a Jewish presence in this world. Our little congregation has never numbered more than thirty some families all year round and yet it has somehow survived for over a century.

For many years we would venture three miles down the road to buy our cherries at Rosenthal's orchard. At first we thought this might be a Jewish family, but on our very first visit we were greeted by a large sign, "Closed on Sundays. See you in church." When we realized that David Rosenthal and his wife spoke with thick German accents and were of the age that might have linked them to the period of the Second World War, we developed another theory: were they former Nazis or at least Nazi sympathizers? That possibility always remained in our minds until one Saturday night, accompanied by dear friends from Houston who were weekend visitors, we drove to the orchard for some fresh cherries. No one but David Rosenthal was there. Emboldened to resolve the issue of the Rosenthals' story, I asked Mr. Rosenthal how long they had the orchard and what was their former home?

At that point David Rosenthal seemed poised and even anxious to share his story. (Let me interject that I don't believe he knew that we were Jews or that I was a rabbi.) David Rosenthal told us they were Germans in Germany during World War II; that as a teenager he was given the honor of being invited to join the Nazi SS Youth. When he shared the news with his parents, his father exclaimed, "If you do that, you will no longer be welcome in our home." David Rosenthal explained that his father was a member of that very small sect of pious Christians who regarded Hitler as the anti-Christ. David then went on to describe how he got himself rejected from the SS by feigning idiocy in words and gesture. Once no longer eligible for this Nazi elite, he was recruited into the regular German army and sent to the Russian front. He described making a vow that if God enabled him to survive the war, he would dedicate his life to Christ. He and the woman who became his wife did survive. As displaced persons, they received help from a Christian refugee agency to leave Germany, resettle in Michigan and acquire a farm.

We thought that was the end of the story until several years later, when a local young woman who helped Joan with housekeeping a few hours per week told us that she worked most of her days at the Rosenthal orchard. By then, the old folks were deceased and their son and his family lived at and ran the orchard. When our aide learned that we were Jewish and that I was a rabbi, she told us the Rosenthals are Jewish; in fact, Orthodox Jews. We retorted, "That can't be so. They may be Jews for Jesus, but…" She held her ground, and we couldn't wait until our next visit to the orchard.

When we arrived, the sign now read, "Closed Saturday." David's son was not there, but Shelly, his wife, greeted us warmly and resolved the mystery. She told us that since he knew of Jews who bore that name, her husband had periodically questioned his father about a possible Jewish connection in the family. Each time, his father flatly said, "No, don't be silly." But on his deathbed, David Rosenthal whispered to his son that his father's parents were in fact Jewish.

That revelation led this generation of Rosenthals to reclaim their Jewish heritage. They were converted to Judaism by an Orthodox rabbi. Each winter, they close the farm for two months, go to Florida and study regularly with another Orthodox rabbi. They keep kosher by securing their meats from Detroit and since they don't drive on the Sabbath, they travel each Friday during the day to Traverse City and worship in an Orthodox synagogue and return after the Sabbath. This is Charlevoix's contribution to the saga of Jewish survival. More than a few Jewish families in Michigan as elsewhere have been lost to Judaism permanently. Then there are those who feel the need to reconnect in some way to their newly discovered Jewish roots.

CHAPTER 7 · THE GIFT OF CHARLEVOIX

Keeping the Ledger Balanced

This memoir is largely chronological. I present these Charlevoix stories here because their setting became part of our lives when we moved to Chicago. The persons we came to know in Charlevoix, and who are mentioned in these pages, are certainly among those who have enhanced my life and deepened my preaching. Reverend Kohn must be included in their ranks.

Harold Kohn was a minister in a large church in Chicago. When he developed some potentially serious pulmonary problems that would only worsen by continued exposure to the polluted atmosphere of the big industrial city, Reverend Kohn accepted a position in the little Congregational church in Charlevoix. He and his wife had grown children. They decided to live in a small cottage in a heavily wooded area. Harold Kohn found many sermon texts by immersing himself intimately in the natural world outside his front and back door.

When I called to introduce myself, he told me of his friendship with Rabbi Mann who had preceded me as a summer resident. I explained to him that because of Rabbi Mann we decided to discover Charlevoix. He invited me to drop by. Our visit included a wonderful walk in his private little forest, enriched by his incisive spiritual commentary on the sermons he found embedded in the natural world.

Reverend Kohn imparted to me that day one of his basic rules for living well. He told me he actually had a special ledger with two columns on each page. One column was labeled, "Income" and the other, "Expenditure." On the income side he included his time for prayer and meditation and just walking around his forested neighborhood. The income column also included spending time with his wife, reading books and periodicals, listening to his classical music recordings, listening to other persons' lectures, or watching a baseball game (this was pre-personal computers and cyberspace).

On the expenditures side of the page, he listed the time he spent working on a sermon or actually conducting a service and preaching the sermon, visiting persons in the hospital, conducting a funeral service and counseling persons in his study. Each evening, Reverend Kohn filled out the page in his ledger and at the end of the week he would see how well his life was balanced between expenditure and income. When he found a serious imbalance, he tried to make some adjustments in the way he conducted his life.

In truth I am not disciplined enough to replicate Reverend Kohn's practice, but I've never forgotten the underlying principle. For me, each summer in Charlevoix has been an effort to rebalance a life that by each spring was too heavily skewed toward expenditure. When the barrel had run dry and needed to be replenished, Charlevoix turned out to be the right prescription. Fortunately, as my family turned to what has become forty years in Houston, Charlevoix has remained very much a part of the rhythm of our lives.

Chapter 8
THE YEARS IN HOUSTON

MOVING TO HOUSTON IN JULY CAN BE a very discomfiting experience. I made several trips in the earlier months without that sensation of oppressive heat/humidity. In fact, in early April, Joan and I came to attend a barbeque reception for the congregation's Board on the patio of the president's home. Its purpose was to extend hospitality to the one who could well be their new rabbi. The climate was delightfully temperate. When I asked the president if the weather was always this nice at that time of year, he answered simply, "Of course." I didn't notice that he was smiling. I believed him because I wanted to believe him, and he took liberties with the truth because he wanted us to come to Houston. In July, Houston offers no exception to the rule (neither do June, August or September): Houston summers are long, almost always swampy and oppressively hot. I learned later that England offers its consular officials serving in Houston the same bonus they offered those who served in India! I also learned that whenever possible, firms did their recruiting during the temperate and often lovely Houston winter.

Happily, we arrived in our new home in July of 1975. The next day we discovered that not only did the air conditioning render our home very pleasant, but also we were greeted by another kind of warmth: a group of lovely women who had filled our refrigerator with goodies and stayed throughout the day to help us get settled.

Beth Israel, like Sinai Congregation in Chicago, was the oldest Reform temple in the state. It seems that I was fortunate to serve old established congregations with history and traditions that were cherished—and renewable. The members of the newly emerging leadership group in Houston were my age, in their early forties. President Alfred Friedlander and Vice-President Melvyn Wolff were particularly effective advocates for our move to Houston. They loved their congregation but realized it was time to chart some new directions.

Fortunately, by temperament and through earlier experience, I had some sense of how to foster change without sacrificing continuity. At the outset, one must defer significant changes until one has earned the trust of the congregation. Even when one is prepared to propose some change, one must do so not by making invidious comparisons between the established way and the new direction; one must do so in the spirit of, "We are standing on the shoulders of those who went before us."

We must acknowledge that the wisdom of life involves striving for necessary change within the context of continuity. No old timers should suddenly feel like strangers in their own home. To realize this objective, it is essential not to use the authority of the rabbi to foist change upon the congregation, but to engage in dialogue with the leaders and members of the congregation. If successful, a critical core of trusted leaders will play a significant role in embracing and advocating those changes.

As indicated in an earlier context, one must be able to show some understanding of why change is hard and how we can respect and even love those who disagree with us. One must be prepared to compromise and be sure to distinguish between core principles and preferences. A group of old-timers, whose families were members of Beth Israel for generations, loved a particular melody to a hymn titled "Ayn Kaylohenu" (There is None Like Our God). As far as they were concerned, the melody was authentically Jewish and as old as the revelation at Sinai! There are melodies I would prefer for that hymn, and I happen to know that far from dating back to Sinai, the cherished melody was that of an old Prussian marching song. To dismiss this preference would be foolish and insensitive. So, more frequently than I would have preferred, we sang to that melody. Apart from being considerate, that concession made it just a bit easier for them to tolerate those things that were changed.

The Basic Principles
In the early 1940s, some changes initiated by leaders of the congregation who felt its Classical Reform principles were being violated, formulated, advocated and passed "The Basic

Principles of Classical Reform" or "Basic Classical Reform Principles." In fact, more than a few of those Principles went back to the Pittsburgh platform, which was passed by the Central Conference of American Rabbis in 1885.

The congregational elders who signed onto this 1940s iteration of those Principles determined that everyone who would claim full (rather than associate) membership in Beth Israel should be willing to formally sign onto them. A bitter split in the congregation followed. Families were divided between the yea-sayers and the nay-sayers. As so often happens in such circumstances, a new congregation emerged from that controversy.

The Principles did elevate the national profile of Beth Israel. A story on them appeared in the pages of *The New York Times* and *Time* magazine. Essentially, the principles denied that we Jews were an ethnic group or a people, and certainly not a nation. Rather, we were united by our faith in the one God who alone is to be worshipped and by our striving to bring closer the Messianic age of social justice, brotherhood and peace.

We must recall that in the 1940s, the Second World War against Hitler took place against the backdrop of what would retrospectively be referred to as the Holocaust. Many Jews reaffirmed the Zionist objective of creating a Jewish state in Palestine for those Jews who desperately needed it. Jews who opposed the rebirth of Israel as a state (who included the proponents of the Basic Principles) argued that such a state would render Jews vulnerable to the charge of dual allegiance and would only increase anti-Semitism in this country.

Once the state was established in 1948—and its continued existence was challenged by five Arab armies—most Jews rallied to Israel's defense. Although my predecessor, Rabbi Schachtel, had endorsed the Principles, once Israel was established, he repudiated the opposition to the state and argued that far from causing disrespect and charges of dual loyalty, the valor of the Israelis had raised the level of Jewish pride and the respect for Jews by our Christian neighbors.

Post-Classical Reform

The other major thrust of the Basic Principles was its depreciation of many Jewish rituals that they felt only served to make us appear different from our Christian neighbors but had no ethical significance. These included the wearing of the tallit, *yarmulke* (head covering) and the dietary laws. I will describe my own participation in the transition from Classical Reform to post-Classical or Neo-Reform, but for now let me explain how I describe it. The new Reform perspective is postmodern, by which I mean that we have a new sense that human beings do not live by reason alone. The non-rational is not necessarily irrational. I have adopted a view of ritual that was in keeping with the new scientific distinction between the two hemispheres of the brain (left, which is the heavily analytical, objective part of us, and right, the more poetic, subjective, emotional and imaginative part of us).

A purely rational (Classical Reform) view of ritual is that it is designed to remind us of ethical truths as the Passover Seder reminds us that God wants all of His children to be free. A postmodern understanding of ritual views it as a connector to the world of religious faith and religious experience. It is a sense that life is not only a problem to probe and solve but also a mystery to embrace.

Post-Classical Reform does not require that we observe all the same rituals. Some need more ritual than others. What would be meaningless to me may be highly significant to my Jewish neighbor. According to this understanding, what makes us Reform is not that we do not keep dietary traditions of Judaism, but that if we keep them it is not simply because they are specifically written in the Torah. If I keep any of the dietary laws, and I do, it is because I find religious significance in some of them for me. A corollary post-Classical Reform principle is that the freedom to discard involves the freedom to reclaim.

I did not wear a head covering during worship in my Classical Reform period in Chicago, I chose not to wear one in Houston and I choose not to wear one even now, but I respect the right of rabbinic colleagues, cantors and Jewish laypersons who choose to worship with covered head. I have no objection to wearing a kippah, but precisely because all our present clergy and a fair number of laypersons do cover their heads in worship, I choose to retain this single link with my Classical Reform legacy; essentially to be in some solidarity with those of my friends who didn't then and don't now feel the need to cover their heads in worship.

A Mini-Crisis

A full six years before I came to Beth Israel, the Basic Principles were abolished. All of this is by way of an introduction to a potential mini-crisis that occurred during a meeting of the President's Advisory Committee which consisted of living past presidents of Beth Israel with the current president as chair and presider. I was invited to sit in on the meeting as a way to deepen my relationship with those former leaders of the

Congregation. In fact, I had proposed to the president that he establish such a committee to enable these former leaders to feel like insiders rather than marginalized outsiders.

In the very first meeting, when the president asked for new business, one of the past presidents who I shall refer to as Mr. Kashman, rose and declared the following, "Mr. President, I have noticed that since the arrival of our new rabbi, more than a few persons in the congregation are wearing yarmulkes. When I go to Beth Yeshurun [a Conservative synagogue where all worshippers are expected to cover their heads], I cover my head. When they come here, they should uncover their head." Mr. Kashman could have mentioned, but didn't, that some of our own members could be seen choosing to cover their heads and even to wear a tallit. He concluded his remarks with these words, "I expect the rabbi to instruct the ushers to tell those with covered heads that they should remove them."

I raised my hand to be recognized and said, "Mr. Kashman, with all due respect, I must respond that if you expect me to insist that all who enter our sanctuary with covered heads uncover them, I'm afraid you'll have to get another rabbi." Without missing a beat, he responded, "Well, maybe we'll need to."

Barely six months after my arrival in Houston, my tenure was in question! Fortunately, Mr. Kashman's retort was greeted immediately with a barrage of spontaneous outbursts from the other past presidents, "He doesn't mean that, Rabbi! Mr. Kashman, you don't mean that!" At that point, the President thanked the committee for coming, thanked me for proposing the group and for coming and adjourned the meeting.

Once that episode was over, I arranged to visit with Mr. Kashman at his home. He was very cordial and said he appreciated my gesture. I told him I was grateful for the significant ways his leadership and generosity had helped the congregation. I also told him that I wanted his friendship. I did not promise to refrain from proposing additional changes. In the years ahead, we did remain on friendly terms and when he died, the family asked me to preside at the funeral service.

Pulpit Attire and Dietary Observance

At Sinai Congregation in Chicago, I wore a conservative suit on the pulpit with no robe. My predecessor at Beth Israel had worn a black robe at Sabbath services and a white robe when officiating at High Holidays and the Festivals. I had grown comfortable with just a dark suit, but I was reluctant to wear an academic robe with doctoral stripes on my arms, which had no Jewish significance. My friend, the Methodist minister, also wore an academic robe but he wore a stole with a cross, which clearly signified that he was a Christian minister. A CCAR committee had actually designed a tapered tallit that could be attached to the robe. When I told the President that I assumed the Congregation would not be comfortable if I just wore an unadorned suit on the pulpit when leading services, he concurred. I then told him that I did not feel comfortable wearing a robe that signified my academic attainments but had nothing to identify me as a Jewish leader of worship. Therefore, I would be wearing a tapered tallit, which I jokingly referred to as an "Ivy League tallit".

I did wear the tallit, and in my column for the next bulletin, I explained why I had felt the need to adorn my academic robe with a Jewish insignia. I had previously informed the Board of my decision. I did not ask for a vote, because this was a matter of principle on which I was not prepared to compromise. Despite a few hushed comments in the congregation and at the Board meeting, the matter became a non-issue very quickly.

The following year, at a meeting of the Ritual Committee, I proposed that for public lunches at the temple, like bar mitzvah receptions, it would be appropriate to observe biblical dietary laws (no pork or shellfish). I explained that I would never preach on the observance of dietary laws. This was strictly an individual choice, and I personally choose to observe a few and not to observe many others. But I felt it was appropriate to make this accommodation to our guests from the larger Jewish community who attend our services for bar mitzvahs and weddings, etc.

The Ritual Committee passed the recommendation with advocacy from some officers of the congregation and members of the Board, who accepted the report of the Ritual and Music Committee. Those families who felt the need for either pork or shellfish at their receptions held them at a hotel instead of the congregation's social hall. Some feared the slippery slope leading to full compliance with all the dietary laws. That never happened.

Relatively early in my tenure at Beth Israel, a contemporary of mine, of whom I was very fond, called to invite me for lunch. During that meeting, he mentioned some of the ritual changes that had occurred already during my watch. He assured me that he liked me personally but felt that he might feel more at home at another congregation, which had broken off from Beth Israel during my predecessor's tenure because they felt Beth Israel was not Classically Reform enough!

I reminded my host that his family had been members of the congregation for generations: "Rabbis come and go. This is your home. Don't make such a decision hastily. Hang around for a while and see what happens." Fortunately, he did, and we became very dear personal friends. In the meantime, my friend had become actively involved in the Jewish Federation, which attempted to represent the total Jewish community in all its diversity. As a leader of Federation, my friend called me one day and said that a Federation committee was meeting for lunch at Beth Israel and he wanted to be sure that whatever we served was strictly kosher. With great delight, I assured him that was all taken care of and I added, in a gently sardonic tone, "Wow, you've come a long way, baby."

The Yom Kippur Symposium

In Christianity, the churches are most well-attended during Christmas and Easter. In Judaism, even the Seventh Day Absentists tend to appear for Rosh Hashanah and Yom Kippur. This is the great penitential observance. Rosh Hashanah is a Day of Judgment when we strive to come to terms with our spiritual failures. Yom Kippur is the Day of Fasting and Atonement when the liturgy affirms God's reconciling love for us. The bridge between the Day of Judgment and the Day of Reconciliation is provided by the ten intermediate days of repentance.

At its best, the liturgy, the music and the messages shared with the congregation set a mood of solemnity, spiritual quickening and renewal. Traditionally, one is expected to spend much of that twenty-four hour period (apart from nocturnal sleep) in the synagogue.

Early on in my tenure in Beth Israel, we initiated the "Yom Kippur Symposium." This became the closest equivalent to what Christians call personal testifying. After consulting with my clergy colleagues and welcoming suggestions from the congregation, each year I would invite four members whose life story was known to me and to my colleagues to share their story with the congregation. This was not to be a time to trumpet one's great achievements in the market place or in other precincts of power. This was the time to acknowledge that like all mortals, you have faced the darker side of life, done your suffering and experienced your crisis of meaning—and somehow emerged with a deeper sense of what makes a life worthwhile. The crisis may result from radical economic reversal, life threatening or life transforming illness, family discord, etc.

Each was called on to describe what in his or her Jewish heritage enabled them to face the abyss and transcend it. These are stories that speak of the triumph of faith over cynicism, love over resentment, hope over despair. During the Yom Kippur day, the total congregation surges and ebbs in number. Each Yom Kippur afternoon, the Symposium draws a large congregation who will invariably be deeply inspired and moved by the stories their friends, acquaintances and strangers in their midst have shared with them. There have been times when I felt the most significant message of the day was given not by one of the rabbis but by one or more of the Symposium participants.

Interfaith Outreach

While most of my preaching, teaching and storytelling was addressed to my congregation, my rabbinate continued to have a significant interfaith component. One of the programs we developed was a high level Jewish/Christian dialogue. This program started as one of the more common interfaith institutes on Judaism for the Christian clergy. This initial paradigm was based on the premise that Christianity has its roots in Judaism. Jesus was a Jew and so were the Apostles. "To fully understand your Christian heritage, you need to appreciate a Jewish perspective on what Christians refer to as the Old Testament, supplemented by an introduction to the teaching of the ancient and Medieval Rabbis."

In honesty, let it be confessed that the subtext of many such programs was: if we educate the clergy to appreciate their Jewish heritage, this could have a geometric effect through their preaching and teaching in the way they portray some of the more sensitive subjects like who crucified Jesus. All of which could result in a reduction of anti-Semitism among our Christian neighbors.

We too began in this more common mold. It was extremely successful. A committee of Jewish and Christian clergy would suggest a topic and we would invite a Jewish scholar to present the topic with ample opportunity for questions and comments. There was a morning session and a brief afternoon session following a great lunch prepared and served by the Temple Womens' Group. Between one and two hundred clergy representing Catholics, various Protestant denominations and rabbis attended. It was so successful that Louis Moore, then religious editor of the *Houston Chronicle*, quipped, "It took the Jews to bring the Catholics and Protestants together."

Fortunately, after a few years, several of the Christian members of the planning committee suggested that we should

CHAPTER 8 ❖ THE YEARS IN HOUSTON

make this Institute a true Jewish/Christian dialogue. With a gentle smile, one Protestant minister suggested that this expanded format would be based on the premise that rabbis have something to gain from understanding Christian perspectives on a spiritual issue.

I felt somewhat chastened for not having proposed this myself. All the more so because in the Central Conference's Journal, I had published an article titled, "Toward a Jewish/Christian Dialogue." In that essay, I bemoaned the danger and unfairness of using the other's religion as a foil for making invidious comparisons and to flaunt the superior virtues of one's own. Thus, there were rabbis who suggested to their congregations that Judaism is a thinking person's religion, while Christianity focuses so much on miracles (as if the parting of the Red Sea in the Hebrew Bible was not a miracle story). By the same token, some Christian clergy were guilty of describing the "Old Testament" as proclaiming a God of wrath and strict justice while the New Testament teaches a God of love.

What I urged upon Jewish and Christian clergy was to judge each other's faith not invidiously but as a different way of dealing with common faith issues like: Why is there undeserved suffering? What are the ways we parse the tension between our obligation to love ourselves and to love our neighbor? How is the Messianic hope formulated in each tradition? etc. The Christian clergy assumed responsibility for identifying a Christian scholar we would invite, and the rabbis designated the Jewish scholar.

The morning consisted of a limited exposition by the Jewish scholar followed by a response by the Christian, and each scholar could address a question to his or her counterpart.

Following a brief coffee break, the Christian scholar would make the presentation, and the Jewish scholar would give a brief response. All this was followed by an extended lunch hour during which questions could be addressed by the assembled clergy to each of the speakers. That's precisely what we did at the urging of our Christian colleagues! The committee jointly picked the topic and chose the scholars. The format greatly enriched the day.

In the article I wrote for the *Journal on Jewish/Christian Dialogue,* I urged my colleagues not to content themselves with the distinction between Jesus the Man and Jesus the Christ. We proudly claim Jesus the man as one of us, a believing Jew. We tend to dismiss Jesus the Christ as a theological construct attributable to Paul whose claims are, to us, alien and false.

I suggested that if we wanted to enter into dialogue with mainstream Christians, we must make an effort to understand the beauty and spiritual power of Jesus as Christ, not only as understood by the rural preacher we hear while flicking the radio dial, but by great Christian theologians like Karl Barth, Reinhold Niebuhr and Paul Tillich.

A significant indication of the change in the Jewish/Christian encounter in our time was the 1990 symposium jointly sponsored by Notre Dame and The Hebrew Union College and held on the South Bend campus of that distinguished Catholic University with a group of Jewish and Christian presenters. The focus of this symposium was the sometimes hurtful words in our respective liturgies and sacred texts.

The symposium was based on the premise that since Christianity emerged out of Judaism, the first Christians were Jews who believed that Jesus was the long-awaited Messiah. Since there is sometimes no more bitter conflict than one within one's family, many of the hostile, deprecating references to the other in our respective liturgies can be seen as an overheated reflection of that time of separation. Jews, by and large, could not and did not accept Jesus as Christ, and that triggered significant resentment among the passionate devotees of the emerging Christian faith.

That symposium was also based on the premise that if we agree that each community is covenanted to God and has a significant role to play in the divine drama on this Earth, we should try to minimize those hostile, hurtful references which do not speak to the contemporary relationship between Christians and Jews. I had the privilege of being one of the Jewish speakers at the symposium. Let me consider one such hostile reference in our Jewish Passover liturgy and the Reform Movement's response to it.

At a certain point in the Passover Seder, the traditional *haggadah* (liturgy) quotes Psalm 79:6-7 which declares, "Oh, God, pour your wrath upon the *goyim* (gentiles)—Christians who knew Thee not." The insertion of those references reflects the period of the Crusades when Jews experienced so much pain and suffering from the Crusaders on their way to Jerusalem. The Reform haggadah removed those words precisely because of their capacity to be misunderstood and because the initial reason for inserting them is no longer felt in our own relationship to our Christian neighbors—especially in America.

At this point in time, if that program were still operative, it would be appropriate to explore opportunities for a dialogue with Muslim imams in our community. Some years ago, St. Thomas University, through its Faith and Culture Center, held a two-day symposium at which a Christian, Muslim and Jewish scholar were asked to select texts in their sacred books which, if they were taken seriously, would promote peace and harmony among diverse peoples.

As the Jewish participant, I focused on the biblical Aaron who in the Rabbinic agada is known as "a lover of peace and pursuer of peace." In one Rabbinic narrative, Aaron knows of two persons who feel wronged by the other and as a result, are totally estranged. Aaron approaches Reuben and tells him that Simeon is very regretful for any upset he caused him and that Simeon would very much like to be his friend. Aaron then went to Simeon and said that Reuben is very contrite for having lost your favor and wants very much to be your friend. As a result of convicting each of the antagonists of unsuspected virtue, Aaron was able to bring them together again as friends. This agada suggests that peace and concord are such great values that one may even stretch the bounds of absolute truth to achieve them.[17]

In another Rabbinic agada, even God shades the truth in order to sustain harmony between Abraham and his wife, Sarah. When, through an angel, God tells Sarah that even though she was post-menopausal she would bear a son, Sarah laughed. She reminded God that she was old and that Abraham was too old to father a son. The Rabbis who were close readers of scripture noted that when God reported Sarah's reaction to Abraham, God mentioned that Sarah felt she was too old but God did not report to Abraham that Sarah had said he was too old! The Rabbis conclude: in the interest of peace between Sarah and Abraham, even God shaded the truth.[18]

No great, momentous, life-changing outcomes resulted from that symposium, but it did present an opportunity for the representatives of the Abrahamic faiths to be reminded of the great core values we share.

Outreach Through the Written Word

Generally, throughout my forty years as a congregational rabbi, I found it less difficult to write a talk or lecture to be heard than an essay or book to be read. During my rabbinate, I did manage to contribute many essays to chapters in books and to see a collection of my essays, sermons and lectures collected in a volume called *The Soul of the Rav*. Over all those years I managed to write only two books that presented an organized exposition of my thinking.

The first volume is *Agada: The Language of Jewish Faith*, which was published in 1980 by The Hebrew Union College Press. In that volume, I contended that through the agada—the stories of God's relationship with the Jewish people that are imbedded in the Bible and in Rabbinic literature—the fundamental questions of life's meaning are expressed or addressed.

The statement by the editor on the inside cover gives the best summary I have encountered of its contents:

> The fundamental question addressed…is whether Agada can mediate the religious consciousness of the contemporary Jew. Through the stories of Agada the Jew understood the meaning of his people's pilgrimage in history. The author contends that Agada continues to offer the most compelling response to the question, who is a Jew…Reflecting on modernity's challenge to the world of Agada, the author argues that it is possible to give legitimate claims of modernity their due without surrendering the Agada's gift of meaning…With some modification, he argues for the retention of the Agadic framework.[19]

In the end, despite my more ambitious hopes, the book was read more by rabbis than lay persons. I did get generous acknowledgments from a goodly number of rabbis who wrote or told me that the volume would be useful to them in their teaching and preaching. Still, there were more than a few persons whose critical opinion I greatly valued from whom I never heard.

Here I must insert a sidebar that illumines our human need for validation: many years after the book's publication, our congregation hosted a distinguished faculty member from the Jewish Theological Seminary in New York City. He had published a number of books that were serious and thoughtful but more accessible to the lay reader than the general scholarly monograph on Jewish theology. I found his work helpful to me in my reflection and teaching.

When I met with our scholar-in-residence for breakfast I told him how much I had learned and gained from his books. He smiled and then told me what had prodded him to write in this genre. He explained that before his first book, the chancellor of his seminary, a distinguished historian of Jewish medieval thought, mentioned to our visiting scholar that he had read a book titled *Agada: The Language of Jewish Faith* by Sam Karff, a Reform rabbi. The president then added, "Why don't persons like you in our movement do more of this kind of writing?"

What the chancellor did not tell his faculty member that day is that many years earlier he was my counselor at a summer camp in the Pocono Mountains of Pennsylvania! I immediately thought how much it would have meant to me to receive such validation from my former counselor!

CHAPTER 8 ⋄ THE YEARS IN HOUSTON

All this leads to my own *mea culpa*: How often have I been favorably impressed by the work of a colleague but failed to take the time to write him or her? Even more indicting is that over the years I had read a book by that leader of the seminary from which I derived much benefit without taking the time to write or call him. The failure to do so may be attributable not simply to inertia, but partially to my continuing struggle to realize that my life is not a zero sum game and that I "am not diminished by the achievements of others." Each morning, in my private prayer discipline, I ask divine assistance to overcome this zero sum mentality. I recite this prayer in tandem with "I thank you for all that you have enabled me to be and do."

In its extreme form, our inability to acknowledge and enjoy the achievements of others without feeling personally diminished can lead to a state of psychological depression. Julian Simon, one of the more gifted members of my Harvard class, became one of our nation's leading economists. He was the acknowledged leader of a school of economics that argued that unlimited immigration was conducive to economic growth. He was frequently cited in the news and opinion pages of our newspapers.

I never encountered Julian after our graduation but more than a few years ago, I came across a review of a book he had published which was not about his economic theory but focused on his battle with depression. I purchased and read it. Essentially, this honest extended essay detailed how he discovered that no matter how high, illustrious and public his achievements, they were never enough to offset the gloom produced by reading about another colleague who won a major prize for economics or who also wrote a book that was well reviewed. He who was at the top of his game felt diminished by the recognition given to a colleague!

It took much courage to write this book. Julian Simon sought professional help from different therapists over the months and years of his suffering. He even tried and found some respite by observing Sabbath rest in a disciplined way. His resort to cognitive therapy, which disciplines you to disarm the self-destructive thoughts and focus on positive ideation, enabled him to tame the monster of over-competitiveness and self-diminishment. I do not know, but I hope he found inner peace in his latter years. Some years ago, I read of his death in a highly validating obituary in *The New York Times*.

Permission to Believe

The second book I authored was titled *Permission to Believe*. Through the years, I had many encounters with persons who cast me as defender of the faith. These discussions were sometimes intense, at times even confrontational. Some would say they are really agnostics because no one can "prove" to their satisfaction that there is a God. Some claim to have been believers until some devastating event in their lives convinced them of the randomness and inherent meaninglessness of life. Others felt that discarding religion and other "security blankets" marked the dawn of their maturity.

In many of those discussions I discovered that in some way, many of my challengers wanted me to win the argument. They pressed their non-belief against my faith with an intensity that betrayed their deep longing for permission to believe. They wanted me to convince them because they intuited that a religious perspective on life offers the most profound response to the glory and pathos of the human condition.

I was not surprised that Abingdon Press, a major Methodist publishing house, accepted the manuscript. As indicated in my preface, my intention was not

> to write a brief for any one religion…When I speak of religion, I am talking about a liberal faith that charts a course between fundamentalism on the right and an amorphous spirituality on the left. Such faith values tradition for its multiple, sometimes conflicting answers to life's deepest questions. It is strong enough to shape the way we live, yet humble enough to respect the religious quests of others…Although I draw largely from my own tradition, the basic issues of belief and faith transcend any particular heritage. Faith is always personal—a personal opening up to whatever affirms the ultimate value of our lives…I write with the hope that this book will be useful to anyone who seeks to discover or recover faith in a world that is broken.[20]

I brought to those pages my own struggle for faith and the realization that even many of the historic giants of the spirit were not spared their religious struggles with a God who is an invisible presence, both hidden and revealed. I maintained, however, that there is a profound difference between a faith journey that is periodically punctuated by doubt, and grounding one's life journey on steadfast non-belief. In this spirit, the cardinal of Milan, in an address at the Harvard Divinity School, once acknowledged that, "There is a believer and unbeliever in each of us."

This volume was an exposition of a pastoral theology that drew inspiration from many of life's wounded I had the privilege to walk with, listen to, and help to reclaim the meaningfulness of the human journey. Those non-believers who wanted me to win the argument were actually seeking permission to believe. They needed a sense that one could remain a first-class citizen of a high-tech, scientifically advanced society and still experience the presence, power and love of God.

My greatest satisfaction from having written the book was to hear from those who found in it a validation of their right to believe or who, for the first time, felt they were given permission to seriously consider a religious perspective on life.

Other Extensions of My Teaching Rabbinate

For some fifteen years in Houston, at the invitation of Lewis Moore, the religion editor of the *Chronicle*, I wrote a weekly column for the weekend religion section. Subsequently, I broadcast an abbreviated version of my Sabbath sermons on one of the popular music stations. To my surprise, that program, taped for broadcast at 6:45 a.m., had as many as nine thousand listeners—including more than a few Christian clergy who listened while getting ready for their early Sunday morning service. This was far more listeners than I reached even during the High Holidays in my own congregation.

Over the years, two listeners stand out. Once I received a note from a Catholic sister who taught at a day school and claimed to be a regular listener. She noted the time her nephew, visiting from out of town, was made a captive audience when she turned on the program with him in the car while they parked in the church lot before attending early morning Mass. She delighted to tell me that after listening to my sermon and attending Mass, they went to a Jewish delicatessen and ordered bagels with lox and cream cheese. Only in America!

Another day I received a call from Dr. Bill Thornton. After telling me that he listened to the program, he asked if I ever made time to counsel with non-members. He acknowledged having an ethical problem that he felt more comfortable discussing with me than with a Christian pastor. We met in my study. It turned out that Bill Thornton was an astronaut, one of the older persons to go into outer space. An M.D. and Ph.D. physicist by training, he helped to overcome the problems of conducting scientific experiments in a gravity-free environment.

He later called to ask me if my congregation would welcome a satellite photo of Israel taken from outer space. That photo was placed in our religious school building and accompanied by a personal visit to the children by Dr. Thornton in full astronaut regalia. We have enjoyed a warm friendship ever since that initial visit.

Teaching at Rice
When we came to Houston, I hoped to be able to teach at least one course in the religious studies department of Rice University. After the chairman of the department, Niels Nielsen, received a letter from the dean of University of Chicago Divinity School certifying that I had taught at that school and might welcome an invitation to teach at Rice, Dr. Nielsen not only invited me to teach, but also asked me to contribute the chapters on Judaism for a textbook on world religions that he was contracted to edit for St. Martin's Press. That text was eventually used by over 200 colleges here and abroad and went into three editions. It was the only publication for which I received even modest royalties.

One of the interesting sidebars to that project was the extent to which it was shaped by the prevailing zeitgeist (or the current forms of political correctness). Thus, by the second edition, women's issues had gained a much more prominent place in college education and in society at large. Living with four strong women whom I dearly loved (my wife and our three daughters), I was delighted by much of the tone of the Women's Movement; but as we contributors were asked to tailor our general treatment of our subject accordingly, I came to appreciate the more earthly concerns of publishers!

In over twenty-two years of teaching at Rice, one of my favorites was a course team-taught with Dr. Werner Kelber, a New Testament scholar, who would succeed Dr. Nielsen as chairman of the department. We offered a full year's course on the history of the Jewish-Christian dialogue—from Jewish and Christian beginnings to the Second Vatican Council and post-Holocaust Jewish and Christian theology.

One of the challenges of teaching religion as an academic subject rather than "confessionally"—especially for me—is that by vocation I seek to impart a deep commitment to Judaism among my students in the congregation. In an academic setting, particularly in a college which is not faith based, my intention must be to expound Judaism in a way that does not possibly suggest I am seeking converts. Generally, I made the presentational shift from defender of the faith to teacher of Judaism as an academic subject quite well, with two notable, if unintentional, exceptions.

One of the Rice students in the course, whom I shall call Laura, was the only daughter of a devout Christian family from New England. At the end of the course she came to see me, described how much she had been affected by the course and announced her intention to become Jewish. Laura was then twenty. I explained to her that such a profound decision should be approached carefully and deliberately. I reminded her that in Judaism you don't have to become Jewish to attain salvation and that we don't actively proselytize; but we welcome those who wished to embrace our faith.

Laura responded that she had considered the matter seriously, had read much more than was on the reading list, had attended our services, and was even planning to spend the next academic year in Israel. I countered, "You're not even twenty-one and you owe it to yourself and your family to re-explore the heritage you received from your parents. You may not have found the right minister or the right church community, but don't leave a faith that is so precious to your parents without reconsidering its claim on you." I told her she was most welcome to attend our services or study groups, but I would not feel comfortable presiding at her Conversion Ceremony at that time.

Laura left my office dissatisfied but more resolute than before, even as she realized my decision was non-negotiable. However, the next year, when she returned from Israel, she declared that she was now twenty-one and more determined than ever to embrace our Covenant. At this point, I could not, in good conscience, refuse her. I invited her to attend the basic course that is given to prospective converts and to see me after she had completed the course.

In the meantime, I received a heart-wrenching long distance call from Laura's mother. Tearfully she explained how crushed she and her husband felt at the prospect of their only child rejecting the heritage they gave her. She assured me this had nothing to do with Jews or Judaism. I assured her mother that I understood her feelings well and would feel the same if a daughter of mine felt impelled to become Christian. I reminded her that I had discouraged Laura initially and encouraged her to embrace the faith her parents gave her. But now that she was twenty-one, I had no basis to rebuff her.

With a sadness in her voice, Laura's mother thanked me for my sensitivity and asked my understanding if she and her husband could not bring themselves to attend the conversion ceremony. She assured me they loved their daughter no less and prayed that her Jewish life would be a blessing. Then the mother asked me to guide her in selecting an appropriate gift they could send Laura in commemoration of her conversion to Judaism.

After graduation from Rice, Laura studied law and passed the California bar. She worked with a major head-hunting firm that specialized in identifying and vetting top executives for non-profit organizations. We kept in touch by snail mail until I received a very welcome phone call from Laura. She told me she had been dating a Jewish young man. After a couple of dates they realized they were becoming serious. When she said, at one point, "But there's something you ought to know about me," he interrupted, "I know, you're not Jewish. That doesn't matter to me. I haven't dated a Jewish girl since high school." Laura responded, "That's just the point. I am Jewish, and it matters to me that we have a Jewish home for ourselves and our children." Whereupon the young gentleman could only exclaim, "Boy, will my mother be thrilled to meet you!"

Some months later, my wife and I flew to California to officiate at the wedding. Laura's parents were there. They had become fully reconciled to this new reality in their life and even seemed to enjoy the occasion as much as the rest of the wedding party. At the reception they even joined in a Jewish folk dance.

A few years later, a second student in the class, whom I shall call Stuart, decided to embrace Judaism. He grew up in a home that was nominally Christian but non-observant, so he was never really raised as a Christian. Stuart was a Rice computer science major who was deeply affected by the course and by his relation to a close Jewish friend. I encouraged him to attend our Sabbath services and to enroll in the course. About a year later, I had the pleasure of officiating at his ceremony of conversion. He had decided he wanted to go through the ritual of immersion (*mikveh*) and undergo circumcision as an adult.

Stuart not only embraced Judaism, but years later asked me to sponsor his application to become a candidate for the rabbinate. He was ordained at my seminary and to my best knowledge is serving on the faculty of a very ecumenical Christian seminary where one of his responsibilities is to guide seminary students on a study trip to Israel.

Fortunately, to my knowledge, my course did not lead directly to any other conversions. Both Laura and Stuart have found much meaning in their adopted religious heritage.

My Most Controversial Project

When I made a proposal to establish a Jewish day school at Congregation Beth Israel, more than a few people who loved our congregation and loved their Judaism were deeply opposed to it, including some of my close friends. The notion of a Reform day school struck them as an oxymoron. Day schools or parochial schools were for Catholics and Orthodox Jews! There was a time I would have agreed with them.

In the lifetime of many of us, our people were still striving to be fully integrated into American society. In those days, many of the fine private secondary schools were not generally accepting Jewish students. Colleges had their Jewish quotas (at Rice, at one point, Jews were limited to 7%). We were generally excluded from the corporate executive suite, and many other exclusions could be cited.

Given those circumstances, we were fully engaged in trying to remove those barriers that kept us and other minorities from fully embracing the American dream. However, that struggle has been won for the most part. Already, a decade or so before I proposed the day school, America was on the way to becoming the most open society Jews have experienced in all our history. Today any Jew who wishes to assimilate and surrender his Jewish identity may do so. We could no longer count on the exclusions imposed by the non-Jewish world to reinforce our Jewish identity. We were all now Jews by choice. That made all the more challenging the need to forge a Judaism that is distinctive enough and spiritually nourishing enough to cause the next generation to choose Judaism for themselves and their children.

Reform Judaism invites each generation to ask, "How can we best sustain and fulfill our Covenant under the conditions of this time and place?" Hence, I made the effort to establish a deeper track of religious education where some of our students could experience and learn about Judaism, not as an after "regular school" weekday or weekend experience, but as an integral part of their education and their human self-discovery. In such a school, a Jewish chapel experience and the study of Hebrew Bible might be preceded or followed by the study of American history or math.

Fortunately, then-President Jack Lapin championed the project with zeal and wisdom. Those who helped me transform a noble idea into a politically feasible project came to share my vision of a Shlenker School that would be academically challenging yet deeply nurturing, whose curriculum, environment and quality of teaching would make students feel sad to leave the school. We hoped that by the time they graduated from the fifth grade and left for middle school, they would indeed proudly and warmly embrace their Jewish heritage, not only as something imposed by their parents' will, but also as an integral and cherished part of their personhood.

While steadfastly committed to being a Jewish school, we would accept students whose parents wanted them to learn about Judaism as the foundation of their own Christian faith. Over the years, a few such students have attended Shlenker.

We wanted our children to have a strong, positive identification with the Jewish people and a recognition of Israel's importance to our people. At the same time, we hoped our pupils would have some knowledge and respect for the faiths of our Christian and Muslim neighbors.

While affirming the validity of the Reform option in Judaism, we wanted to instill respect for those who embrace Orthodox and Conservative Judaism. In selecting charitable projects that affirm our responsibility to the vulnerable and needy among all peoples, our administrators would be sure to also include assistance to charities and causes outside the perimeter of our Jewish community. We wanted our students to embrace the concept of *tikkun olam*—our responsibility to help repair the brokenness in that tiny corner of God's world entrusted to our care.

The project would include commitment to a building a new edifice that would be used by our religious and Hebrew school students as well as the Shlenker School. This very ambitious project would not have materialized were it not for a core of highly respected leaders in the congregation who bought into it, partially out of their knowledge of how deeply invested I was and their willingness to trust my judgment. For others, including some dear friends, it remained a hard sell.

To counter the sense that such schools were only for Catholics and Conservative and Orthodox Jews, I could point to the fact that the main line churches, including large Episcopalian and Presbyterian congregations were now committed to this deeper track of day school education—and for many of the same reasons that I was advancing in support of a Reform Jewish day school.

These main line Christians also realized that society is so open and so much more secular than Christian that they needed to inculcate Christian beliefs and values in a more powerful way than was provided solely by the traditional Sunday school. In a society where there is so much religious mobility, via inter-marriage and mixed marriage, they also felt they needed to sow the seeds of Christian loyalty more deeply.

Some critics within our community feared the day school would not prepare Jewish children to live effectively in a predominantly non-Jewish world. My most effective counter argument was very personal and could not be given without the prior permission of my wife, Joan, which she happily granted. I contrasted the way Joan and I were raised. She was brought up with only a marginal relationship to her Jewish heritage. She never experienced a Passover Seder until she married me. Joan was sent to a Christian boarding school for her high school education. By contrast, I grew up in a home that was palpably Jewish. We observed the Jewish holidays in our home. I even had a private tutor as a child to introduce me to the great religious stories told by the ancient rabbis.

What was the result of our contrasting forms of our Jewish identity? Joan grew up without pride in her Jewishness, seeing it more as an obstacle to acceptance in the larger community. More significant, Joan felt very insecure in the company of Christians. She felt she was walking on eggs and feared she might be rejected. I, on the other hand, have always felt extremely comfortable and natural in the company of Christians. The difference is that I entered the larger society as a proud, self-respecting Jew. I knew who I was, and I embraced my Jewish identity as a precious heritage.

Fortunately, while the Shlenker School was established without receiving overwhelming or enthusiastic support from many in the congregation, it has since blossomed into a crown jewel of Beth Israel. Virtually without exception, children graduate from the school with a robust pride in their heritage and some wistful sadness at having to leave the Shlenker environment. Some of the very friends who had deep reservations about the school now become misty-eyed as they describe its positive impact on the lives of their grandchildren.

Encountering the Political Arena

Our years in Houston included my several years as president of the Central Conference of American Rabbis. In that capacity I got my first and only invitation to attend a Chanukah party in the White House. President George H. W. Bush was our host. Our delegation presented the president with a Chanukah menorah as a ceremonial gift. One of us chanted the Chanukah blessings over the menorah that had been given to a previous president. Students from a local Washington Jewish day school sang songs and illustrated for the president and Vice-President Quayle how you play Spin the Dreidl. Both the president and vice-president accepted a turn spinning the dreidl. I found this to be the most humorous spectacle I had witnessed in a long time.

When President Bush was nominated by his party to run for a second term, the Republican Convention was to be held in Houston. Ken Lay, then chair of the local Welcoming Committee, invited me to serve on the committee and be responsible for planning a prayer breakfast the morning before the president would give his acceptance speech. After thanking Mr. Lay for the invitation, I informed him, in the interest of full disclosure, that I was not a Republican but an Independent, to which he responded, "Remember, Rabbi, you are not being asked to serve because you are Republican or Democrat, you are being asked as a citizen of Houston to welcome one of our nation's great political parties to our city."

The service was intended to be ecumenical. Not surprisingly, even with our efforts to make it so, it ended predominantly more Christian than neutral. I did manage to invite a member of our congregation, who was the CEO of the Texas Commerce Bank, to read a selection from the Jewish morning liturgy.

That service produced a very memorable, unscripted comment from President Bush that was never reported in the press. Earlier that morning, the president went to Convention Hall to rehearse his acceptance speech. Apparently, he concluded his rehearsing earlier than expected, and he asked to be taken to the Hoffheinz Pavilion where the prayer breakfast was in progress. When he entered the room he was widely cheered, and the Chair invited him to make a few remarks. He was obviously unprepared to do so and found himself speaking these words from the heart: "Friends, I must confess that I feel a little uncomfortable at this event. You see, for us Episcopalians, religion is a private thing." Those few words immediately distanced him and Barbara from their son, George who was a born-again Christian and attributed his recovery from heavy drinking to the rededication of his life to Christ.

In the year 2000, about four weeks before the inauguration of George W. Bush as president of the United States, the Inaugural Committee invited me to participate in a special service that Sunday morning of the inaugural weekend for the president, vice president, their families and their guests, to be held in the majestic Washington National Cathedral. Joan and I were guests of the Republican National Committee. They arranged for our travel, saw that we were met at the airport, taken to our hotel, given reserved seats for the inauguration on Saturday afternoon and for all the inaugural balls that Saturday night.

The weather in Washington that weekend was cold and rainy. As it turned out, we never left our hotel until that Sunday morning when we were picked up and taken to the Cathedral. We had planned to attend the inaugural ceremony Saturday afternoon, but decided we would not be missed and could watch it much more comfortably on TV. We had brought formal clothes for the inaugural events, but we happened to tune in to an interview in the late afternoon of Sally Quinn by Larry King on CNN. When he asked her which ball she would be attending that night, she responded, "None. That's for tourists. You stand in long lines to check your coats, stand in long lines for the buffet dinner that is not very good, and then find little room to really dance." Hearing this, Joan and I immediately decided to enjoy a quiet cozy evening meal at the hotel. We never got to wear our formal clothes.

The next morning, a limo transported us to the Cathedral. Joan took her seat in one of the reserved pews and I was escorted to the robing room where I was introduced to the other participating clergy. The service was very structured. The Episcopal rector of the cathedral had edited the liturgy. Each of us was assigned special parts to read. Mine included a psalm and some verses from the book of Jeremiah which Laura Bush had requested be read in Hebrew and in English. That may well have been the first time Hebrew scripture was read from the altar of Washington National Cathedral in Hebrew. It was a beautiful service with the president and his family, the cabinet and the Supreme Court justices seated in a reserved section in the first few rows. I felt genuinely privileged to be there.

After the service, I witnessed another unscripted moment. Much to the chagrin of the Secret Service, the president lingered to greet the worshippers and sign the program upon request. I was standing about five feet away from the president, when a young African-American lad (who Joan told me later had played a violin solo prior to the service) offered his program to the president and asked for an autograph. President Bush obliged and after signing, he put his hands on the lad's shoulders and said, "Someday, son, you may grow up to be president." The lad responded, "No sir! Not me!" Whereupon the president spontaneously responded, "Trust me, son. If I can do it, you can do it." This was not a disingenuous comment but an honest expression of humility from someone who, at times, wondered himself, how come I'm here? Brother Jeb was supposed to be the political heir in the family. The comment, of course, was also portentous. Now that an African-American is president that lad would have greater reason to say, "Yes, I can!"

Within a week after our return to Houston, I received a hand-written note from George H. W. Bush on his personal stationary:

> Dear Rabbi Karff,
> I am sorry I did not get to tell you today how much my whole family appreciated your participating in today's service at the cathedral. It was ecumenical and the service sent out a strong message of faith and God's love. My respects, sir—Barbara and I send you our family's love.
>
> George H. W. Bush   January 21st, 2001.

Although it was peripheral to the core of my rabbinate, I am gratteful for this public, quasi-political aspect of my years in Houston. The majestic service that morning at the Washington Cathedral was certainly more Christian than neutral. Of the twelve leaders of the service, I was the only non-Christian on the altar, and it was held in a church rather than neutral ground.

On the separation of church and state issue, I have been more a moderate than a purist. I am certain that such total separation of religious expression from the public sphere is not possible, and it may not even be desirable.

This service was designated as a liturgical event, essentially for the president and his family. We were all praying for the proper flourishing of his term in office. On more than a few issues I would strongly disagree with the president and find a proper venue to register dissent, but this was an occasion to wish him and our country well.

When the president's father called the service "ecumenical," he referred in part to my presence and inclusion in it. As I joined in the recession from the altar, I was noticeably moved by the obvious delight registered by body language and even some verbal expressions by the assembled congregation when it was my turn to march down the aisle.

Ideally, the service might have included other non-Christian participants but there is arguably a special Judeo-Christian component in the history of our nation. My only uneasiness on this score appeared in the conclusion of the prayer given by Pastor John Kirby Caldwell, also from Houston, at the Inauguration itself. After giving a prayer that was manifestly Christian, he ended by inviting all who agreed to say, "Amen." I felt denied inclusion in his prayer and made a point of taking him to lunch when we returned to Houston. I asked him how he, an African-American, would feel if I gave a similar prayer on such an occasion which ideally should embrace all Americans and concluded, "Let all who are white say 'Amen.'" Pastor Caldwell conceded the appropriateness of my criticism and said he might do differently on subsequent occasions.

My other moment of uneasiness came when Franklin Graham, substituting for his ailing father, gave a homily that explicitly denied salvation to all but those who embraced Jesus Christ. I recognize that those who espouse other religions or no religion could feel similar uneasiness.

I see no simple feasible solution to the church-state conundrum. I think that we are destined as a nation continually to wrestle with the meaning of church/state separation. Those comments notwithstanding, I am grateful for the privilege of being where I was at the Inauguration that day.

Houston is Our Home

Our years in Houston now exceed four decades, which is much longer than my years anywhere else. We have been here long enough to observe the city attain the status of a major metropolis with all the opportunities and challenges such growth entails. The city is at the cutting edge of the global economy. It mirrors the ethnic and cultural diversity that is rapidly becoming the new American norm. Houston is a vibrant and progressive city.

We came to Houston in 1975 and in retrospect, I can say that, for me and my family, "our lot has fallen in pleasant places." Here I will spend the remaining days of my life. In my years as an active congregational rabbi, Beth Israel provided a nourishing community to live my vocation. In retirement, it remains an embracing, warm, and loving place. My family and I have been blessed by precious friendships.

Some of my rabbinic colleagues have felt it is not possible or wise to cultivate close friendships with those who become lay leaders. In my own experience, I have felt a natural affinity for those who care enough to devote time and energy in its service. Some of our dearest friends are former lay leaders of the congregation.

I am genuinely heartened by the knowledge that the synagogue I served for twenty-four years of my life continues to flourish under the leadership of my successor, Rabbi David Lyon. Someone asked me which I would prefer: to be told that the congregation is flourishing under my successor, or that I am missed. My honest response was both.

Our Houston years coincided with my efforts within the congregation and in the national Reform movement to influence the transition from classical Reform to a post-modern Reform. To those efforts we now turn.

Chapter 9
LIVING & INFLUENCING THE CHANGE TO POST-MODERN REFORM

My SPAN OF FORTY YEARS AS A CONGRE-gational rabbi saw changes in the tone and tenor of Reform Judaism. That should not be surprising in as much as the basic reform question remains always, "How can we fulfill our covenant with God as Jews in this time and place?" Changes in the larger American culture provided the context for a post-modern Reform Judaism.

I use the term post-modern to signify the shift from Moses Mendelssohn's notion that he could separate his Jewishness from his personhood. Thus a biographer could write that Mendelssohn "despised apostasy as dishonorable but would gladly have joined his (Christian) friend Lessing in a society where there were neither Jews nor Christians."[21] Optimally, in post-modern Reform, we would view the Torah at its best as the means whereby someone who is a Jew cultivates his or her humanity most authentically. In this view we don't shed or aspire to shed our Jewishness in order to enter a neutral human sphere; rather we make our distinctive contribution to the larger American culture by reflecting the noblest forms of our Jewish identity.

This shift was reflected in the larger culture as America became more self-consciously a pluralistic society—multi-racial, multi-ethnic and multi-religious. The Civil Rights Movement that affected the status of all minorities in America was a re-affirmation of pride in our distinctive identities ("Black is beautiful"). In this era, Jews with Jewish-sounding names, even in high-profile professions like journalism and the cinema were more likely to retain their given names.

Another manifestation of a cultural shift is that science was no longer considered the final arbiter of all kinds of truth. Science can tell us how to build a nuclear bomb; it cannot tell us whether or not to use it. Not all that can claim to be true is demonstrable by the methods of science. Scientism is a vain effort to "materialize the subjective." Science helps us analyze and control the world. It is not applicable to the great meaning questions such as: What is the deepest source of meaning in our lives? Why should I be good even if there is no tangible reward for being so? What is the ultimate ground of my hope?

Another sign of a cultural change which occurred during my lifetime is the deepening of the "hunger for the sacred," or the renewed interest in religion and spirituality on college campuses. When I was in college, the study of religion was marginalized. Now there are over 300 Jewish Studies departments in American colleges and universities. General courses in religion are generously subscribed and well attended. A course on Hebrew scripture at Harvard taught by an Orthodox Jewish professor has enrolled 125 students. A general course on ethics is similarly fully subscribed. Generally, our culture has become more sympathetic to the proposition that not everything in life is a problem to solve; life is also a mystery to embrace.

Perhaps most significantly, America has become the most open and freest society we Jews have ever lived in. Many of us are old enough to remember the time in the United States when Jews were generally excluded from the corporate suite, Jewish doctors were prevented from practicing in more than a few hospitals and Jewish lawyers knew not even to apply to the large firms. We could not live in certain posh neighborhoods. Jewish professors were denied tenure in many universities, and a Jewish president of an Ivy League university was an impossible dream. How radically different is the American environment today.

This ripening of America is also evidenced in the account by pundit Max Lerner of his life story. He confessed that he left Brooklyn for Yale and married out of the faith in part to escape from his Jewish identity. His children also married non-Jewish spouses—not to escape from a disadvantaging Jewish identity but because in an open society they fell in love with non-Jewish persons. While the rate of intermarriage has increased in this open society, some Jews have been brought closer to Jewish religious life by their marriage to a non-Jew. One of them is *New York Times* pundit David Brooks. In an interview, which appeared in *The Jewish Times*, Brooks acknowledged that after three years of marriage his wife converted to Judaism, insisted that they keep a kosher home and that their children attend a Jewish day school. Their social lives "are less involved with Washington's power brokers and journalists, but rather built around weekly Shabbat dinner with friends from their shul and their kid's schools."[22]

A Revaluing of Ritual

Another of the characteristics of post-modern Reform is a much more positive view of ritual. Classical Reform defined us essentially as stewards of the "message of Israel" which was embodied in "ethical monotheism." A faithful Jew bears witness to God by zealously rejecting all substitute objects of worship, by righteous and loving deeds and by daring to hope that God's dream for creation will ultimately be fulfilled.

Ritual was intended to hold that noble vision in protective custody. Ritual was designed to unite the Jewish people, preserve our sacred memories, and symbolize the ethical ideals for which we stand. Public worship is such a ritual as is the celebration of the Passover Seder.

Many rituals were discarded as non-essential and even as distracting us from our primary mission. Some were discarded as irrational or superstitious. Generally our classical Reform elders believed that Judaism at its best is a legacy of ideas more than a richly symbolic style of life.

But America in the sixties and seventies valued lifestyle over conceptualization; it was an age of body language and sensitivity training, of proclamation by demonstration, of folk song and dance more than extended formal oratory, an age to celebrate the mystery rather than to demythologize it.

This more positive valuation of ritual was abetted by the fact that many of the main line churches, in response to the new cultural zeitgeist, also gave more emphasis to ritual. Even more portentous was a new look at the words of a Rabbinic sage who imagined God saying, "If they were to forsake me (by not believing in me) I should forgive them if they may yet keep my Torah (including ritual as well as ethical commandments). For if they forsake me but keep my Torah [the Torah] will bring them closer to me."[23]

The wisdom of this ancient sage is evidenced in the contemporary research of world-class cultural anthropologist, Clifford Geertz, who, on the basis of studying many cultures around the world, concluded, "ritual observance has been a significant way of engendering religious faith."[24]

The Return of Herman Gollub

Ritual can play a significant role in promoting spiritual growth. Herman Gollub opened himself to the spiritual dimension of life when he contemplated his retirement from a long, distinguished career as a book publisher. In his memoir, *Me and Shakespeare,* Gollub acknowledges a deep hole in his life. His stressful working years were characterized by "competitiveness...the self-absorption of careerism...the emotional sterility of operating, for the most part, in a critical, analytical mode, in the thrall of the intellect."[25] Essentially, he had lived the life of the mind but had starved his inner spirit.

Growing up in a non-religious family, Gollub never had a bar mitzvah, although at the insistence of a relative, he underwent a perfunctory confirmation service. Seventeen years later Gollub returned to the synagogue for his wedding ceremony. Although well-schooled in Western secular literature, he was totally ignorant of his religious heritage.

After his wedding, Gollub was absent from the synagogue

for another twenty years—until he was invited to attend the bar mitzvah of a friend's son. He came to the synagogue that day only to honor his friend, but he discovered he could not remain a passive observer. One of the ritual high points of the Shabbat service was an invitation for the congregation to rise as the Torah scroll is ceremoniously taken from the Ark. Certain prayers are sung involving the congregation and the cantor and one of the officiants leads a processional with the Torah scroll down the aisles of the synagogue, so when it passes your row and you are near the aisle, you may kiss the fringe of your prayer shawl and then let the fringe touch the Torah.

In earlier days, Gollub would have regarded such a ritual as quaint and interesting, but that morning he found himself kissing the fringes of his tallit and touching them to the Torah scroll. At that moment, he knew he had crossed a significant threshold. He started reading books on Judaism and observing some of the Sabbath rituals at home. He and his wife joined a neighborhood synagogue where Gollub began to study for the bar mitzvah he had missed in his youth.

Of his adult bar mitzvah, Herman Gollub wrote,

> Came the big day, I didn't feel like a performer, holding the Torah, I felt a sense of joy, a mystical sense of being with the Divine, and for the first time understood that God had made a covenant not only with the Israelites but with all the future generations. I was standing at Sinai with an aching humility and a feeling of innocence and beauty that brought me close to tears during the ceremony.[26]

Post-classical Reform teaches that the freedom to discard rituals which became meaningless includes the freedom to reclaim those which, in our present frame of mind and spirit, can help us connect to our deeper selves, our community and God.

Reform vs. Orthodox View of Ritual

In this new context, how do we distinguish between an Orthodox and Reform perspective on ritual? For the Orthodox Jew, the ultimate warrant for keeping a kosher diet is that it is commanded in the Torah and/or the rabbi insists that I should. A Reform Jew who keeps kosher chooses to do so because he or she finds this to be a meaningful spiritual discipline, but will not regard another Jew as less authentic if he or she does not find keeping dietary laws as a way of deepening his or her Jewish spirit.

Reform continues to recognize that not all of us will be drawn closer to our covenant by performing all the same rituals; nor is a Jew who performs the most rituals necessarily the more authentic Jew. By temperament, a Reform Jew is more comfortable retaining a greater measure of personal choice, although, as we suggested earlier, there are boundaries beyond which the exercise of freedom lapses into irresponsibility. In the final reckoning, ritual propriety can never become a substitute for ethical conduct in our relationships to ourselves and to other persons.

Authentic Judaism Holds Truths in Creative Tension

Over a span of forty years as a rabbi, I have lived through and played a role in the Reform Movement's transition from classical Reform to its current post-classical mode. Yet I am deeply disturbed when some colleagues who entered the rabbinate quite happily when its classical mode was dominant now make invidious comparisons which belittle our classical roots even as they proudly describe the rightness of our Movement in its present post-classical mode.

I expressed such concern during a talk given to faculty and students at our seminary, The Hebrew Union College-Jewish Institute of Religion in Cincinnati in December of 1974, just six months before I was to begin serving Congregation Beth Israel in Houston. I titled my talk, "The Legacy of Classical Reform." That night, I suggested that rather than snidely depreciate the classical Reform under which we entered the ranks of professional Judaism, we should acknowledge that our classical Reform elders earnestly and successfully met the spiritual needs of many Jews in their time, even as we are seeking to do the same for our generation. We are Reform Jews, not reformed Jews; change is of the essence in Judaism as each generation asks: How can we best serve God as Jews under the conditions of this time and place?

Let us acknowledge that we are standing on their shoulders. Let us also recognize that in a period when we seek to enrich our Jewish styles of living, we ought not neglect the distinctive "message of Israel" we carry with us. Even as we attach more spiritual resonance to the ritual deed, we must be able to tell the Jewish story. Even as we seek to revitalize Jewish worship, let us not denigrate the value of a good homily or D'var Torah. Even as we unite to defend ourselves against those who challenge our right to be, we must also build bridges to the many persons of other faiths who acknowledge that the life and witness of our people is still needed in this world.

For those within our ranks who propose a more disciplined *halachic* (governed by Jewish law) rigor within our Movement, I had this message,

> As far as I can discern, even the most fervent neo-traditionalist among us is not anxious to surrender the freedom to wend his own way through the labyrinths of *halachah*. The early Reformers struggled to establish the authenticity of non-Orthodox Jewish options. That battle is not yet fully won in some circles. Must we now say to Reform's detractors, you were right in condemning our elders but we are different! To regard classical Reform with such condescension is not only unbecoming but unwise.[27]

I concluded that talk to the faculty and my future colleagues at the seminary,

> As we struggle for a valid understanding of liberal Judaism today, feel not compelled to file an evil report on classical Reform, or imagine their legacy is expendable in our time. We are at our best when we hold up both the vision of our elders and the vision of the neo-traditionalists among us and rediscover with some humility and grace that "these and these are the words of the living God."[28]

The Current Challenge to our Reform Seminary

During my years in Chicago and later in Houston, I was privileged to participate actively in leadership roles within our Movement. These were the years when my essays appeared regularly in the *CCAR Journal,* the periodical published quarterly by the Central Conference of American Rabbis. From 1981 through 1984, I edited the *Journal*. A few years earlier, to mark the centennial anniversary of our seminary, I edited a volume titled *Hebrew Union College-Jewish Institute of Religion: At 100 Years*.

My introductory essay focused on the role of the college institute in training Reform Rabbis for this post-classical era. Written from the perspective of the needs of a new generation of congregants, the essay suggested that

> [By] now this role of Rabbinic apologists has diminished considerably. The American Jewish community has come of age...moreover, the level of overt anti-Semitism has considerably ebbed.
>
> Neither is the liberal American Rabbi still cast as the broker of the best in American culture to a constituency deprived of a college education. The overwhelming majority of his congregants...most appreciate the Rabbi's mastery of Judaism and his capacity to transmit it effectively...They are not in need of a Rabbi to further their acceptance in American society but to offer them, within the life of the Synagogue, that nurture of the [Jewish] mind and spirit not readily available in the mass media or the market place. Less than ever can the American Jewish community afford mediocrity in its Rabbinic leadership. More discerning than ever before is the constituency whose respect and responsiveness the Rabbi covets.
>
> In a culture with increasingly specialized roles, great physical mobility, and intense fragmentation, the Rabbi is commissioned to foster a sense of the whole. He is enlisted to help Jews find in the wisdom and the symbols of

their heritage the power to perceive their lives as part of a significant story. More than ever will the conscientious Rabbi feel the need to draw upon the classical texts. More than ever will he need to wrestle with the possibilities and limits of halachic and agadic change. He must grope for that balance between revision and re-appropriation which alone can grant him the grace of authenticity. That task must surely be initiated within the walls of the college institute. The tone and temper it assumes will provide an operational definition of the word *Reform*.[29]

Some Heady Recognition for a Young Rabbi

The year 1967 was marked by the Arab-Israeli "Six Day War." The Reform congregations in North American belong to an organization then known as the Union of American Hebrew Congregations (recently re-named The Union for Reform Judaism-URJ). Reform rabbis are part of an organization known as The Central Conference of American Rabbis (CCAR). The seminary that ordained me and most other Reform rabbis was known as The Hebrew Union College until, in 1948, it merged with The Jewish Institute of Religion and became known as "HUC-JIR or The College Institute."

In the spring of 1967 I was invited to deliver the ordination address at my seminary. The invitation was extended by then president Nelson Glueck who, although ordained as a rabbi, was internationally known as the archeologist who discovered King Solomon's copper mines. (You may recall the incident described earlier involving his invitation to novelist Saul Bellow to visit the HUC-JIR.)

The Chairman of the Board at URJ was always a layman, but its president was Rabbi Maurice Eisendrath, who was generally considered the titular leader of the Reform Movement. That summer, I received an invitation from him to be the banquet speaker at the Union's biennial convention that November in Montreal. This international conclave drew more than a thousand delegates even in those years. The previous biennial speaker was Martin Luther King.

Two such invitations within a few months of each other were heady stuff for a rabbi only thirty-five years old! Before I left Montreal, Rabbi Eisendrath asked me to consider joining the Union staff with the possibility that "somewhere down the line" I might be asked to succeed him.

A year later during part of a summer in Israel, I was taken around Israel in Dr. Glueck's jeep. He spent nearly every summer digging in the Negev region. During our ride, he took me to an Arab antiquities dealer with whom he had done much business. He made a point of securing for me that day (at no expense to himself) a little oil lamp that was thousands of years old, which I still treasure. In the course of our ride, Dr. Glueck suggested to me that he was close to retirement and would like me to be a candidate to succeed him.

Initially, I truly felt that I was most suited by temperament and would find most meaning in remaining a congregational rabbi. I knew even then that the majority of a college president's time is expended in fund-raising and that the Union position, if available, would sentence me to considerable travel alternating with administering a bureaucracy in an office building in New York City. The even greater strain on my availability to my wife and children in either position struck a cautionary note within me.

I easily declined the invitation to join the Union staff, but several years later when the actual search for Dr. Glueck's

CHAPTER 9 ❖ LIVING & INFLUENCING THE CHANGE TO POST-MODERN REFORM

successor began in earnest, I was pressured by some members of the faculty and by Dr. Glueck to become a candidate. The major inducement was that as president, despite the heavy burden of fund-raising, I would have the opportunity to shape the mind-set of future rabbis and help forge a vision for rabbinic education in our seminary. I allowed myself to be a candidate. I knew there were search and selection committees but Dr. Glueck's word would be decisive.

At the same time, the CCAR was creating a committee to assess what needs of future rabbis were not being adequately met by the current curriculum at our seminary. When asked by the then president of the Conference to serve on that committee, I gladly accepted. Hearing of my participation, Dr. Glueck summoned me and told me he considered the existence of this committee an act of disloyalty and expected me to resign. I tried to persuade him that he and the members of that committee shared the same goal and that, rather than oppose it, he would do better to embrace and eventually co-opt us. Dr. Glueck was not persuaded, and when I refused to resign, I knew that my candidacy as his successor would no longer bear fruit.

Still, by now my ego was engaged and I stuck it out—only to discover that my initial conclusion was correct. Not having lost many professional goals I seriously pursued, my losing this one was painful at the time. Yet, in retrospect it was the best thing that could have happened to me and to the College Institute.

With the passage of the years, I became more certain than ever that I was destined to remain a congregational rabbi. As such, I would be taking an increasing role in the leadership circle of the Conference culminating in a two-year term as its president. In that context, let me describe three major changes our Reform Movement instituted.

Women Rabbis?

Over the centuries, Judaism has made a clear distinction between men and women's roles in religious life outside the home. In the synagogue, men and women sat separately. Men led the worship service even as all priests in the ancient Temple were men. Men recited blessings over and chanted the Torah. Women had religious duties in the home including, for example, blessing the Sabbath and Festival lights. But because of the prominent role of tending to the children, women were excused from religious obligations that must be performed at an appointed hour.

David Gelernter, an eloquent defender of modern Orthodoxy, celebrates this asymmetry in gender roles. Religious life is properly "partitioned, like the Temple. Men are in charge of public religion. Women take precedence in private religion at home."[30] Duly acknowledging that the non-existence of female rabbis has taken on "for some women the force of tragedy" Gelernter responds that

> Judaism can sympathize but can't do anything about it… the roles of reader, singer and officiator at Synagogue were conceived for men in the same sense that the stage roles of Hamlet or Henry V were. A woman can say the words, as a man can play Rosalind or Lady Macbeth, but when it happens, the result is less than satisfying and everyone knows it.[31]

With all due respect, that sensibility makes me especially pleased to be a Reform Jew. There have been two stages in the process of reappraising the role of women in Jewish life. The first came with the dawn of the Reform Movement in Germany in the nineteenth century. At the very first Reform Jewish service in 1810, the *mechitzah* (partition dividing male and female worshippers) was removed. Family pews were instituted with men, women and children sitting together for worship.

Women were counted as part of the quorum of ten persons required for public worship. In the Reform religious school, boys and girls studied together. Reform introduced the Confirmation service as a Covenant renewal ceremony for teenaged boys and girls.

The second stage in the evolution of the woman's role in the synagogue was the Women's Movement in the latter part of the twentieth century. It was then not uncommon for a woman to become bat mitzvah, which included blessing and reading from the Torah and offering a brief homily explaining how that Torah portion applied to her life. It was not uncommon for women to serve on the Board and even become president of the congregation.

Then came the ultimate step. In 1974, our Reform seminary ordained a woman rabbi. Reform's attitude on this and other gender issues is formed, ultimately, not by the precedents of halacha but by the changing roles of women in society. Again, we are reminded of the operative principle of Reform: How can we best fulfill our covenant with God under the conditions of this time and place?

Because of technological innovations in the home, and the availability of daycare, women's options have expanded.

We felt Jewish women should not be excluded from choosing to use their gifts to provide spiritual leadership for our people. If men and women's creation in the divine image is the basis for the inalienable dignity of each, why not expand within the Jewish community a woman's opportunity to find fulfillment and opportunities for service not only in the home, but also in the synagogue?

There was some initial push-back within our congregations. The first women to crash the male rabbinic boundary had to be like Jackie Robinson when he broke the color barrier in baseball. They had to demonstrate their equal or superior competence and not become overly defensive when some overt or subtle resistance was evident.

By now, most of our people are not only comfortable with female rabbis and cantors; they take this monumental change for granted or are expressively grateful that the rabbi pool has been so significantly expanded and enriched. To be sure, like their male counterparts, women rabbis vary in their competence and suitability for the role, but taken as a whole, it can be said that the addition of women to our rabbinic ranks has significantly elevated the overall quality of rabbinic preaching, the depth of rabbinic spirituality and our poetic sensibility.

No doubt women in the congregational rabbinate face the same juggling act as women in other professions. Some who realize that it is impossible to have it all, to be exempt from paying a price for our vocational choices, have taken non-congregational positions, leaves of absence during their children's younger years, or gladly withdrawn from aspiring to senior rabbinic responsibility.

All in all, the fateful decision to ordain women rabbis, (followed ten years later by the Conservative Synagogue Movement in Judaism) has immensely enriched our Reform Movement.

This change was led by our Seminary with the encouragement of the Central Conference of American Rabbis and the Union for Reform Judaism. As I told our congregation when we engaged our first woman rabbi, it was not because we expressly sought a woman, but because we felt that this particular person could best meet the needs of our congregation at that time. We had no reason to regret that choice. Rabbi Carole Meyers was a fine preacher, a gifted teacher and a great comforter to persons who had faced the darker side of life.

The Issue of Inclusive Gender Language

With the rise of the Women's Movement in America, it followed naturally that the emergence of women rabbis would become a probability in the Reform Movement. Not surprisingly, the issue of inclusive gender language in our prayer book was also raised—and not only by our women rabbis.

The emergence of this issue helped me hone my own sensitivity to the need for more inclusive language in our next prayer book. The raising of my own consciousness had already made me uncomfortable in retrospect with the lack of such inclusiveness in my book, *Agada: The Language of Jewish Faith*, published by the Hebrew Union College Press in 1979. I was invited to be part of the initial discussion group that processed a number of issues raised by the projected publication of a new Reform prayer book. That discussion included the need for more gender inclusive language.

The impulse to actually change the language of ancient prayers bumped up against the feeling of many that such time hallowed linguistic traditions have acquired a sanctity which should not be tampered with. Ultimately we concluded that biblical texts were canonized and never altered, whereas prayer books went through many editions that included some variations in language. Thus we would not tamper with "He leads me beside the still waters." (Psalm 23) but would feel more freedom to make additions to prayers in our classic liturgy.

In illustration of that editorial privilege, we may point to the Amida, that central prayer of the daily, Sabbath and Festival liturgy which was changed from, "Blessed are you, Adonai…God of our fathers, God of Abraham, God of Isaac, and God of Jacob," to "…God of our fathers and mothers, God of Abraham, God of Isaac, and God of Jacob, God of Sarah, God of Rebekah, God of Rachel and God of Leah."

A related issue was exclusively masculine God language. Literally, God transcends gender differentiation, and in our Kabbalah, or mystical tradition, God is both masculine and feminine. The broadly used term to connote the immanence of God's indwelling presence was the feminine noun, Shechinah. The solution of those who actually edited our latest prayer book, published in 2007, was to avoid gender specific names for God in favor of such neutral or inclusive terms as Eternal One, Sovereign, etc. The editors did not alter Biblical references in the prayer book even when they were explicitly masculine.

Over the years, I have been invited to give many invocations and benedictions. Generally, I favored exclusively gender-inclusive or gender-neutral language for references to the Divine. By way of illustration: "You who are the Source of our being," or "Holy One."

Who is a Jew? The Issue of Matrilineal/Patrilineal Descent

Since the end of the nineteenth Century most Reform rabbis in the United States did not require adult circumcision and immersion in the ritual bath (mikveh) as a pre-condition for conversion to Judaism. At the CCAR conference held in Phoenix in March, 1979, I was asked to debate the Reform requirement for Jewish status with Rabbi Dow Marmur, a distinguished colleague. Rabbi Marmur then took a position that in the interests of Jewish unity and survival, we Reform rabbis should not deviate from the traditional criteria for Jewish status; that adult converts should be required to undergo circumcision if male and ritual immersion if female. Moreover, he called for retaining the traditional standard for Jewish status—someone born of a Jewish mother is Jewish and someone whose father is Jewish but whose mother is not must undergo conversion to be considered Jewish.

I countered that prospective converts should be made aware of the traditional standards for conversion as a living option but not as a requirement. Some or even many may choose to undergo these ritual procedures but for many males, adult circumcision is a psychologically heavy procedure that engenders critical anxiety without offering a meaningful, positive symbol of what is central to a mature adult's embrace of Judaism.

To those like Rabbi Marmur who say that without those physical bodily rituals the conversion ceremony would be shallow in meaning, I countered that to study Judaism, to adopt a Hebrew name, to hold the Torah scroll while reciting the Sh'ma Yisrael prayer, to formally pledge to embrace our faith and our people under all circumstances and conditions and to be blessed by the rabbi—all this carries more than enough gravitas and emotional resonance.

Most controversial of all has been Reform's claim that to have one Jewish parent—mother or father—and to be raised as a Jew, makes one a Jew without need for a conversion ceremony. In advocating this position, we need only restate the operative Reform question: How do I best perform my covenantal responsibilities to God and the Jewish people under the conditions of this time and place?

Why the matrilineal criterion of Jewish status all through the centuries? In the age of the Bible, and in the early rabbinic period, descent was traced through the male. During the period of the Greco-Roman Empire, if a Roman soldier fraternized with a Jewish woman and a child emerged from that relationship, there was no civil marriage. They would return to their own people and the woman would take the child to her family. Moreover, in situations where paternity was in doubt, maternity was far more easily established. That was the probable origin of matrilineal descent in Jewish life.

In the period following the Jewish emancipation from the ghettos (eighteenth century) until at least the middle of the twentieth century, maintaining the matrilineal criterion for Jewish status was sustainable. Prior to that time, most Jews and Christians vigorously opposed interfaith marriages for their children and such marriages were relatively uncommon. But as our American society became much more open—as Jews and Christians of marriageable age had much more social interaction in the workplace and the university—they were much more likely to fall in love with each other. In many instances this was not intended as an act of disloyalty to their given heritage, but a natural result of propinquity.

Once the percentage of interfaith couples increased to as much as 50%, new conditions required, we believed, a different response. As a member of the CCAR, I was part of the committee that established that Jewish status can be conferred on the basis of paternal or maternal Jewish heritage, if the child is raised as a Jew.

In an age of interfaith couples, the religious identity of the child is likely to be determined by the parent who feels more strongly connected to his or her heritage. I know of many situations in which the Jewish male's insistence on the children being raised Jewish was agreed to by the non-Jewish mate. In still other situations, it was, paradoxically, the non-Jewish woman, unprepared to convert to Judaism herself, who not only acquiesced to the children being raised as Jewish, but insisted that the Jewish mate establish a Jewish home and see that the children got a Jewish education!

One of the counter-arguments made by Rabbi Marmur and some colleagues is that in the name of the unity of the Jewish people, we should observe the requirement that if someone has a Jewish father and the mother is not Jewish, the child's Jewishness should require formal conversion. On similar grounds, they contended that we should require of gentile converts that they undergo adult circumcision or immersion in the ritual bath.

My response to that argument in the debate was and remains to this day that adopting a more stringent conversion procedure or demanding conversion where there is patrilineal rather than matrilineal descent would not make us kosher in the eyes of the Orthodox Jewish authorities. Nothing short of complete surrender of our independent Reform authority would satisfy. I concluded that our prevailing Reform policy in the United States "is not thinning the ranks of Jewry, nor does it violate the imperative of Jewish survival." I also suggested that,

> The most elemental common denominator of Jewish status in a post-Holocaust world is a sharing of fate and destiny. The ultimate hallmark of Jewish legitimacy is neither the *milah* (circumcision) or mikveh (ritual immersion) certificate, but a willingness to affirm in word and deed, "'Your people are my people and your God, my God.'"[32]

I concluded,

> By all means, let us focus on the larger concerns: We must imaginatively address the issue of preserving Jewish vitality and continuity in an open society—a society in which we are numerically a miniscule minority and in which one can, if he chooses, totally distance himself from the mainstream of Jewish life…let us make our distinctive contribution to Jewish survival as self-respecting Reform Jews who claim full partnership in the household of Israel.[33]

It takes considerable courage and humility to modify one's initial position. Subsequently, on the basis of his experience with offspring of mixed marriage, Rabbi Marmur has since endorsed the acknowledgment of patrilineality as a legitimate ground for Jewish status. In an article, Rabbi Marmur has acknowledged, "Many children of mixed marriages who otherwise might have been lost to Judaism are now active members of Jewish communities and are raising Jewish children because Rabbis and congregations put people before principles—liberal Judaism at its best."[34]

Gays, Lesbians and the Rabbinate

In the late 1980s, the issue of ordaining gay and lesbian rabbis came to the fore in our conference. We all knew closet gay students in our seminary who were our friends. That friendship alone made the ordination of gay and lesbian rabbis un-evadable. In 1986, the president of the conference appointed a committee to study the issue and produce discussion and action by our conference plenum. Though appointed to that committee, I had no inkling at the time that I would be presiding as president of the CCAR at the historic 1990 convention when that report would be presented for action by the plenum.

Our committee was a cross-section of major stakeholders. It included some rabbis who were known to be gay or lesbian, those of us who had no official standing on the issue, representatives from the URJ (our lay body) and from the seminary faculty. We realized the seriousness of the issue and how deeply fraught with repercussions it would be.

We began by examining the relevant biblical references. Leviticus 18:22, "Do not lie with a male as one lies with a woman; it is an abhorrence." The second relevant verse was Leviticus 20:13, "If a man lies with a male as one lies with a woman the two of them have done an abhorrent thing; they shall be put to death—their blood guilt is upon them."

Next, we considered what we know now that our ancestors did not know which would have a bearing on our deliberations. The key issues revolved around our biblical ancestors' view that homosexual expression was a choice—an evil choice—but one that could be resisted. For them homosexuality was an act or series of acts—not a state of being.

Our consultation with texts and experts in the social and biological sciences showed at that time an absence of consensus on these critical issues. The scholarly opinions seemed to be divided between finding the ideology of homosexuality in one's given nature and attributing it to psychodynamic factors in one's primary relationships. Even in the latter case, it may still be an irreversible condition. At the time we formulated our report, the jury was still out.

Certain things did seem clear to the majority of the committee; the fact that the Bible labels such conduct as a sin worthy of death does not mean that our tradition gave the Bible in its literalness the last word. We read that if someone has a "wayward and defiant son who does not heed his father or mother or does not obey them even after they discipline him...he shall be brought into the public square and stoned to death" (Deuteronomy 21:18, 21). Apparently, our Rabbinic sages could not accept such a decree, so they simply concluded that there never has been a son in Israel who fits that category![35] If one is unable to accept the biblical notion that homosexuality is an evil choice that can and ought to be resisted, there is no lack of ways in our tradition to counter the impact of such biblical literalism.

The crucial consideration is that we have come to believe that, for many, homosexuality is their given identity and fate. If one doubts that this is so, one must ask: Why would anyone but a masochist actually choose a way of expressing his human sexuality which resulted until relatively recently, in so much hardship, discrimination and the urge to remain in the closet? In 1990, after four years of small group discussion throughout our Movement, we were ready to present to the plenum a report that the overwhelming majority of our committee could endorse.[36]

That report stipulated, "It is clear that for many people sexual orientation is not a matter of conscious choice but constitutional and therefore not subject to change."[37]

Given the positive valence Judaism gives to human sexuality in the context of faithful, loving relationships, imposing celibacy on Jews incapable of feeling heterosexual attraction seems inappropriate if not outright *hutzpah* (audacity). The report does affirm that there can be spiritual significance and holiness in such same-sex relationships. Helpful to me in processing this situation were two Talumdic principles that I apply in a more expansive way than an Orthodox legal authority. The first was enunciated by Rabbi Simeon ben Gamaliel: "A rabbinic court should not decree for a community more than they are capable of observing."[38] I take that to mean that we, who understand that homosexuality is more a fate than a choice, ought not to expect such a person to fulfill that which is not possible.

Another Rabbinic principle affirms the centrality of affirming and respecting the dignity of all human creatures. Thus, we learn that "*Kvod Habryiot* (the honor of God's creatures) is so important that it suspends a biblical law"[39] Again, our interpretation is more expansive than a strict Orthodox halachic scholar would allow, but I take it to mean that imposing mandatory celibacy on a homosexual person—denying such persons any "kosher" expression of their human sexuality—would be a violation of their essential human dignity.

A corollary of that principle is, "To the extent that sexual orientation *is a matter of choice* the majority of the committee affirms that heterosexuality is the only appropriate Jewish choice to fulfill one's covenantal obligations." In other words, for those capable of fulfilling it, monogamous, heterosexual relationships are the Jewish norm.

From this we went on to discuss whether persons who by fate and by destiny are homosexual should be eligible to be ordained as rabbis in the household of Israel. In consultation with our seminary, then-president Alfred Gottschaulk clarified that "HUC considers the sexual orientation of an applicant only within the context of the applicant's overall suitability for the rabbinate, his qualifications to serve the Jewish community effectively and his or her capacity to find personal fulfillment within the rabbinate." Our report endorsed that HUC-JIR admittance policy.

After viewing the text of the report approved by the majority of the committee, a small number of members felt constrained to issue a minority report. In essence it declared, "equal possibility of covenantal fulfillment in homosexual and heterosexual relationships. The relationship, not gender should determine its Jewish value as *kiddushin* (the term for a Jewish marriage)." The minority was not prepared to link our legitimation of homosexual relationships to situations where there is no choice.

My reason (and most of the committee's) for privileging heterosexuality where there is choice was both personal and political. Most of us felt this way and we also felt that the only way to avoid a highly divisive floor battle once the report was up for discussion and vote, and the only way to ensure its passage by an overwhelming majority of the plenum, was to formulate the issue in those terms. Namely, that to the extent there is choice, heterosexual monogamous marriage is the Jewish norm.

I did preside at the Seattle convention in June of 1990. It was very well-attended. Much to the relief of the overwhelming majority who were there, we had no floor fight. When the minority report was presented it was quickly rejected. The vote, in favor of the majority report, passed by nearly 95%. Notice of our decision appeared in the press all over the world. Alas, the nuanced form of the resolution was totally lost in the transmission to all but the religious writer of the *Houston Chronicle* who had received an extensive briefing from me.

How much the cultural environment and my personal stance has changed since then! It is now virtually consensual that whether homosexuality is the way we are born or significantly affected by our primary relationships in the family, it remains more a fate—the way we are wired or if we prefer, the way God made us—than a choice. Moreover, it is a state of being that cannot be and should not be attempted to be changed by therapy.

In our committee's deliberations at one point, I raised the question: "We know that feeling some attraction for persons of the same sex or even having experimented with a homosexual episode does not necessarily make one gay or lesbian. Suppose a teenager came to see you and expressed deep anxiety about feeling such attraction. What would you counsel him?" The majority of the committee appeared to agree with me when I responded, "I would first make it clear that having such feelings is not that unusual and in itself does not make one gay. I would then counsel the person to discuss his sexual feelings with a therapist and if, as a result of that interview, it becomes clear that you are gay, you should proudly affirm who you are, respect it and live it responsibly. If, however, there is a professional feeling that you could go either way, because of the cultural situation if nothing else, your potential heterosexuality is worth striving for."

Now, twenty-five years later, I would not make that referral. Really listening to the person should make his or her sexual orientation clear, and I would strongly encourage the person to embrace and cherish who he or she is. Twenty-five years later, there is an overwhelming consensus that our sexuality is who we are and who we are intended to be. The final arbiter of our sexual orientation is the person.

A number of other changes are noteworthy: first, the sheer rapidity with which the cultural attitude toward homosexuality has changed within the mainstream of our culture. In addition, thanks to the options of surrogacy and in vitro fertilization, same-sex couples can procreate and parent. While there is some evidence that, all things being equal, growing up with two parents rather than one is preferable for a child, there is no evidence that parenting by heterosexual parents is better than being raised by two loving parents of the same gender.

If the entire issue we dealt with then were to be deliberated on and voted now, the minority report's contention that, not the gender but the quality of the relationship qualifies it as kiddushin, would pass overwhelmingly, my vote included.

Today, I feel that a colleague could serve my congregation without dissembling about his sexual identity; and, if by character, skill set and spiritual commitment, he or she stood strong and true, that person would be accepted. Alas, he or she might still have some difficulty receiving the initial invitation.

CHAPTER 9 ❖ LIVING & INFLUENCING THE CHANGE TO POST-MODERN REFORM

Some years ago, our Conference endorsed civil marriage for gay and lesbian couples. More than a few of our colleagues conduct commitment ceremonies, not marriage. Others make no distinction between them. All in all, our culture and our Conference have come a long way since 1990—and on the whole, I am pleased.

Joan and I are standing on a balcony that overlooks the old city of Jerusalem, faintly visible in the background, during one of our many visits to the Holy Land.

Chapter 10
ISRAEL & ME

My connection to Israel is lifelong and natural. My mother was born and grew up in Jerusalem and my paternal grandfather for whom I am named migrated from Czarist Russia to Palestine to become one of the first generation of settlers in Tel Aviv. We spoke modern Hebrew in our home, and the hope for restoration of a Jewish homeland in the British mandated territory of Palestine was a basic part of my cultural heritage.

Already in the late nineteenth century, with the resurgence of a rabid European anti-Semitism, the biblical hope of Israel's restoration in Messianic times ("the end of days") was transformed among some Jews into an activist Zionist movement that aimed to establish a Jewish state by human effort in our time. Initially, that movement was opposed by the European Reform Movement, which saw no need for the restoration of the Jewish Temple in Messianic times or the re-gathering of Jews currently in the Holy Land. They felt that wherever Jews lived, whether Berlin or Paris, was the Jewish homeland.

The early Reformers called their synagogues "Temples" as a way of repudiating any Jewish aspiration for the rebuilding of the Temple in Jerusalem. To be sure, the activist Zionist movement was sparked mostly by non-religious Jews who had no interest in rebuilding the Temple now or in "end of days." They were concerned with putting an end to the Jew as stranger in countries that tolerated and sometimes encouraged anti-Semitism.

Theodor Herzl (1860-1904), widely regarded as the father of political Zionism, was overwhelmed by European anti-Semitism and concluded that the heart of the "Jewish problem" was that we were an alien people to our gentile neighbors and could only find a solution by recreating our own state and putting an end to Jewish powerlessness and homelessness. Whereas the Reformers, who opposed Zionism, felt that Jews needed to try even harder to be loyal, patriotic citizens of the European countries in which they dwelled.

In the 1930s in the United States, Jews were heavily divided on the Zionist issue. By 1937, with the rise of Hitler and Nazism in Europe, the Reform Movement officially took a more positive stance toward the efforts to rebuild a homeland in Palestine, but American Jews remained divided.

In the early 1940s, long before I got there, that Zionist/anti-Zionist controversy caused a split in Congregation Beth Israel in Houston. A group within the congregation promulgated and passed the document called "The Basic Principles" which, as part of its stance on membership and other issues I mentioned previously, went so far as to proclaim that those who espoused Zionism were only eligible to be associate members. The controversy had resulted in a significant minority leaving the congregation to form a new synagogue.

I was a sixteen year old in Philadelphia when, in 1947, my parents joined those many American Jews who prayed that the United Nations General Assembly would vote to partition Palestine into a Jewish and a separate Arab state. By that affirmative vote, Israel was born—only to be attacked by five Arab nations seeking to abort its life. As of this writing, Israel has become a very strong, viable entity, but its right to exist is still not formally conceded by large segments of the Arab world. My first rhetorical opportunity to defend Israel's right to exist came in my senior year in high school, just a year after Israel's creation, when I was invited to be a speaker at high school commencement and chose to speak about Israel's rebirth.

When some years later, for reasons I have already explained, I decided to enter the Hebrew Union College and become a Reform rabbi, I had to come to terms with the earlier anti-Zionism of large segments of the Reform Movement. I could apply to the Reform seminary because I was satisfied that anti-Zionism was a markedly declining sentiment in its ranks, and I knew that two of the greatest Zionist leaders in America, Abba Hillel Silver and Steven Wise, were Reform rabbis.

Although details of the magnitude and horror of the Nazi Holocaust came trickling out early after the Second World War, not until 1960, and the Eichmann trial, did our community and the world contemplate the full story of Hitler's intent to destroy the entire Jewish people. In 1967, during the first few days of the Arab/Israeli War, when it seemed quite plausible that the Arab armies would destroy the fledgling state, many segments of our community all over the world suddenly realized the full measure of our Jewish stake in Israel's survival.

I was a rabbi at Chicago Sinai Congregation at the time. I vividly recall the response of a group of Jewish professors at the University of Chicago who were generally lukewarm about Israel and took its existence pretty much for granted. When they contemplated the real possibility of Israel's destruction, their adrenaline flowed and they were galvanized into the most concrete form of expression available to them. They dipped into their bank accounts to make sacrificial monetary gifts to the Israel Emergency Fund! This scene was replicated all over the United States.

The Issue of Dual Allegiance

Following a talk at a Rotary luncheon in Houston on what Israel means to me, one questioner raised the issue of dual allegiance: "Rabbi, I recognize your love for Israel, but you are an American citizen and you indicated this is your home. What if there were a war and Israel and the United States were on opposite sides of the conflict? With whom would you stand?"

I found myself responding to this obviously unfriendly question as follows: "Sir, I will answer in two ways. First, I will tell you that my ultimate loyalty is not to any state but to the Lord, my God. I would make the choice after considering which state's policies were more consonant with the commandments in Scripture.

"But let me now answer, not from my rational calculations of whose cause is more just, but from the feelings in my gut or soul. Let me say first that if that day ever came, it would be the saddest day of my life. You are asking me a question that is analogous to another: Suppose a building was on fire, my three children were trapped inside and circumstances were such that I could only save one. Which one would I save? Sir, I cannot tell you in advance which daughter I would save on that tragic day."

Without a pause, my questioner responded, "I know which one of my children I would save," to which I replied, "If that is your response, I'm afraid I have nothing more to say."

The Moral Challenges for an Empowered, Thriving State of Israel

By the end of the Six Day War, a victorious Israel found itself in control of what in biblical days was called Judea and Samaria. This became known as the West Bank, a territory largely populated by Palestinian Arabs. At first a growing restiveness and resistance to the new reality took the form of non-recognition of Israel in its expanded territory. Under Yasser Arafat, that opposition became a violent, terror laden effort to expel, intimidate and ultimately, to destroy Israel.

As the year progressed, a growing number of Israelis and Jews in America became concerned about the dehumanizing effect of Israel's role as an unwelcome occupier. The effect of suicide bombings, as part of what became known as the First and Second Intifada, hardened positions in both the Jewish and Arab camps.

When, under new leadership, the Palestinian authority rejected the terrorist strategy of Arafat, strove to build a West

Bank infrastructure in preparation for statehood and committed itself to a "two state" solution of the Arab/Israel conflict, a significant segment of Israelis and Jews in America became committed to this resolution of the conflict.

What loomed as a formidable obstacle to this plan was a militant Jewish settler movement grounded in the notion that God gave Israel that entire territory and a right wing Israeli government's acceptance of an ever expanding Jewish presence in that predominantly Arab part of the country.

During this period, American Evangelical Christians opposed the partition plan because they believed the New Testament's prophesy that Jesus' return must be preceded by a Jewish nation that is sovereign in the entire territory promised Israel in the "Old Testament."

At the same time, a growing segment of mainstream Christians began to view the situation in the Middle East as a drama casting the powerful Israel as Goliath and the Palestinian Arabs as an oppressed people in need of their active support. Some went so far as to advocate the boycott of Israeli companies and products.

More than a few rabbis, including me, were unwilling to endorse all policies of the Israeli government. We favored a two-state solution and were deeply concerned about the expansion of Jewish settlements in a region that would, in all likelihood, naturally fall in to the Arab portion of a two-state reality. At the same time, we soberly realized that Hamas, the Arab political entity in control of Gaza, is still formally committed to Israel's destruction. What is more, the recent turmoil in Egypt, Syria and other nations surrounding Israel did not, at least at the present writing, portend peaceful co-existence between Israel and her neighbors.

CHAPTER 10 ❖ ISRAEL & ME

A Talk to the TCC

In February of 1988, I was invited to speak on the Arab/Israeli situation at a gathering of the Texas Conference of Churches that was scheduled to meet in Houston as guests of my congregation. I was asked to address the leaders of the conference at their dinner meeting. Before I spoke, I was aware of a resolution to be considered by the Conference that, from my perspective, would be strongly anti-Israel. I was being invited to address the gathering before they discussed and voted on that resolution.

My address that night acknowledged that the Arab/Israel conflict was the tragic clash of two just claims. Recognizing this, the United Nations in 1947 partitioned the Holy Land into two states. The leaders of the Jewish community in Israel accepted the plan. The Arab response was for five Arab armies to attack the Jewish settlement, fully intending to destroy it. Between 1947 and 1988, Israel was forced to defend its right to exist in five different wars, each ending with Israel victorious in battle, but resulting in an uneasy armistice, continually violated, rather than a peace treaty. (Since that conference, a peace treaty was signed with Jordan and Egypt.)

In my address I described the birth of Israel in 1948 as a desperately needed sign of grace for a Holocaust-scarred people. I acknowledged that there is a

> Palestinian Arab community...who also have a claim to that same small land...It is painful to see some Jewish leaders who refuse to acknowledge there is a conflict here between two just claims...It is painful to see some critics of Israel who fail to place this tragic conflict in

perspective, who see it as a simple morality play in which the more powerful Israel wears the black hat.

What would we ask of our American Christian neighbors in these parlous times? Not that you endorse all that a given Israeli government stands for; we don't make that demand on ourselves. Not that you disavow your concern for the plight and yearning of Palestinian Arabs. Many of us share that concern. We would ask you to be aware of our people's past and of the history and context of the Middle East conflict. We would ask you to try to understand why your Jewish neighbors are so intensely concerned about Israel's survival and security.

Earlier in the talk, I said, "We need Israel to live. We know that power may corrupt but we know only too well that powerlessness destroys."

My words that night fell on deaf ears. The anti-Israel resolution passed overwhelmingly. With sadness I sent a letter to the chairman of the Conference which expressed my disappointment and dismay:

> Surely you and we are called to assail injustice, and there is enough injustice in the Middle East status quo to evoke our prophetic and compassionate response. But to deserve to be taken seriously, our words must preserve a respect for nuance and complexity, not to mention the facts of history. The sixth "whereas" (in the resolution) implies that a Jewish state, by its very nature, is an unjust intrusion on the Middle East. What would constitute a "Jewish nation state acceptable to Christians and Muslims?" The resolution consistently signals to our people that there is no place in the Middle East for an

empowered Jewish community with the right to exercise the joys and burdens of living as a Jewish majority, and to create an unconditional refuge for a people so desperately in need of it, especially in a post-Holocaust world.

Does not elemental truth require a "whereas" to state that each war was initiated by Arab leaders bent upon Israel's destruction…A few weeks ago I sat with members of my family in Jerusalem. They have been there for six generations. My aunt, who lives in Tel Aviv but was born in Jerusalem, said to me, "Maybe we shouldn't be here. The world doesn't seem to think we belong here."

Your resolution is sensitive to the aspirations of the Palestinian Arabs but shows no appreciation for the pain of a people which is surrounded by hostile nations who, if they could, would deny their very existence in that part of the world. I shudder to think that the resolution, in its present form, represents the considered judgment of the Texas Conference of Churches…

Fortunately, there are mainstream Christians in my American experience who marvel at Israel's achievements and appreciate its challenges as a robust, contentious and thriving democracy in a very tough neighborhood. We must be careful not to equate all non-Jewish critiques of Israeli policy as a resurgence of anti-Semitism.

Some speak of the rising anti-Jewish and anti-Israel feeling, particularly in Europe, as the new anti-Semitism. So much depends on the spirit in which the judgment is made. Is it within a context of respect and commitment to Israel's survival? Or is it a vestigial resentment that the Jewish people, especially in Israel, have become, not a helpless victim, but an empowered, thriving, high-tech nation? Perhaps it is some of each.

Memorable Vignettes

After all my many returns to Israel, the individual trips merge in my memory. Yet, in my total Israel memory bank, three events remain most vividly etched. The first was related to me by my cousin, Tiki. At the time, she lived with her husband in Tiberius, a town along the coast of the Sea of Galilee. They lived on the outer edge to accommodate Tiki's love of animals. One of her favorites was a baby pig, or piglet. Tiki's mother was to visit from Safed. Her mother was so strictly kosher that she brought her own utensils and prepared her own food during such visits.

Anticipating her mother's horror upon encountering a quintessentially forbidden animal in her daughter's home, Tiki farmed out her piglet to the family next door. Unfortunately, the little creature was accustomed to sleeping in Tiki's bed and responded to the strange surroundings with a virtually incessant and quite audible squeal. When her mother inquired about the strange noise, Tiki dismissed it by saying that the family across the way had a pet of some sort.

That response would have put the matter to rest, were it not for the fact that at the time, Tiki's teenage daughter was quite upset with her mother over some request that Tiki had denied her. The daughter seized the opportunity to roil the domestic waters by telling grandma that the strange creature next door was a baby pig, which actually belonged to her mother!

Hearing the word "pig," Tiki's mother reacted with a fainting spell. Once revived, her mother assailed Tiki with a plaintive, "How could you bring this un-kosher creature into your house?!" Once the issue was joined, Tiki was defiant: "First of all, this is my home, not yours, and my life, not yours, and I'll live as I chose! What's more, I'm keeping it as a pet, not eating it!" Tiki brought the creature back home to her bed. (This predilection of Tiki's may have had more than a little to do with the break-up of her marriage.)

Early the next morning, when Tiki entered her kitchen, she was shocked. Her mother was peeling potatoes and just disposing of the skins by leaving them on the kitchen floor for the piglet! Tiki accused her mother of hypocrisy: "One minute you're horrified that I have a little pig as a pet and the next moment you're feeding it!"

Her mother's response was classic: "I thought you said it eats anything. While the Torah commands us not to eat *chazir* (pig), the Torah also teaches us not to cause pain unnecessarily to any living creature."

When this episode occurred, the Israeli Supreme Court had been asked to rule on whether it is possible for Father Daniel, who was assigned by his Church to a parish in Israel, could be regarded as ethnically part of the Jewish people even though he was religiously a faithful Catholic. The court decided that ethnicity cannot be totally separated from religion in a legal definition of a Jew.

David Ben Gurion, then prime minister of Israel, decided to use this controversy as a basis for inviting any Jew to respond to the question: "Who is a Jew?" Many of the responses were published in Israel's leading newspaper. Tiki, by now fully reconciled with her mother, proudly submitted her mother's response as an example of who is a Jew.

My Companion on a Public Bus

My visit to Israel in the summer of 1968 enabled me to attend our CCAR Rabbinic Conference in Jerusalem and, as it turned out, to be at my cousin Hani's wedding in Tel Aviv. It was a small wedding in her family's apartment. Hani's parents had a long-standing friendship with Menachem and Aliza Begin. In those years, Menachem was a minister without portfolio in the Israeli Cabinet. His duties kept him from attending the ceremony, but Aliza came alone.

After the wedding reception, she and I needed to return to Jerusalem. I had taken for granted that a cabinet minister's wife had a special car which brought her, so I asked if I could "hitch a ride" to Jerusalem with her. She responded that I was welcome to join her on the public bus back to Jerusalem.

That was one of my most memorable bus rides. Aliza Begin welcomed the opportunity to speak about the years they spent in Russia and Poland before emigrating in 1942 to what would become Israel. She vividly recalled the years when her husband, Menachem, was head of the Irgun, a right wing underground movement. During the latter years of the British Mandate, in order to end British rule, the Irgun attacked British military installations and personnel. Although the Irgun, unlike the more radical, "Stern Gang," tried to spare civilian lives, it was considered by many critics as a terrorist organization.

Aliza spoke of the years in hiding when Begin employed several disguises to elude the British authorities while her family actually lived in the apartment building where the wedding occurred. Those were the years Hani's parents and the Begins became close friends. When I asked her if her husband hoped someday to be Prime Minister of Israel, she responded that he had given up such hope. His only goal as leader of an opposition party was to keep the ruling coalition honest. Little did she or I realize at the time that Menachem Begin was destined, not only to become Prime Minister of Israel, but also the Israeli leader who would shake hands with Yassir Arafat when President Bill Clinton spearheaded the Camp David Accords.

I found Aliza Begin to be a down-to-earth unpretentious woman who loved her husband deeply and was proud that son, Benjamin, was a member of the Israeli Parliament (Keneset). That she, a cabinet minister's wife, had no compunctions about traveling between Tel Aviv and Jerusalem in a public bus said much about Aliza Begin—and perhaps about Israel as well.

The Power of a Word

During one of our many trips, I tried to visit my cousin Sarah Pearl in Safad whenever possible. Sarah and husband Moshe owned and lived in the Hotel Herzliah. In its courtyard is a two-thousand-year-old olive tree. During one of these visits, when I got off the bus, I knew I was near the hotel, but could not discern which way to walk.

Fortunately, I spotted a group of young street urchins, perhaps ten years old, playing nearby. They were dressed in the traditional black and white garb of Hasidic Jews and sported the traditional side curls and kippah. I addressed them in Hebrew and asked them to direct me to the Herzliah Hotel. Instead of responding immediately, they huddled and conspired to have some fun with a stranger.

When they emerged from the huddle, I repeated my question. They responded in unison with the word, "There," but each pointed in a different direction, and they broke into jovial laughter. At first I was more amused than annoyed; but, with mock seriousness, I replied in Hebrew: "Oh! I am so surprised at you. It says in the Torah that you should not oppress the stranger. It's a mitzvah."

I had uttered the special word, mitzvah! Instantly, one by one, they asked for my forgiveness and dutifully led me to Cousin Sarah's hotel. "Mitzvah" triggered an immediate awareness that there are certain things we are commanded to do by Hashem (God) and God's commandments must be observed.

We sometimes quip that the Decalogue consists of ten commandments—not suggestions. I have used that incident to illustrate one of the strengths of Orthodox piety at its best. The challenge to us more "liberal Jews" is to sustain that sense of holy commandment—within our greater sense of autonomy!

A Challenge Closer to Home

Over sixty years has passed since World War II. The generation that survived the Holocaust and has personally testified to its horrors is rapidly dying out. Many of the visceral cues to which my generation responded no longer resonate with the younger Jewish generation today. The Holocaust is ancient history, and in the United States Jews are growing up in the most open and embracing society for Jews in all our experience through the ages. The impact of this new situation upon Jewish communal fund-raising is already being felt. Even when the younger generation has the capacity to match or exceed the generosity of its elders, that level of giving is not forthcoming.

In spite of the many pilgrimages to Israel for young and old, observers of the Jewish scene note a certain emotional distancing from our brothers and sisters in that part of the world. Some polls have quantified this diminishing sense of Israel's importance for American Jews. They are uncomfortable with scenes of Israelis playing the role of unwelcome occupier of Arab territory or with Haredim, Orthodox zealots, who would, if they could, radically limit the role of women outside the home and whose males exempt themselves from serving in the armed forces and expect state support for their permanent role as "students of Torah."

This is not to ignore the beautiful models of a modern Orthodoxy that combines ritual and ethical piety with active acceptance of the normal burdens and responsibilities of Israeli citizenship and respects those Israelis who do not share their form of religious expression. Still, it is difficult for any insightful observer to ignore the challenge of an increasing emotional distancing of many American Jews from the older narrative of American and Israeli Jewish solidarity. As an elderly Jew whose deeply rooted emotional connection to the land and its people derives from my parental heritage, this challenge is quite sobering.

As one deeply invested in Israel's survival as a Jewish and democratic country, I join those who view the status quo as unsustainable. We must hope that leaders within the Israeli and Palestinian Arab community will be able to show adequate regard for each other's interests and concerns. Each side must be so committed to transcend the status quo and what it portends that they will take the necessary risks and make the necessary compromises to make a two-state solution a reality. Many have acknowledged that Israel cannot remain both a Jewish state and a democracy without such a resolution.

Playing the Game of "What If?"

During my adult years, I have visited Israel at least twelve times; once with my entire immediate family, a number of times with my wife, Joan, and occasionally alone. I also led congregational trips to Israel during our years in Chicago and Houston. Each time my fluency in modern Hebrew returned, although my American accent was obvious. On those occasions when I remained for more than a week I began to dream in Hebrew. With each visit, I was viscerally reattached to the land and its people.

At no time, however, did resettling in Israel loom as a real option for me. While there is a growing Reform movement in the country, I have always felt that for Progressive Judaism to flourish in the Holy Land, it must become an indigenous reality and not remain largely an American transplant.

Fortunately, that has begun to happen. Native born Israelis are choosing to become rabbis, lay educators and youth leaders within the Movement. A branch of our Reform seminary was established many years ago, first as a school for archaeological research and fieldwork, then as the classroom for all American Reform rabbinic students during their first year of seminary study. More recently a full-fledged Reform seminary for Israelis has been established on that Jerusalem site. At this writing, that Jerusalem branch of our seminary has ordained a number of classes of Israeli Reform rabbis.

Unfortunately, for Reform and other non-Orthodox rabbis,

the struggle to gain the privilege to solemnize marriages and bury the deceased has not yet been granted. I am confident that struggle will ultimately be won. At present, many couples go to the Orthodox rabbinate to get their marriage license and complete the technicalities, but then invite a liberal rabbi to actually conduct what they regard as the more meaningful ceremony. The current lack of full recognition rankles but would not have deterred me from moving to Israel.

In truth, however, my reason for not making the move in my younger years is deeper. I have felt too strongly rooted to life and work in this country. My personal mission has been to make Judaism a spiritually vibrant and important part of Jewish self-consciousness in this great land.

I sometimes wonder what I would have become vocationally if I had made the move in my younger working years. Would I have become a rabbi in the Israeli Progressive Movement? Obviously such idle imaginings are of limited value.

I can say with certainty that I have been able to take much pride in my paternal and maternal family in Israel. Generally they have embodied the *sabra* (the native born Israeli) at his and her best. Although I do not see them often, I do feel bonded to them. A number have attained a distinguished high profile in their country. A first cousin, Moshe Margalit, is a leading Israeli architect. Many years ago, Jerusalem mayor, Teddy Kolleck, designated him to design the public space in the area that both separated and could serve as a bridge between the predominantly Arab and Jewish parts of the city. More recently, Moshik (as he likes to be called), was commissioned to reconstruct the old Jewish ghetto in Shanghai.

Another first cousin, Asher Grunis, served as the Chief Justice of the Israeli Supreme Court, which has, on occasion, made difficult and important rulings to safeguard the legitimate rights of Arab/Israeli citizens when those rights were being violated.

Those American/Israeli familial bonds have been renewed in the next generation through my daughter, Amy Halevy. About twenty-five years ago she married a high school friend from Houston, Amir Halevy, whose roots in Israel go back many generations. Amir's grandfather traveled from Israel to be at that wedding. He was seated next to my mother. As they conversed with each other, it became evident that they had been in the same class in a Jerusalem first grade some seventy years earlier!

In 1974, after returning from a trip to Israel, Alfred Kazin, an American Jew and a distinguished author and literary critic, published a diary of his trip in the *The Atlantic Monthly*. His last words then still resonate with me even now:

> All I really know about Israel is that a great many people around the world would like to see it vanish, sooner or later. So that if someone had been ridiculous enough to ask me to contribute one more thought to the political wisdom already tormenting Israel, I would have shouted with all my might, "'Brothers, friends, live!'"[40]

This picture with my friend Jeremy Tucker was taken the day he signed the contract for the publication of his book "Before A Canyon" It was a very happy day for him and for me.

Chapter 11
DEFENDING THE FAITH IN A SECULAR AGE

CONVENTIONAL WISDOM HAS CORRELATed the advance in science and technology with a continual, irreversible diminishment of religious belief. My experience in forty years as a "Defender of the Faith" has not validated that thesis.

In the United States, every poll finds that the overwhelming majority of Americans affirms a belief in God and most regard religious faith as their ultimate support in time of critical, life-threatening illness. In Eastern Europe, under the Communist regime, despite the attempt to suppress religious expression, organized religion has experienced a subsequent revival. In large parts of Europe and Asia, a robust, sometimes militant Islam, is very much in evidence.

In the course of my own rabbinate, I have observed a resurgence of interest in spirituality, mysticism and religion. Books on these subjects have proliferated, and courses in religion (including Judaism) on college campuses have mushroomed, especially in our "elite" universities.

Yet, the term "secular age" is still apt to define the context of my rabbinate. In the United States, religious practice and freedom from religious belief are equally protected. Religion is able to flourish as a voluntary act, but without coercive support from the larger culture. Indeed the culture is sufficiently secular so that in many ambiences the one who processes life religiously may not assume that those around him resonate to the message.

There was a time when it was difficult to separate one's identity as a person from one's membership in a religious group. Today, in what many have called a post-modern world, I would prefer to say that my Judaism remains inseparable from my personhood. My covenant with God as a member of the Jewish people is the most profound expression of my personhood. It is my way of becoming fully a mensch. That does not mean that it is the only way, or that everyone must follow this way, but it is my most authentic way of expressing my humanity. Because this is a secular age, I cannot assume even that my fellow Jews parse their world in those terms, any more than I can assume that they define themselves as religious Jews.

Signs of the Sacred in a Secular Age
As a teacher of Judaism, I found it helpful to identify experiences in the life of a person who might not define herself as religious, but which parallel the experiences of the traditional believer.

CHAPTER 11 ⁂ DEFENDING THE FAITH IN A SECULAR AGE

In the 1960s, the late Abraham Maslow taught psychology at Brandeis University. He conducted interviews with eighty persons and received written responses from 190 subjects to whom he gave the following instructions:

> I would like you to think of the most wonderful experience or experiences of your life; happiest moments, ecstatic moments, moments of rapture, perhaps from being in love, or from listening to music, or suddenly being hit by a book or a painting, or from some creative moment. First list them and then tell me how you feel in such acute moments—how you feel differently from how you feel at other times; how you are at that time a different person in some ways...[41]

Once initial resistance to the assignment was overcome, a large number reported what, in Maslow's terms, were basically religious experiences. He called them "peak experiences." They turned out to be associated with great moments of love (a mother fondling a newborn infant), moments of aesthetic appreciation (observing the spray of the sea on rocks at dawn or dusk), moments of peak creativity (some meaningful and difficult task adequately performed) or great moments of insight or discovery.

"In the wake of such experiences, persons may report feeling wonder, awe, humility, surrender, and even worship. They recall feeling that they are the recipients of gifts, owe for what they have been given, and under obligation to repay with acts of goodness."[42]

My role as rabbi involved trying to evoke, identify and respond to such teachable moments. I vividly remember making hospital rounds one day and visiting two mothers in different rooms on the maternity floor who had very recently given birth to their infants. In the first room the father was also present. As I walked in and wished them a Mazal Tov, the father pointed to his son in his wife's arms and exclaimed, "Well, Rabbi, what do you think? Take a good look because with college tuition being what it is these days, he'll probably be our last!" I did not see a teachable moment here and after some exchange of small talk, excused myself.

As I walked into the second room, the mother was in bed with her infant. Seeing me, she found herself saying, "What a miracle, Rabbi! What a gift!" As she wiped her tears, I echoed her sentiments and found a natural segue to the recitation of a prayer that is familiar to many Jews: "Praised be thou, O God, sovereign of the World, *shehecheyanu*—who has kept us in life, sustained us and enabled us to reach this moment." In that context, no mere words would have carried the powerful resonance of that traditional prayer. It was truly a teachable moment.

That prayer has acquired special resonance in the life of our people. It should be recited when a new and blessed milestone has been attained. It presumes that there is a Divine role in such attainments. In shorthand, it is known as The Shehecheyanu Prayer.

Here let me share a teachable moment experienced with Jeremy Tucker, a young man from Congregation Beth Israel, during his college years at Yale. On his visits home for semester breaks, Jeremy would call me and we would have lunch together. At one of our more memorable get-togethers, after we had done our more mundane catching up with each other, Jeremy blurted out that he didn't think he believed in God. I remember responding that even for believers like myself, there are moments of doubt. He responded that for him this wasn't an occasional moment but a firm conviction.

I then asked Jeremy if he felt driven or compelled to live in a certain way. He thought for a moment and said that he felt driven to use his life and skills as a physician to heal children, especially those underprivileged children who would tend to be ignored by society. When I asked him why he felt such a passion to help underprivileged children, he could give no carefully formulated reason.

At that point I found myself saying that "I [find] little difference, Jeremy, between being driven to help sick, poor children and feeling commanded by God to use our gifts to help repair the brokenness in that tiny corner of God's world entrusted to our care." I asked him to forgive me if under those circumstances I could not regard him as an atheist. Jeremy smiled approvingly and we went on to discuss other things. I do not mean to suggest that I convinced him or that he was thereafter a closet believer, but I had found a teachable moment to bridge the gap between our views of the world, without pressing him to define himself in my terms.

"Signals of Transcendence"

Sociologist of religion, Peter Berger, like Abraham Maslow, also finds what he calls "signals of transcendence" in our so-called secular culture. Berger contends that the human tendency to order our experience "is grounded in the faith or trust that ultimately reality is in order...[and] in this fundamental sense every ordering gesture is a signal of transcendence."[43] Similarly, he finds the human propensity for play, which included entering into game time, as an intimation of eternity. Moreover, the importance of humor in our lives is for him a sign that we are captives of hope. With our laughter we proclaim in some sense our triumph over the dehumanizing aspects of our lives.

Years ago, I found inspiring validation for this perspective. When I began to visit Henrietta Bowman in our local home for the elderly she was in her nineties, hearing impaired, eyesight so diminished that she could not read her beloved newspaper even with a magnifying glass and limited to her bed or a wheelchair. But when I walked into her room one day, she greeted me with an animated recitation of all these losses while she laughed heartily. I took this gesture not as denial or self-diminishment but as a sign of her inalienable dignity.

Psychologist Kenneth Pargament describes a visit to the Grand Canyon with his twelve-year-old son as a sacred experience. "I believe it contained qualities that are often used to describe the divine by theologians, philosophers, psychologists and artists. They include aspects of transcendence, boundlessness and ultimacy." Transcendence describes something that is "out of the ordinary...something that goes beyond our everyday lives and beyond our usual understanding." Boundlessness "involves a perception of endless time and space." Ultimacy refers to "the foundation of all experience...it has to do with what is perceived as really real."[44]

Pargament finds that the healing relationship of therapist and client is itself sacred: "Seen from the perspective of the sacred, the therapy office is more than a room; it becomes a sacred vocation. The relationship between client and therapist is more than a professional working alliance; it becomes imbued with sacred power."[45]

In my counseling I have found that to lift such experience to a person's awareness, whether or not the person feels comfortable attaching a divine cause, is still to open that person to his or her own religious sensitivity. That was my sense of Jeremy's pleased response to my statement that I could not define him as an atheist or non-believer.

The Scientific World View as Warrant for Non-Belief

There are still persons who feel they must choose either the scientific perspective on reality or the religious perspective. In my defense of the faith I would sometimes invoke the authority of prominent scientists who have comfortably affirmed that they are religious believers. For example, I might refer to a statement by William Phillips who was both a Nobel laureate in physics and a devout Christian:

> A scientist can believe in God because such belief is not a scientific matter. Scientific statements must be "falsifiable"…by contrast religious statements are not necessarily falsifiable. I might say, "God loves us and wants us to love one another." I cannot think of anything that can prove that statement false…there is no requirement that every statement be a scientific statement. Nor are non-scientific statements worthless or irrational simply because they are not scientific.[46]

For many years now, I have preferred the concept that science and religion deal with different kinds of questions. Some of life's most important questions are not subject to empirical resolution. For example, what gives human life its deepest meaning? How are we intended to live? What is my ultimate source of hope?

In my preaching and teaching I have suggested to my congregations that reality is too complex to be caught in the net of only one symbolic language system. I need the language of science and I also need the language of religious story.

At one point in a Sabbath Eve homily, I suggested how I navigate between these two approaches to reality,

> As I work on an essay or a chapter in a book I find at times that the word or concept I am seeking to expound does not come to me. My mind is blank and I may set the project aside with a sense of frustration and inadequacy. Then, when I least expect it, at maybe five in the morning, when I am barely awake, the thought comes, the light bulb goes on in my mind, insight and clarity are accessible and I will often be spurred to recite the traditional prayer, "Baruch atah Adonai, Praised are you, Adonai, giver of knowledge."
>
> Now I know this process of cognition can be described in the language of brain science, and I don't deny the validity of such analysis; but there is a deeper level in which I receive this knowledge as a gift from the source of my being and the ultimate source of knowledge. You see, the language of brain science is powerful and useful, but I also need the language of religion (agada) to fully capture the depth and meaning of living in this world. Abraham Heschel spoke of the religious mindset as "being able to see a divine margin in human attainments"' When asked to explain the mystery of his artistry, Marc Chagall would respond, "I work for art; God does the rest."
>
> Judaism teaches us that God is not only a creator and helper. God also makes known to us the way we are intended to live. The ritual commandments which call

upon us to observe the Sabbath or Yom Kippur or to pray regularly are all part of the spiritual discipline intended to open us to intimations of God's presence, but the most important commandments are those which call us to respond to the needs of other persons in our lives.

If we are religious we may hear echoes of God's call to our ancestors—*Ayecha*, where are you? The call does not come to us as a deep baritone voice from Heaven; it comes through our consciousness of the needs of another and a sense that we must respond.

The greatest sense of God's presence in my life are moments when I encounter a person in need and am impelled to help and heal. At such moments I may feel that what I am doing is at the heart of why I am here— L'chach notzarta—for such a moment were you created.

We don't need thunderclaps or bursting flames from Heaven to experience the reality and nearness of God. If we are attentive, mindful, and receptive, we too may discover as did our ancestor Jacob: "Behold, God is even in this place and I did not know it" (Genesis 28:16).

The Evolution of My Personal Theology

As I indicated earlier, my personal acknowledgment of a relationship to God preceded by many years my theological reflection on its implications. God's presence was very real, personal—and narcissistic. Over those years, I struggled to come to terms with the ineluctable truth that my God was also the God of the Universe and God's concern was not limited to my personal agenda!

The first semi-disciplined reflection on the nature and implications of my faith did not really come until

I became part of that study group conducted by Maurice Zigmond, the Harvard Hillel rabbi. He introduced me to Mordecai Kaplan's *Judaism as a Civilization*, which expounds a "Reconstructionist" theology, presumably most rational and acceptable to sophisticated, modern Jews like me. In Kaplan's theology God becomes more an energy or force for righteousness within me and the Universe than a God who is more person-like. For a time, Reconstructionism became my theological preference—my way of living as a religiously sophisticated, modern Jew.

Yet in time I realized there was a disconnect between the theology I now espoused and the actual relationship to a personal God which was my lived reality. Once I read the thought of Martin Buber, Franz Rosenzweig and Abraham Heschel, I found a way to re-appropriate my covenant with a personal God, who is conscious of my presence, who is aware of my prayer directed to him. This God is the source of my being (Creator), teacher of the way I ought to live my life (giver of Torah) and a benevolent, loving and redemptive presence in my life and in the world. At that point, I became more a Religious Existentialist than a Reconstructionist.

In my first book, *Agada: The Language of Jewish Faith*, I suggested that we finite beings can best gain some access to ultimate reality or the ultimate One through the narratives we find in the Hebrew Bible and in Rabbinic literature.

On the issue of so called anthropomorphism I wrote, "For many 'modernists,' an anthropomorphic God is primitive, childish, immature. On the other hand for many believers, myself included, the image of God as energy or force diminishes the grandeur and intimacy of faith."[47] Our consciousness of God is a sign of our unique place in creation. Our inability to find adequate words for our religious experience is a sign of our finitude. But speak we must. The Agada speaks of God as if He were a person. In doing so, it reminds us that the Torah speaks in the finite language of the human person.

When we use personal, poetic symbolism to reference God, we are declaring that our creative power, our consciousness, our freedom and our moral passion are gifts from the ultimate reality in the Universe. I wrote in *Agada*:

> In our human experience we associate such qualities with persons rather than forces. Such anthropomorphic language is the best way, or the least inadequate way of imagining and speaking of the qualities that are linked to the highest rungs of the evolutionary scale. The age of sophistication does not require us to abandon speaking of God as if He were a person. It requires sensitivity to the symbolic quality of all human language, especially that language by which we seek to express our relatedness to the transcendent mystery of life.[48]

The Covenant Theologians: Sharing My Beliefs with Colleagues

Six years after my ordination, in my early thirties, I received a most welcome invitation to attend the annual gathering of a group of like-minded, mostly young, mostly Reform rabbis, all of whom had been influenced by Buber and Rosenzweig.

Rabbi Eugene Borowitz, who would become an influential theological mentor to my generation, was one of the founders and leading spirits of this group. In a *Journal* article to which I will make further reference below, Borowitz describes the group as persons,

> Who enunciated a liberalism which was yet seriously religious, a modernity which was pious, an intellectual sophistication which made Jewish observance significant… they do not hesitate to use religious terms such as revelation, sin, fear of God…one might simply describe their position as seeking to take the Jewish religion with full personal seriousness, but not literally.[49]

I was a latecomer to the group. They were all at least five or more years older. In 1957, when they first met I had recently been ordained. In 1963, at a CCAR conference that was to meet in Philadelphia, an entire morning program was given over to theological discussion with papers presented by some members of the group. With gratitude and some trepidation, I accepted the invitation to be one of the presenters that morning. This was the first time I was invited to address a group of my colleagues at our national convention.

I titled my presentation, "Agada as a Source of Contemporary Jewish Theology." It was based on my recently accepted doctoral dissertation. Before sharing with you a bit of the content of that talk, let me place it in context. Shortly after the conference, that article to which I have already alluded appeared in *Judaism*, a quarterly journal of Jewish thought. The article was titled, "The Reform Rabbis Debate Theology: A Report on the 1963 Meeting of the CCAR." Its author used the pseudonym Ben Hamon (one of the multitude). The author, we learned years later, was Eugene Borowitz, who himself was one of the presenters that morning. This pseudonym enabled him to assess the presentations more candidly, including his own.

When Borowitz came to my presentation, he wrote,

> Rabbi Karff had chosen [to speak on] the place of Jewish sources in contemporary Jewish theological method. This pairing of man and theme aroused some special interest. Rabbi Karff is young by Rabbinic standards—in his early thirties, and while he has been widely touted…his invitation to speak was almost certainly linked to his recent eye-browsing selection as successor to Rabbi Louis Mann at Chicago's large and prestigious Temple Sinai…no one, however, could resist the good sense, the balanced judgment, and the personal commitment that lay behind Rabbi Karff's paper…it was a personal success as well as an intellectual contribution.[50]

Such validation from one of my mentors was of course deeply encouraging.

The presentation I gave that day had its actual origin in the agada I studied with my tutor, Dr. Bethlachmi, at age eleven. At seminary, I would come to fully realize that these were more than just good stories. They were nothing less than the way those Rabbis did theology. Agada was the language in which the Rabbis expressed spiritual truth—their understanding of the nature of God, the human creature and the Covenant between God and us as well as the divine relation to all God's children. If Christianity's basic story is rooted in the "Christ Event" at Calvary, the Jewish story is rooted in the "Torah Event" at Sinai. Both Jewish and Christian theologians turned to biblical accounts as revelatory events.

As a liberal Jew, I believe that all biblical accounts of God's revelation at Sinai are not literal transcriptions but verbal traces of an actual divine/human encounter. Agada reduces the ineffable moment of revelation to writing. The Rabbis who reflected on the nature of the covenant between God and Israel drew their conclusions from the Biblical text, the creative stirrings of their religious imagination and from their personal experience of the living God.

My own particular theological interest focused on the nature of the covenant relationship between God and us. In the paper for my colleagues that morning in Philadelphia, I posed the question thus, "Are we confronted...by a paternal-filial bond of unconditional love...or is the covenant essentially a conditional, functional partnership between God and Israel?"[51]

I contended that both dimensions, however seemingly contradictory, are embedded in the Agada. The divine dilemma may be clarified by this analogy: the CEO of a corporation is looking to engage a very competent junior partner who can help lead the management team to a higher level of market share, profitability and contented stockholders. The contract drawn up is essentially conditional. This junior partner will be subject to annual review and the contract is revocable if either party fails to fulfill its conditions. There is one complication: in this particular instance, the junior partner is also the CEO's beloved son whom he loves unconditionally and wants desperately to make it in the company. Similarly, the people of Israel are not only an accountable covenant partner but also God's beloved, bound to the divine parent in unconditional love.

In my doctoral study I identified certain bridging concepts that help sustain the creative tension between conditionality and un-conditionality, God's justice and love in the divine/human relationship. Through *zechut avot* (the merit of the ancestors) God places on the scale of judgment not only

Israel's merit alone but also the merit of righteous ancestors; the concept of *teshuvah* (repentance) provided opportunities for the penitent acts which restore the viability of the relationship once it is endangered. The unconditional component of the covenant makes such second and even third chances possible, while the conditional component makes such acts necessary prerequisites to acceptance. There is also the concept of discreet leniency: thus one agada describes how God sees Israel as penitent even when Israel does not regard itself in a penitent mode!

In my paper I concluded:

> What may to a casual observer appear as an exercise in verbal gymnastics reflects a profound truth. The Rabbis evoked and lived by a covenant grounded in an enduring tension between God's demanding justice and unconditional love, between man's creativity and creatureliness, which although logically untidy, was welded together in the poetry of Agada and the concreteness of life.[52]

The image of the covenant between God and Isreal which I discerned in the Agada has a broader relevance. It applies to virtually all sustainable human relationships. A good marriage is lived in that creative tension between mutual accountability and unconditional love. The art of parenting also involves unconditional acceptance and the accountability inherent in "tough love."

No wonder there is a Rabbinic agada which describes God's various attempts to establish the foundations of the world. At first, God intended to establish the world on the foundation of strength and justice, but God saw that it could not stand. So God tried to create the world on the foundation of love, but God saw that it could not stand. So God then created the world on the dual foundations of justice and love.[53]

That morning offered me the first of what would be many opportunities to expound and defend the faith not only to my congregants but also to my rabbinic colleagues. I regarded this as a special privilege for which I have been grateful.

Chapter 12
THE RABBI AS A SPIRITUAL GUIDE

During my decades as a congregational rabbi, I had the privilege of addressing audiences in "high profile" events. In retrospect; however, the encounters that have meant the most were one-on-one time with persons who in some way were threatened by a crisis of meaning.

In the context of such events, I found myself more than occasionally echoing the Rabbinic dictum, "For this you were created." These were times when I felt I was just where I was intended to be, doing what I was intended to do. I suggest at the outset of this memoir that I ultimately chose (and was chosen by) the rabbinic vocation because it provided the most opportunities to confront and address the great meaning questions of life. No dimension of the rabbinate offered more such opportunities than the pastoral.

Understanding Our Capacity to Heal

Especially in the earlier parts of my rabbinic life, one of the most difficult and threatening aspects of pastoral work was the sense of my own impotence. However much I earnestly wished to resolve the life crisis and make things alright, so often I felt like a personal failure with my mission not accomplished.

During the middle years of my rabbinate, I was part of a group in our conference whose members felt we who were called upon to deepen the spiritual life of our people may ourselves be more spiritually undernourished than we recognize or can respond to adequately. So we planned a weekend gathering of colleagues at a retreat center in Mohonk, New York. At that retreat, one of our colleagues, Rabbi Jerome Malino, offered me the most powerful response to my sense of inadequacy in those pastoral encounters. Rabbi Malino told of a tragic auto accident on an icy Pennsylvania turnpike which resulted in the instant death of a couple from his congregation, who at the time were visiting the wife's family in Pennsylvania. The funeral was held in Connecticut and Rabbi Malino, then very young, presided. The most difficult part of this pastoral challenge was not the funeral itself, but the mourning period that followed.

Rabbi Malino described for us his feeling of total impotence when he visited with the mother who had lost her son. He had actually rehearsed some remarks to make or questions to ask; but his mind went blank, and he felt like a complete failure. The grieving mother and the rabbi sat in silence. At one point he extended his hand and the bereaved mother began to sob and Rabbi Malino wiped tears streaming down his own cheeks. After what seemed like an interminable interval of silence, he said no more than "I'm awfully sorry," and quickly, feeling very awkward and unsuccessful, hastily retreated from the grieving mother's home.

Rabbi Malino returned at varying intervals through the following months. Each time he fumbled for words and felt inadequate to the challenge. He felt somewhat relieved by the fact that the mother appeared regularly at the Sabbath service during those months. In the midst of her congregation, she dutifully recited the Kaddish, or mourner's prayer.

Eleven months after the death, when it was time to conduct an unveiling of the stone at the cemetery, that Friday night, the mother from Pennsylvania whose daughter died in the crash had come to Connecticut for this formal end to the traditional period of mourning. Following the Friday evening service, the family and close friends gathered at the local mother's home for a reception. Rabbi Malino overheard the mothers talking in the kitchen. The out of town mother was asked by the local mother how she was doing? He overheard her reply, "Terribly. I just can't get over it. I haven't stepped foot in my home synagogue the whole time since the funeral." When she asked the local mother who had lost her son in that crash, "How about you?" Rabbi Malino overheard this reply, "Oh, it's been terribly difficult. I couldn't have gotten through it without our rabbi. His regular visits were so comforting and it was somehow comforting to attend the Sabbath services he conducted in the synagogue and to recite the Kaddish prayer."

I believe that every rabbi present at that retreat left with an unforgettable message. We may feel so impotent as would-be comforters, but in truth to be a healing presence for those who have experienced life's darker side, we need only be present to them, ready to listen to their story, validate their pain and, to whatever extent possible, share some of it.

The Symbolism of Being a Rabbi

We heal not only by our presence, but also by the symbolic significance of being a rabbi. Milton Steinberg, one of the greatest rabbis America produced—and one of my important rabbinic mentors—got many things right about the rabbinate. However, in his slender, but exceedingly rich volume, *Basic Judaism,* Rabbi Steinberg defined the rabbinic role much too narrowly when he wrote, "In the end the rabbi differs from his Jewish fellows (in his day all rabbis were male) only in being more learned than they or more expert in the tradition they all share."[54] In other words we are teachers—not priests.

We may be tempted to embrace this definition because it places less of an existentially central role upon us. I know colleagues who resent and deny any priestly role and with it, the burden of being a role model. Let me suggest from my personal experience some occasions when I possessed religious authority that did not depend only on my deep knowledge of Judaism.

One High Holy Day season I made hospital rounds a few days before the great fast day of Yom Kippur. I had been alerted by the hospital chaplain office that a patient, whom I will refer to as Becky, had informed her physician she had fasted her entire life and intended to fast, even though her physician told her that to do so was hazardous to her health. When the physician suggested the compromise of consuming only liquids that day, she vetoed the plan. She told the doctor that she did not observe many Jewish rituals during the year, but from reaching the age of religious maturity she had fasted completely on Yom Kippur. Most of her life was behind her, and she was not going to change now. When the doctor suggested there must be a religiously sanctioned exemption in situations such as hers, she just shook her head negatively. The physician did not even gain her consent to be infused with liquids in order to avert dehydration. What made this so strange is that this woman did not define herself or live as an observant Orthodox Jew, but this was her practice on Yom Kippur.

I visited, introduced myself as a rabbi and told her that even the most Orthodox rabbi would agree that it was a mitzvah, a religious obligation, for her to eat and that it would be a great sin for her to fast if she would be threatening her life and her health. Hearing these words from a rabbi carried the day, and she agreed not only to drink, but also even to eat lightly on Yom Kippur day. The same instruction given to her by a learned professor of Judaism at a local university would not have altered her determination to fast.

Respecting Boundaries

One of the great hazards of the ministry is its highly symbolic role. To our congregants we are moral exemplars, expected to embody the values we teach and assume the burden of practicing what we preach. When we counsel vulnerable female congregants, the charisma that often enhances effective leadership also makes us potential figures of symbolic sexual significance.

We may allow ourselves to be cast or cast ourselves as rescuers for a troubled woman counselee, which may trigger sexual feelings in us for the person we counsel. Under these circumstances, we must be sure not to trespass boundaries in word or deed. Our most precious asset is the trust we inspire. We must steadfastly guard against betraying it.

Sometimes we are the source of such sexual feelings; at other times we are targeted by the other. One of the most disquieting experiences in the first few months of my rabbinic life occurred at a congregational event before Joan had entered my life. Without warning, the wife of the congregation's president asked me to be her partner for the next dance. On the surface that seemed harmless, but on the dance floor she placed herself much closer to me than was appropriate under the circumstances, and as if that were not intimidating enough she whispered suggestive language in my ear. I countered with physical distancing, made a totally unrelated comment and politely but firmly extricated myself during a pause in the music.

Our ancient Rabbinic elders wisely understood the primal energy which is strongest in effective leaders. That *yetzer* is double-edged. It empowers us to do many loving and creative acts in this world but it also makes us especially vulnerable to lust.

In Rabbinic literature we read the agada of Rabbi Abbaye. When he saw a couple not betrothed to each other walk together along a path in the woods, he followed them in order to prevent any inappropriate behavior. As it turned out, when the couple reached a crossroads they parted innocently.

However, this episode triggered high anxiety in the Rabbi as he mused, "If I were in that man's place, I'm not sure I could have acted with such restraint." Just then, the Prophet Elijah appears to Abbaye and comforts him, "Do not despair; the greater the man, the greater the yetzer (the more the temptation to violate sexual boundaries)."[55]

Ritual, Anxiety and Hope

When we humans reach and mark each phase of the life cycle, from birth to death, each such transitional occasion is accompanied by some anxiety and the need to reaffirm hope in the presence of a future we do not fully control. This is true of parents who hold their baby at a religious naming ceremony, when they know they cannot fully protect their infant daughter from the hazards of life. It is true of a couple that stands at a wedding ceremony and cannot help but realize that the future is uncertain and no one knows how they may be tested. A rabbi's recitation of the traditional prayers on such occasions has special valence. Religious ritual is a way of coping with the anxiety and affirming hope for the future.

What is the distinctive significance of the rabbi's prayers? Our words are precious to our people, not because we have intrinsic influence with the Holy One (though they may persist in thinking so), but because they know us to be formally committed to that transcending hope they wish to embrace: we are not alone. The source of our being, the God who created us, is with us in our journey as our ultimate source of hope. We are, on such occasions, thrust in the priestly role of mediating a peoples' openness to the experience of a sacred moment.

The obligation to visit the sick is operative for every Jew capable of doing so. An ancient rabbi said that that such a visit may take away 1/60th of the illness.[56] We have had a special lay visiting committee at our congregation for many years. The sick persons often appreciated the visit, which on Friday afternoon included some challah, the traditional Sabbath bread, and grape juice for the Jewish patients. Invariably; however, those patients also wanted a visit from a rabbi not only because they would thus be spared the suspicion that if they were more prominent members of the congregation, such a visit might be forthcoming—but also because, when I offer the traditional Jewish prayers for the sick or offer a variation of Moses' prayer for the healing of his sister, the rabbinic recitation of that prayer has special resonance. Incidentally, when congregants imply that my prayers are more effective than theirs, I usually respond with "remember I am in sales, not in administration."

During the transitional moment that marks the end of the human journey on Earth, the liturgy and the eulogy by the rabbi are needed to articulate the shared grief of the survivors and to affirm faith in the abiding value of a particular life that has ended. Most Jews, however secularized they appear, need some relation to the religious symbols through which that faith is expressed.

The Rabbi and Jewish Guilt

Our priestly role is also evident when our people acknowledge that not all guilt is a neurotic syndrome that needs to be processed and disarmed by psychotherapy. Some guilt is the mark of our humanity. We call those types, who seem incapable of feeling guilt for violating the basic order of decent human life, psychopaths.

When a person has reason to feel guilty and needs a religiously symbolic way of both acknowledging and relieving it, we can play a central healing role. A couple came to me for counsel in anticipation of their forthcoming marriage. Each had been married before. Their "courtship" was in essence an affair that took place while the woman was still married and living in the house with her current husband and their children. When the secret affair was exposed, their conduct brought grief to the husband and the children who felt betrayed.

This couple wished to embark upon a new life, free from the burden of that guilt. During our counseling session, the woman explained that the marriage had been troubled for years. Some time ago she and her husband had gone to a psychotherapist to explore how to save the marriage. The underlying issues were never resolved. Leaving the marriage became nonnegotiable, but she deeply regretted how she did it.

In our time together, I indicated that I regarded her feelings of guilt as a hopeful sign. I explained the distinction between irrational or neurotic guilt and normal human guilt, which is the badge of our humanity. One of the goals of psychotherapy is to help free us from irrational guilt feelings, those distorted images that derive from formative experiences with the primary figures in our lives. But, religion helps us acknowledge and address guilt that results from actions that pursue our personal agenda without proper regard for the harm they cause others.

I encouraged the woman and her future husband to put their relationship and marriage on hold so that she could spend considerable time with her children, acknowledge that sometimes divorce is the proper option, express regret for the improper way she ended the marriage and ask for their forgiveness. She needed to reassure them that they were innocent bystanders, not the causes of her failed marriage. This woman did work hard during this period to regain her children's trust and reassure them that her love for them was everlasting.

She also made an attempt to express similar regret and ask forgiveness from her husband. Following this interval, the most significant gift I gave this woman and her new partner was my willingness to officiate at their marriage. The children attended the ceremony. The rituals of the occasion were exceedingly poignant and meaningful to the couple. My counseling and officiating offered them a gift no therapist or judge presiding at a civil ceremony could bestow.

One of the Rabbinic teachings I have found so fraught with wisdom is Rabbi Hillel's dictum, "If I am not for myself, who will be for me? But, if I am only for myself, what am I? And, if not now, when?"[57] That woman whose secret affair deeply hurt her husband and her children, needed to acknowledge the spiritual resonance of Hillel's dictum in its totality. She needed to place her plans for the future thoroughly on hold in order to address the hurt to both her children and her husband. She was responding to the part of Hillel's dictum that declares, "If I am only for myself, what am I? And, if not now, when?"

The Rabbi as Giver of Permission

A woman I shall call Joycelyn, also needed the totality of Hillel's dictum. Jocelyn and Carl were happily married and enjoyed many common interests, including a love of classical music. When a medical exam revealed that Carl had an inoperable cancer and was expected to live no more than a year, their life was radically and abruptly changed. Within a month, Carl was confined to his bed at home. Jocelyn took leave from her job as a nurse supervisor to be with him and nurse him. Fortunately, his pain was minimal, but his weakness was progressive. Being Carl's caregiver was very wearing for Jocelyn, especially as he was very demanding, sullen and intolerant of her absence from the room, much less the house for more than a brief interlude.

Jocelyn loved Carl and nursed him tenderly. She understood how much he needed her and much of the time felt good about being there for him at this last stage of his life. After six weeks of absence from her job, Jocelyn received a call from her superior at the hospital and was told that if she did not return within a week, they would have no choice but to seek another nurse supervisor.

At that point, Jocelyn got a neighbor to stay with Carl and came to see me. As she described her plight, she sobbed openly. She explained that she was grateful for her marriage and their years together and that she loved Carl and understood his emotional and physical dependence on her. She wanted to be there for him, but she was also concerned about her future. Carl had lived well on his salary, but never saved. He had virtually no life insurance and could leave her no monetary resources. She loved her job and explained how difficult it would be to find another at the same level. Visibly uneasy, she confessed that it had become virtually intolerable to nurse Carl without any break. She was exhausted and she felt guilty about her resentment, but felt terribly worried about giving up her present job. "Rabbi," she said, "I am terribly confused and don't know what I should do."

As I pressed her, Jocelyn acknowledged that she wanted to provide a caregiver for Carl and return to work, but she feared doing so would make her feel terribly guilty. She felt trapped, and she wanted and needed my guidance. Jocelyn felt surprised, but terribly relieved, when I told her that if she were a saint, she could be expected to ignore her personal needs and focus only on her husband's, but the Torah does not command us to be saints; it expects that we be loving to others without ceasing to love and care for ourselves.

I told her she needed to set boundaries: she should go back to work to preserve her job and find some relief from her round the clock nursing at home. She could provide a suitable caregiver while she was on the job and be there for Carl when she was at home. If that became a burden she could not handle alone, she could seek additional help.

The woman in the secret affair needed to remember "If I am only for myself, what am I?" Jocelyn needed to affirm, "If I am not for myself, who will be for me?"

Responding to a Crisis of Meaning

In my four decades as a comforter of those who are experiencing a crisis of meaning, two kinds of events have most precipitated such a crisis. They are the death of a child, and a medical condition which suddenly and radically transforms a human life. Let me describe the first. Early on in my rabbinate I received a call from parents who had just learned that Jane, their eleven-year-old daughter, stricken some weeks earlier with a life-threatening illness, was dying. She had been in a coma for eight days. The mother told me the medical history and broke down. She told me she had always tried to believe in God and taught her daughter to believe. She reported that last week in the hospital, before the coma, her daughter Jane turned to her and said, "I don't think I can pray to God any more. God has let me down."

I listened. Before they left I stood close to them. I offered a prayer. I hugged them and found myself tearing up with them. Then we sat in silence. Some days after that visit they called to tell me Jane had died and asked me to conduct the funeral and burial ceremony.

In the funeral chapel, I read a few psalms and shared with the congregation some of the memories of Jane's life which were most precious to them. I spoke of the joy Jane had found in her childhood friends, in reading, in time the family spent hiking on wooded trails and of the generous spirit Jane had shown by her concern for others in need. I affirmed that she had so lived in her brief life that she would be cherished in memory and deeply missed, even as we affirm in our tradition that her soul will be linked to God forever. We concluded the service with the chanting of the traditional prayer entrusting Jane's soul to God.

At the brief burial ceremony, there were many tears. After the casket was lowered, we recited the traditional Kaddish prayer, which affirms our trust in God at a time when such trust is both most difficult and yet most deeply needed.

Many years later, I remember another instance of an eleven-year-old child's death. Jack and Linda's son, Nicholas, was eleven when one day his father asked him to retrieve a tool from the garage that he would be using in trying to do some repairs on his car. Nicholas dutifully proceeded to the garage, but as he reached for the tool a ladder fell on him. He was knocked to the ground. He never regained consciousness. I remember the vigil in the hospital and the moment when life-support systems were removed and how Jack cradled his dying son in his arms as he sobbed bitterly.

In both Jane's and Nicholas' dying there was so much grieving and healing to be done with their parents. During the early stages of mourning they did not need theology. They did not need for me to share the narratives that had become part of my way of trying to understand undeserved suffering, especially the death of children. They needed my presence, hugs, love; my readiness to listen to the outpouring of their hearts. But the time came some weeks after the death when in each case the parents came to see me and asked the why question. At that point, I felt they needed some response. Up until that time, they needed their sense of great loss to be validated, rather than for me to present what would have been a premature redemptive theology, one that would clear God and enable them to reaffirm their relationship to the Source of their being.

Stories to Help Mend the Estrangement

Now the time had come in each case, separately, because these episodes occurred many years apart. At this point I found enormously helpful the narratives that I had turned to in my own crises of meaning as I confronted the darker side of life. At the outset of this discussion, I told the grieving parents that if they have gone through or are still in a mode of anger and bitterness in their relation to God, they are not alone. Some of the greatest spiritual giants of our tradition, including psalmists and prophets, had their arguments with God when they could not understand why there was so much undeserved suffering, especially when that suffering was theirs or belonged to those they loved. I would then go on to suggest that sometimes we move from God the enemy to God the companion and friend by going through that confrontational mode. God can handle our negative thoughts. It is not blasphemous in our tradition to utter hostile feelings toward our Creator in the freshness of our grief and suffering.

I would also tell the parents what I found so helpful in my study of the Jewish Agada. I discovered that there are different narratives and what may make sense or be compelling to one person may not have that meaning for another. I suggested that when we confront the issue of undeserved suffering our sages tended to offer two alternative stories to help them reaffirm their relationship to God and the meaning in their lives.

One is embodied in the book of Job. In that book, God is described as both infinitely powerful and just—and yet there is undeserved suffering. Job refuses to believe he deserved the suffering that he endured, but if God is good, loving, powerful and caring why should there be undeserved suffering? The author of Job ultimately responds that to be human is to ask questions, which are beyond our power to answer and so, in the end, we must either conclude that there is no meaning, that life is absurd, or we must live with the mystery, acknowledge that our covenant with God has hidden clauses, and we must strive to trust that beyond the mystery there is meaning.

In keeping with the sense that God is totally in control, we have the Talmudic story of Rabbi Meier and his wife, Bruria. We are told that one Sabbath, Rabbi Meier went to the synagogue; his wife remained home with their twin sons. While Meier was gone Bruria went to check on the children and she found, much to her horror that they were in their crib, lifeless (we might now call that infant death syndrome). In addition to being numbed by her own grief, she began to think how she would tell this terrible news to her husband when he returned from the synagogue.

When Meier came back, Bruria told her husband this story: "Some time ago dear, someone left me two precious jewels for safe keeping and I took good care of them, but then the giver came back and said that it was time for these jewels to be returned to him, what should I have done?" Rabbi Meier responded, "Of course, you need to return them." At that point Bruria led Meier to their children's room and when he saw their lifeless forms, Meier and Bruria wept bitterly and clutched each other. In time, Rabbi Meier realized that these precious children had been entrusted to him and his wife, and now, for reasons beyond their power to understand, it was time to return these darling sons to God.[58]

An Alternate Story

If we study Rabbinic literature, we discover that not all the Rabbis were content to accept that story. Other Rabbis responded with a different story. In the book of Deuteronomy, we are commanded to show sensitivity to all God's creatures. So if a person sees a nest with a mother bird hovering over her young chicks, the hungry person may retrieve the young birds from the nest, but only after shooing the mother bird away so she does not have to witness this act. Furthermore, the Torah promises that if you obey this law you will be granted long life and prosper (Deuteronomy 22:66).

The sages then recall an incident where a Jew sought to be faithful to God and strictly observe this commandment, but as he was on the ladder leaning against the tree and began to shoo away the mother bird, the ladder collapsed and the man fell to his death. So there is a debate among the Rabbis, "How come? Here he did what he was supposed to do, and for that he gets not a reward, but death." One of the Rabbis responded, "When it says that you will have long life, the Torah does not mean in this world, it means in the world to come. So what is denied this man here on Earth will be granted to him in the life beyond." But Rabbi Elazar heard this and he paused before saying, "I can't accept that." And, when he was asked, "So how would you explain it?" Elazar replied, "It must have been a rickety ladder." In other words, not everything that happens in God's world is God's will.[59]

Another expression of this alternate theology is the Rabbinic story about a dishonest farmer who crossed the road and stole some wheat plants from his neighbor's field. By right, when he plants such stolen wheat it should not grow. In fact; however, this wheat grew just as robustly as the honest farmer's wheat. How come? The Talmud responds, "The world follows its natural way."[60] This is to suggest that God is self-limited by giving us a world of dependable law, which can be a great blessing. Imagine a world in which we could not depend on water always quenching thirst, and sometimes it burned our gut? There are laws of nature through which God chooses to guide our world.

By extension, Maimonides, a rabbi and physician, taught that disease may not be directly willed or controlled by God. Viruses are no respecters of human character. They follow the laws that govern viruses and our vulnerability to so many diseases is the price we pay for being embodied persons who can think and feel and love and create.[61]

In a similar vein, not all that we do is what God would want us to do. God has given us the dignity of having free choice so that we can act even against God. If we were puppets on a string, there might be many less wrong decisions on our part and much human suffering in this world might be prevented. But if we were puppets on a string, we would lose that freedom which is at the heart of human dignity. It follows from this that a Rabbi Hanina observed, "All is in the hands of heaven except the fear of heaven."[62]

A poignant example of this is found in another Rabbinic story. Rabbi Simeon ben Yochai pondered the story of Cain who was jealous of his brother, Abel, and allowed this jealousy to erupt into an act of murder. God confronts Cain and asks him where his brother is, and Cain replies, "Am I my brother's keeper?" The Rabbi extends that biblical answer and imagines Cain challenging God, saying, in effect, "You are my brother's keeper. Why didn't you prevent me from killing him if that was your will? Surely you had the power to do so," and God does not respond to Cain's question.[63]

According to this alternative view, God limits the divine self in order to grant human creatures the dignity of real freedom, rather than be puppets on a divinely controlled string. God also limits his micromanaging of the universe by giving us dependable laws of nature. This means the saintly and the evil-doer are equal-opportunity potential victims of disease; but a lawful universe, a world which follows its natural course, also empowers us to hope that someday researchers, by understanding these laws, can discover a cure for many diseases to which we are now vulnerable.

Martin Buber once described his theology in these terms, "You need God in order to be, and God needs you for the very meaning of your life."[64] This, I take as God's divine self-limitation, for it is through our sacred tasks, through our partnership with God in helping to repair the brokenness in this world, that we find the deepest meaning of our lives.

Finding Comfort in Different Stories

In separate meetings with me, many years apart, the parents of eleven-year-old Jane and the parents of Nicholas were groping for ways to reaffirm their trust in God and in the meaning of life. When I shared these stories with them, they found comfort and meaning in different narratives. The parents of Jane knew their daughter died because she was assaulted by a rare disease for which presently there was no cure. Her parents felt they could relate more easily to a God who was self-limited by giving us a lawful universe and the gift of freedom.

If God did not control everything and did not visit this tragedy upon them, where was God in its midst? They were more able to relate to a God who shares our pain and as it were weeps with us, who gives us strength to carry on in the midst of such tragedy. They found God to be present in the love, comfort and support extended to them by so many in their world, in their family and by friends and sometimes even by strangers.

God became the source of their power to feel the abiding presence of Jane's spirit in their minds and hearts. God enabled them to heal their own pain by finding ways of healing the pain of sick children as they volunteered in a local children's hospital. They found consolation in Judaism's hope that while Jane's body was returned to the earth, her soul finds its eternal home with God.

Jack and Linda went through many bitter moments long after the funeral and burial of their son, Nicholas, but the time came when they too were seeking within their tradition some help to cope with their sorrow and to reaffirm the meaning of their lives. I did not know which story they ultimately chose until the following High Holiday season. I have mentioned elsewhere that it was customary during the long Yom Kippur day for a number of members of the congregation who had experienced serious suffering to share with the congregation how they coped and how Judaism helped them return to life and reaffirm its meaning.

I invited Jack to participate in that symposium. He began by telling us about the great struggle to rebuild his faith. He spoke of the rawness of grief and confessed that the mourner's prayer, the Kaddish, by which we proclaim trust in God in the face of tragic loss, was for him, in the beginning, an empty exercise, but as time passed he began to find comfort in its recitation. Jack's next words to the congregation revealed which story he had embraced:

> Through introspection I visit Nicholas and I can find beauty in his smile. I was fortunate to have spent incredible time with my son in the ten-and-a-half years God bestowed upon us. I am grateful I did not miss the opportunity I did have. If I were given the choice to never have known Nicholas or to have known Nicholas at the price of suffering by losing him, the choice would be simple. I am forever thankful for being Nicholas' father. I am grateful that although he is no longer in my stewardship, he is in God's hands. I have let him go.

CHAPTER 12 ▫ THE RABBI AS A SPIRITUAL GUIDE

Jack had retold the story of Bruria and Rabbi Meier.

In my role as spiritual guide, I was able to share with my people diverse answers to the question of life's tragic dimension. The narrative that proved more meaningful to Jane's parents did not satisfy Nicholas' parents, but I helped them understand that despair may not be given the last word in the story of our lives. We Jews must rekindle and satisfy our passion for life's meaning.

Jeremy and Me

I have already mentioned a teachable moment with Jeremy Tucker during his college years. From Jeremy's days in religious school I had come to know him as a child and later a teenager who embodied a precious combination of an exceptionally fertile mind and a deeply caring heart.

Jeremy grew up loving the music and the liturgy of the synagogue, the biblical and rabbinic stories and, later, Reform Judaism's Greene Family Camp. My first memorable encounter with Jeremy occurred when it was time to prepare for his bar mitzvah. He told his parents he didn't want to become a bar mitzvah. At this stage it would be, for him, strictly social rather than a spiritual rite of passage. His parents required that he convince me before they would honor his decision—fully expecting that I would exert the power of rabbinic persuasion to bring him on board the original program.

Much to their surprise, and Jeremy's delight, I accepted his position and said that it did not affect his status as a Jew and that he could become bar mitzvah at a later date, when he was ready. Jeremy was an outstanding student in religious school and in his secular studies. No one was surprised when he was accepted to Yale or when he distinguished himself as an academic star. He intended to become a pediatrician, but majored in English literature and graduated summa cum laude.

Jeremy's academic record at Yale again left no one surprised when he was accepted to Harvard Medical School. I was also not surprised when he deferred his medical studies to "Teach for America" in a Phoenix, Arizona barrio. Jeremy not only taught at risk children in the classroom, he bonded with fourteen-year-old Victor Villanueva. Victor's father was totally absent. His mother cleaned motel rooms and physically abused him. Until a recent move, the family had lived in one of Phoenix's most violent neighborhoods where murders were a weekly occurrence and the "Wetback Power" gang shot at anyone who wore rival colors on their street. Victor's neighborhood was a breeding ground for gang membership, drugs and violent crime.

Somehow Jeremy got permission to take Victor and his younger brother on a trek through the Grand Canyon. As a burgeoning writer Jeremy kept a full journal account of the experience, including the arguments and the generous use of four letter words. These two weeks were punctuated by deeply bonding experiences and angry confrontations. Jeremy kept periodic contact with Victor by phone while he attended medical school, where he again distinguished himself academically. When his M.D. Degree was obtained he was wooed by Dr. Ralph Feigin of Texas Childrens Hospital to return to his native Houston for the residency years.

A Life Radically Transformed

After completing his first year of residency, Jeremy's life was abruptly transformed. He was operated on for a malignant brain tumor and emerged from the surgery with greatly impaired speech and confinement to a wheelchair. While still in the hospital, he asked Dr. Feigin to call me in Charlevoix. I could understand very little of his garbled speech on the phone, but promised to visit with him when we returned to Houston. During many months of rehab, including speech therapy, physical therapy and occupational therapy, no one worked more diligently and determinedly than Jeremy. He still held on to the hope of walking again and resuming his medical training.

Before long, Jeremy realized he could not realistically plan to resume his pediatric residency. Just studying for and taking the qualifying examination would require more accommodations than could possibly be granted. Even the somewhat less rigorous path of child psychiatry was beyond his reach. This realization, coupled with what appeared to be a permanent inability to stand on his own feet and walk, catapulted Jeremy into deep despondency. As far as he was concerned, his life was essentially over.

One cannot overstate the magnitude and depth of Jeremy's loss. He, who had bonded with Victor, a child handicapped by life circumstances, was now himself a conspicuous member of the handicapped community. He who had encouraged Victor to envisage and strive for a new life, was now challenged to embark upon a similar journey. His family and some friends were there for him. He knew we cared deeply, but only he could decide whether or not to "choose life." Once we returned to Houston, I began visiting with Jeremy each Sunday afternoon. His parents arranged for him to live in his own apartment with a group of rotating aides. Eventually he mastered the skills necessary to be alone at night. Physical therapy had strengthened his hands and his speech became much clearer.

During our visits, he initially censored his thoughts and speech to accommodate what he thought a rabbi would tolerate. Once he tested my limits and found them much broader than he anticipated, Jeremy spoke more freely. Within a few months he considered me as much his friend as his rabbi. He delighted in calling me "Sam" and came to realize that my regular visits were by now more an act of friendship than rabbinic duty.

During those early months of our weekly visits, no matter the subject we were discussing, Jeremy almost invariably found a way of reminding me that his life had lost its core of meaning and that death seemed a more reasonable option than life. I did not argue with him. My standard response was, "I hear you and it's your choice, but I sure hope and pray you choose life."

Jeremy's Struggle to Reclaim Meaning

At some point, when he spoke warmly of his times in our congregation, I encouraged him to attend. His aides delivered him to us for the Sabbath Eve service and I, now Rabbi Emeritus, pushed his wheelchair to the aisle next to where Joan and I were seated. He found himself singing some of the Hebrew prayers and reading aloud the familiar text with the congregation. He enjoyed listening to the cantor and appreciated the rabbi's homily. At the reception (Oneg Shabbat) following the service, Jeremy eagerly interacted with congregants who introduced themselves and chatted with him.

Some months later at the High Holiday season, Jeremy wanted to attend the Yom Kippur Eve service. We had planned to attend the early service. He found it easier to attend the later one. I called his father. Jeremy's parents were, of course, terribly shaken by the traumatic transformation in their son's condition. In fact, they had not been able to step foot in the synagogue since the surgery. Jeremy's mother, who had been a regular attender, found it impossible to return. I called Jeremy's father and told him that his son wanted to come and shouldn't be sitting alone with his aide on Yom Kippur eve. The father, Jeff, agreed to attend with Jeremy. The next day I received an email in which Jeff recounted that during the Kol Nidre chant, one of the signature and hauntingly stirring cantorial solos, the congregation was asked to rise. Jeff remained seated with Jeremy and they held hands. Shortly after the lights were dimmed and the cantor began to sing, Jeff recalled bursting into an uncontrollable sob. It was the first time he cried since the surgery. Jeff added that this was the closest thing to a spiritual experience he had ever had.

In one of our conversations, Jeremy asked how I, a rabbi, and therefore a teacher of Judaism, understood the problem of undeserved life-transforming traumas like his own. I offered those two responses that I found embodied in biblical and Rabbinic story. When Jeremy asked which narrative theology I accept, I told him that I embrace each at different times. He liked the notion that the faith journey may include periods of doubt and even angry confrontation, all of which can sometimes lead to a deeper faith and closer intimacy with our God.

I also shared with Jeremy the great story told by the Jewish mystic, Rabbi Isaac Luria. His version of Kabbalah teaches that when God created the world, God's glory overloaded the vessels that received it, and the vessels cracked. So in the very act of creation, the world sustained a cosmic brokenness, which we must help repair as God's partners. Isaac Luria provides one of the most powerful narratives of a God who really needs us to help repair the brokenness in that tiny corner of God's world entrusted to our care. By our acts of *tikkun* (repair), we fulfill the deepest meaning of our lives.

Jeremy resonated most to the notion that we can argue with God, and that God would rather be challenged than ignored. He also resonated to the notion that God needs us to help repair the brokenness in our world. When I suggested that Jeremy might want to read the Torah portion assigned for study, offer his own interpretations and even attend the weekly Saturday morning Torah study at the synagogue, he did it for a while and enjoyed it; but it was not sustained, partly because the class was early in the morning and, unlike me, Jeremy was a nocturnal guy whose energy was renewed at the very time I am ready for bed.

Something subtle, gradual, and wondrous was happening to Jeremy. Somehow, after months of grieving his losses, he began to focus more on what he still possessed. He recognized with gratitude that the brain tumor surgery that so diminished his physical mobility did not impair his great cognitive prowess. His passion to help underserved children also remained undimmed. His quirky sense of humor resurfaced, and with his aide, he began to indulge his great love for movies. Each week, I would receive his incisive review of a film or two with his recommendation that I see or skip it.

While after the surgery Jeremy found it difficult even to sign his name, he could comfortably tap on the keyboard of a word processor. Seizing a teachable moment, I encouraged

CHAPTER 12 ⁂ THE RABBI AS A SPIRITUAL GUIDE

Jeremy to return to his journal of *A Backtrack Through the Grand Canyon with Victor* and to transform the journal into a full-fledged book. With great discipline and enthusiasm, he became totally engrossed in this project.

After some considerable rebuffs, a publisher was found and, as Jeremy put it, he was no longer just a writer, but he was about to become a published author. The actual signing of the contract became instantly a day for celebration and the first day since the surgery when his parents flashed a radiant, tear-filled smile.

As Jeremy was cleaning up the manuscript before submission, he realized he couldn't write the end of the book without reuniting with Victor. Accompanied by his aide, Jeremy flew to Phoenix. The reunion was both poignant and wonderful. After seeing that Victor, now twenty-four years old, was honorably employed, married, the father of three children, and—far removed from a life of gangs and drugs—Jeremy realized that he had helped repair the brokenness of a human life. I waited impatiently for some word from Phoenix. When it came and I read the message sent from his mobile phone, I was moved to tears: "My journey was great. I think the change in a person from child to teen to adult is a miracle. The ways we change, the ways we don't. It's a miracle of life's journey. Witnessing life is...a blessing!" This was the most compelling sign that Jeremy had indeed re-embraced life. Surely his struggles were not behind him, but that email was Jeremy's *l'chaim*—his toast to life.

Healing Oneself by Healing Others

Fortunately, Jeremy would soon be given an opportunity to discover that when we ourselves have been deeply wounded by life, our truest path to healing is to help heal the wounds of others. One of our congregational members was a major underwriter of the KIPP schools. These charter schools have demonstrated significant success in educating and restoring the self-confidence and academic competence of children whose life situation has been dysfunctional. Through my contact, Jeremy and I secured a meeting with Mike Feinberg, who lives in Houston and is one of the founders of the KIPP schools.

As I expected, Mike was very taken and impressed by Jeremy and found a place for him in one of the schools. Twice a week Jeremy spent half a day tutoring individual students. Later he was assigned the task of meeting one-on-one with "problem students." His magical rapport with children, his wry humor and his obvious disability gave him moral authority with them. He would tell his students, "Look, we're all in some sense disabled; some have more visible disabilities than others, but you and I have stuff to deal with and which we must strive to overcome. Even as I have been able to cope with my disabilities, you can, too."

Jeremy was loved by those students, and they gave him an opportunity to indulge his passion to help the marginalized, disadvantaged children in our world. They in turn validated and helped heal him.

The most precious gift I received for my eightieth birthday was an extensive letter Jeremy composed on the word processor printed, and managed—with considerable effort—to sign personally. The letter began:

Dear Sam, At first you were my rabbi, so I called you Rabbi Karff. Slowly as we grew from a formal relationship to friends I started to call you Sam, and now I always say Sam and I think Sam. But, you are a rabbi, my rabbi, a rav, a teacher, a man who, like the Hebrew origin, is abundant. Abundant in what? Knowledge in sermons? Yes, but more than that. Abundant in wisdom and kindness, humility and humor, truth and story. Abundant in love. Love for Joan, for your daughters and their spouses, for your grandchildren, for many other people I am unable to name—and now for me. Your love abounds.

In the acknowledgment section of his book, *Before a Canyon,* Jeremy wrote:

> He gives me great advice and helps me go down the bumpy road that is my life. He uses powerful words such as blessing, and balance, and beauty; he talks with me about both philosophical issues and current movies and we often discuss both the daily challenges and funny moments of our personal lives, our jobs, and our limits... but most of all I like Sam and I care deeply about him.

I wish I could end the story of Jeremy by telling you that he lived a long life, enriched by an intimate, loving life partner and that he had the privilege of testing his great love for children by relating to his own. This was not to be. Some eight years after the life-transforming brain surgery, Jeremy faced another medical crisis, which would lead to his dying at age thirty-seven. His death was a devastating loss to his wonderful parents, his loving sister, his doting grandmother and to all of us who were so profoundly touched by his life.

The service to mark his life's end became both a time for deep grieving and a time to celebrate the life of a remarkable person. To me, he was like a son I never had.

There is a price to be paid for allowing other persons to deeply enter your life, but there is a much weightier loss for not allowing one's life to be so touched. Perhaps the reader will now more fully appreciate why, of all the facets of life as a rabbi, I cherish most the privilege of being a spiritual guide.

Being With Persons Who Know They Are Dying

To be human is to live life with the consciousness of our mortality. Meaning-seeking creatures that we are, we may raise questions, experience crises of meaning and moments which are especially meaningful. If death does not come instantly and we are aware that we are dying, the question of meaning becomes front and center.

Elsewhere I have suggested that we may die with the consciousness that our life has been meaningful. We know we have loved and been loved, were engaged in work that gave us the sense of being needed and useful and are able to die with the sense we will be remembered and will be missed. For those of us who have lived with a sense of God's presence, there is the additional hope that, while dust returns to dust, the soul returns to God for Eternal Life.

As a rabbi I have had the privilege of spending time with those who knew they were dying and who knew that I knew they were dying. Such moments are drenched in authenticity, no pretense nor posturing, no small talk. When devoid of physical pain or discomfort, this period of life can bring with it peace, trust and hope. To share such moments is the highest privilege, the pinnacle of a rabbi's pastoral role.

In most of the Hebrew Bible, the primary source of meaning in dying is to know that one has lived, not perfectly, but well and that we have been part of a larger story that our descendants whom we have nurtured and taught, will now carry on. In Rabbinic Judaism, there is a full affirmation that death is not the end. A classic Rabbinic prayer we continue to recite refers to the soul which lives within us and at our death returns to its source in God. While our tradition certainly includes a belief in the ultimate resurrection of the dead, most of our people, including me, resonate more easily to the image of the body returning to the Earth and the soul returning to God.

A faithful Jew may embrace one or both these envisagements of our post-mortal destiny. Many years ago, I embraced the narrative description of the soul's post-mortal destiny found in the teachings of the great twentieth century Jewish mystic, Rabbi Abraham Isaac Kook. In his stunning metaphor Rabbi Kook regarded life as an inverted tree with its roots in Heaven. The trunk and branches of the tree represent our deeds on Earth, while its roots are in God. The more we are nourished by the roots in this earthly life, the more we fulfill God's commandments and cultivate our relation to our creator and the more soul we will bring to the soul of souls after our life on Earth has ended. Such is the second kind of hope Judaism offers me as I contemplate the end of my days.

What of those whose life is snuffed out in infancy or early childhood (as was the case for Jane and Nicholas)? Those circumstances are addressed by the ancient Rabbinic statement that some persons acquire eternity through a life of striving and doing while others acquire it in a single hour.[65]

My life as rabbi has been blessed by being in the presence of persons who knew their life on Earth was ending. Not all were members of my congregation or even persons I had known in earlier days. The M.D. Anderson Cancer Center in Houston has earned the highest distinction in its field with patients not only from the local metropolitan area, but also from other states and around the world.

Joan Robbin was an elegant older woman who, after being assaulted by a chronic form of leukemia, became a periodic visitor to M. D. Anderson. She would receive treatment for weeks at a time as an outpatient and was able to visit with new friends she had made, eat in our town's finest restaurants, even go to theater, and was periodically buoyed in spirit by visits from her out-of-town family. Joan was a strong, matriarchal and commanding presence who took pride in her family and in the beautiful home, which became her precious anchor of security. The assurance of being loved was central to her wellbeing. When visits from her out-of-town family seemed less frequent than she needed, Joan felt hurt. The source of her greatest joy was seeing them in her hospital room.

After several months back home from her most recent visit, Joan was told that her leukemia was now acute. Some weeks after she returned to M. D. Anderson, Joan lapsed into a coma. When her family received the news and the medical expectation that life was rapidly coming to an end, they rushed to Houston. They requested that she be allowed to do her dying in a hospital room, in their presence, rather than the ICU. Contrary to expectation, Joan emerged from the coma and reported a near-death experience.

Emotionally fragile after this episode, she resisted any further "experimental treatment" but found great difficulty coming to terms with her death. A sensitive, competent and deeply compassionate woman who served as the lay Jewish Chaplain at the hospital asked if Joan would like a visit from a rabbi. When she nodded approvingly, I was invited to visit with Joan and her family. Early in our visit it became evident Joan was not worried about a painful death. She feared death itself. She was made anxious by the thought of entering the great unknown without faith in a personal God. She had lost that faith after the death of her young son. Absent that faith, Joan was overcome by a fear of dying.

In such circumstances I would take my cues from the person, rather than seek to impose my faith. Here my initial task was to help Joan reaffirm the meaningfulness of her life on Earth. When I asked her what she was proudest of in her life, she spoke of her children and grandchildren and of being able, after a difficult divorce, to build a new life with her current husband, Harry. She marveled at the successful blending of the two families and took some credit for it. I assured her that she would be vividly and lovingly remembered by her family, in that she had so much to do with the kind of persons they had become.

When I asked permission to read aloud the 23rd Psalm, she listened intently; and when she asked me if I believed the words of the psalmist, "I shall fear no evil for thou art with me"—I responded, "Yes, I do." Then I shared with Joan the experience of a dear congregant whom I visited on the Saturday that turned out to be the day before her death. When I asked her, "Knowing that your life on Earth is ending, what are your thoughts at this time?" She told me of an experience as a young child. She and her sister had been brought to the hospital for the removal of tonsils. The mother held the hand of each child. Since Harriet was older, she was asked to go first. She pleaded with her mother to go with her. The mother insisted that she must remain behind with the younger sister, but assured Harriet that she could trust the nurse, who at that moment had taken her hand and was leading her through a doorway to an unknown land. Later, when Harriet awoke, she saw her mother and realized that all was well in this new land.

That memory became for Harriet a metaphor of her need to trust as she prepares to make her journey to that unknown land. Harriet expressed trust in the Source of Being. She was grateful for the joy, including the love of her husband and her children and the joy of grandchildren she had experienced in her life.

Following this half hour interlude, Harriet dismissed me as courteously as she could. She said, "Shalom." That was the last time I saw her before conducting her funeral service two days later. Joan listened earnestly to Harriet's story, and it seemed to me she was deeply moved.

Joan's daughter, Amy, told me that the doctor had granted permission for them to take their mother back to her beloved home. Some weeks later, I learned that Joan was able to die at home, "her spirit at peace." The funeral service was conducted by a local rabbi. In her letter to me, daughter Amy recalled that, after I left her second meeting, "Mom kept asking us to repeat what you said. It gave her a lot of comfort. I remember lying with her on the bed, cuddled, holding hands and talking about what we believed. A precious moment of love I will always remember. That day was the beginning of her renewed faith, and mine."

As a rabbi, I have cherished the opportunities to preach, teach and serve noble causes in the larger community and to preside at lifecycle ceremonies, which enable transitional moments to be invested with sanctity. I loved teaching in the congregation and at a university level, but no facet of my rabbinate has been quite as meaningful to me as the opportunity to be present to persons struggling with life's darker side and to help them recover the precious gift of meaning.

Joan and I are standing on the shore of Lake Charlevoix which for over half a century has been the site of our summer cabin in beautiful Northern Michigan.

Chapter 13
RETIREMENT & MY SECOND VOCATION

IN MY EARLY SIXTIES, I BEGAN TO THINK seriously about retirement. It seemed that more than a few colleagues never fully adjusted to that new status. These were usually the kinds of retired rabbis who brought much heartburn to their successors. I was determined not to become one of them. When would I retire? Hopefully before my congregation became anxious for me to do so! How would I know it was time? As it turned out, about halfway through my sixty-eighth year I received a sign that the time had come.

In a congregation of some two thousand families, it was not unusual for me to have two or even three afternoon meetings with a bar/bat mitzvah candidate and his or her parents. These meetings lasted about forty-five minutes to an hour. Since I was not directly involved in teaching the child to read/chant from the Torah scroll, lead the prayer service and help him or her write a talk based on the Torah reading, I used that time to learn about the child's interests and special gifts and to elicit from the parents some comments about their son or daughter. This conference and my subsequent notes enabled me to speak to and bless the child at the service with some personal knowledge.

The reason it was not unusual to have three such back-to-back meetings on at least several afternoons a week is because the children were schooled until mid-afternoon. On this particular day I had concluded the second family meeting and was on my way out when my secretary gestured that a third family was waiting for me in the sitting room next to her office. Hearing that, I uttered an audible sigh. I took that sigh as an unmistakable sign that the time had come to retire. Pondering that reaction after I got home, I felt it did not apply simply to that day and that child but to a general tiredness. I had reached a point when the arduous schedule of my congregational rabbinate had become too much. I was almost sixty-eight and ready for a much less demanding schedule.

When the president, also a personal friend, urged me at least to extend for an additional year, which would mean the congregation would have had only three senior rabbis in one hundred years, I did not reconsider—I knew it was time. For twenty-two years I had also taught a three-hour seminar at Rice University in the Religious Studies department each Monday night. I decided to give this up as well.

CHAPTER 13 ⸙ RETIREMENT & MY SECOND VOCATION

As I began to focus on all the things I would miss, relief at the prospect of an easier life was eclipsed by anxiety over an uncharted future. To be sure, retirement did not mean I somehow stopped being a rabbi, but it did mean in relation to my congregation I would become rabbi emeritus. Many rabbis were very content with their new life, but more than a few were deeply discontented. I had observed that the happiest retired rabbis I knew had either been unhappy in their work and viewed their new status as a great liberation or, they were very fulfilled congregational rabbis who now found the primary source of their validation and fulfillment outside their congregational sphere. I hoped to join the ranks of the latter group, but I could not be certain that this would be possible.

My Counsel to Others

Over the years, I was asked to counsel with members of my congregation who were facing retirement. They exhibited in varying proportions the same combination of joy and anxiety at the prospect of that easier life! I would tell them that generally the happiest retirees I knew had a two-dimensional life. On the one hand, they gave themselves opportunities to do more of the things they enjoyed but didn't get a chance to do enough of during their working lives.

Now was the time to indulge such interests and passions without guilt. On the other hand, I suggested to these prospective retirees the need to find some activity outside the home "that will give you the continuing sense of being needed and useful. It needn't be an income producing job but it needs to be meaningful and satisfying."

At the core of my religious perspective is the belief that life is a sacred vocation. We find our deepest fulfillment not simply by self-indulgence, but by accepting our lifelong vocation to help heal some of the brokenness in that tiny corner of God's world entrusted to our care. Now the time had come when I was challenged to practice what I taught others about a good retirement. As a retired rabbi, I needed to symbolize my change of status within the congregation. My predecessor sat on the bimah next to me and had a standing invitation to offer the benediction at the conclusion of the service. He continued to officiate at any life-cycle functions when families invited him. When I retired, I did not accept this practice for myself. Many persons asked, "How long did it take you to get used to sitting in the congregation?" I replied, "About three minutes." All those previous years I was separated from my family. For the privilege of sitting with my family I gladly surrendered the honor of sitting on the bimah.

I also decided to limit my preaching and teaching in the congregation to no more than one or several each year—if invited by my successor. During the first few years, I accepted invitations from congregants to participate in lifecycle rituals; at baby blessings, weddings and funerals—only with the consent of my successor and only if he presided at those events.

After a number of years in this mode, I wrote an open letter to the congregation expressing my decision no longer to participate in any lifecycle functions except for members of my family. I would attend some as a friend but declined to officiate or co-officiate. Here is an excerpt from that letter to the congregation:

CHAPTER 13 · RETIREMENT & MY SECOND VOCATION

Until now, if I was close to a member of the congregation who died, I did accept the invitation from my successor and the family to give a eulogy at the service. I believe that the time has come to change my role. First because this role properly belongs to an active clergy member and especially to the senior rabbi. Fortunately you and I are blessed with a senior rabbi and other clergy who sensitively fulfill this role. An additional reason has influenced this decision. At this stage of life, the need to be both mourner and eulogizer weighs too heavily upon me. In the years ahead, while I hope we shall share more joys than sorrows, I will want to be with you at those times of loss to comfort you as a friend rather than specifically as an officiant. So please know that this decision represents no diminution of my love and respect. As the Good Book teaches us, "For everything there is a time…"

This decision would spare me from choosing to officiate for some families and declining to do so for others. It would also prevent me from even the appearance of assuming a role that now more properly belonged to my successor.

This new reality left unresolved the second aspect of a good retirement. I had no problem identifying those things I planned to do more of—like indulging my love of baseball. I intended to indulge even more widely my love of reading newspapers, seeing movies, extending our travel experience in and outside the country and of course, spending even longer summers in Charlevoix.

An Offer I Could Not Refuse

What of the need to find something to do outside the home that would give me a continuing sense of being needed and useful? It is said that when one door closes in our lives, God opens another. As my retirement day was only a few months away, I had no clear idea what shape the second dimension of my retirement would take. To my surprise, a phone call from Dr. David Low opened the door to my next vocation. David Low was then president of the University of Texas Health Science Center, which consisted of schools of medicine, nursing, dentistry, public health and biomedical research.

At our lunch, Dr. Low invited me to join the faculty of the UTHSC (since renamed UT Health). He wanted me to create and teach a program that focused on the non-biomedical or relational dimension of being a healing physician. I accepted the appointment half-time in the Department of Family Medicine, but I had not the foggiest notion what I would actually be teaching. Speak of an act of faith! Since Dr. Low was trained as a neuroscientist, his conviction that there was an important non-biomedical component to healing gave instant credence to his claim. That summer, I devoted all my study time to an intense immersion in reading and reflection. I devoured just about every book that was recommended to me in the relatively new field of "medical humanities," or what some called, "spirituality in medicine."

Twenty-five hundred years ago the Greek physician, Hippocrates, taught that if the patient liked and trusted his physician and believed in the efficacy of the treatment that medical intervention would be more effective.[66] In short, there is potentially healing power in the doctor/patient relationship itself.

Over the centuries, physicians practiced this relational medicine. How the physician related to the patient—the trust and caring he inspired—was considered part of the doctor's healing power. Until the middle of the twentieth century, the old-fashioned family physician in the United States had a relatively limited medical arsenal. I'm old enough to remember the family doctor. He wrote his prescriptions in Latin and made house-calls, and he relied heavily on what today's generation would call placebos. Yet in every poll, doctors were rated at the top of the list of admired and trusted professionals. So they must have done some healing after all!

Biomedicine and Its Limits

Following the Second World War, antibiotics were discovered which could "zap" many conditions an earlier generation of doctors could merely palliate. These "wonder drugs" ushered in the age of biomedicine and with it a new paradigm in medical education and practice. Medical professors would now allow their students to conclude that their primary task was to learn, master and then practice the biomedicine because, at the end of the day, that alone was relevant to medical outcome. Under this model of medical teaching and practice there would have been no open door for a clergyman to teach future medical students, but some thirty years later there were growing signs that the pure biomedical model was inadequate. What were some of the factors that led to a reconsideration?

Polls that in earlier years had rated physicians as the most admired professionals began to place them lower on the list. There were complaints that modern medicine was becoming essentially a detached exchange of medical knowledge and skill for compensation. Many patients felt too much contact with the cold steel of diagnostic tests in relation to the time actually spent speaking to and being heard by a physician.

During this time, alternative and complementary medicine emerged as a major factor in a patient's choice of therapy. A growing number of patients consulted alternative therapists for acupuncture or herbs without even telling their primary physician. Observers of this phenomenon saw it in part as a consumer rebellion against the perceived coldness and impersonalism of so much mainstream American medicine. Many people it seems wanted a competent clinician who was also a healer.

Perhaps the most significant factor that contributed to the eclipse of the biomedical model was a seminal article published in 1977 in the eminently respectable journal, *Science*. Its author was Dr. George Engel, a physician and psychiatrist at the University of Rochester Medical Center. Dr. Engel argued that the biomedical model needed to be replaced with a bio-psycho-social model. Engel wrote that, "Even with the application of rational therapies, the behavior of the physician and the relationship between the patient and physician powerfully influence therapeutic outcome for better or for worse." He noted that the "insulin requirements of a diabetic patient may fluctuate significantly depending on how the patient perceives his relationship with his doctor."[67]

This emerging new model of medical education and practice did not belittle the tremendous advantages of the biomedical age. We should all be grateful for its benefits and would not want to return to that earlier age. But, in this new model, the physician must also seek to connect to the patient as a person. She must seek to understand how the person is experiencing the condition, what effect it has on the person's life and spirit; most significantly, that the quality of the doctor/patient relationship can affect medical outcome!

In 1999, the new paradigm became official. That was the year the American Association of Medical Colleges (AAMC), which grants medical schools their accreditation, issued the following guidelines: "Patients have a fundamental right to considerate care that safeguards and respects their cultural, psychosocial, and spiritual values."[68] That same year I retired from the senior rabbinate of Beth Israel and began teaching at the Texas Medical Center. At that time there were only a few medical centers with required programs in medical humanities or "spirituality in medicine." My task was to create and teach in such a program at the University of Texas Medical School.

My Mission: To Teach a Relational Medicine

In the religious story that has defined me, God is the source of our being, the giver of the way we are intended to live. God is active in our lives and in history to fulfill the divine goal for creation. I fulfill God's purpose for me by being faithful to my peoples' covenant with God and by striving to repair the brokenness in that tiny corner of God's world entrusted to my care.

While God has given us humans the power to heal, God is the ultimate healer. God's healing is mediated through the health care giver, the clergy who comfort our troubled spirits, the scientist who discovers healing substances in the laboratory, and the healing power implanted within our minds and bodies. Sometimes God heals in God's own way, which we call a miracle. In my religious story, disease is not inflicted by God as punishment for our sins but is, as Maimonides insisted, the price we pay for the privilege of being sensitive and embodied persons.

That is the pastoral theology that has informed my preaching and my life. I was now entering a different world by teaching at a state-sponsored medical school that observes the separation of church and state. Moreover, I brought to my vocation no biomedical skill, knowledge or credibility. Yet I was asked to teach future physicians and nurses.

Clearly I was being invited to bring to these students the benefit of my experience with persons who have faced life's darker side—serious, life-threatening, chronic or terminal illness. One of the issues I would be asked to address with medical students is what is the role of the physician in end of life care? Or, how can one be a healer of the human spirit when you can no longer function as a healer of that patient's body?

My initial act was to form a committee of faculty representing the medical school, the school of nursing, the school of public health and the school of biomedical research. Easily, the committee members agreed with this core principle of the new paradigm: *there is healing power in the doctor/patient relationship*. We called our initiative the "Health and Human Spirit Program" and agreed that the program should help students appreciate the importance and acquire the skills to practice what I came to call *relational medicine*.

While the UT Medical School is not religiously funded or "faith-based," it is not coincidental that the new model of medical teaching and practice has reintroduced the term "spirituality" to the medical and nursing school world. In most polls, a significant number of Americans, when asked about their ultimate source of support in times of illness, will refer to their religious faith. Others may claim not to be religious but would agree they are spiritual. Clearly, we needed to fashion a program which was user-friendly for those like myself for whom religion is the deepest expression of their human spirit and those who might refer to themselves as spiritual but not religious, as well as those who simply consider themselves not religious.

Sensitivity among some faculty members about the term "spiritual" or "religious" was reflected in how they introduced me to their classes. Some would prefer to call me Doctor rather than Rabbi. To be sure, I have a doctorate in rabbinic studies but given my lack of biomedical accreditation and the nature of my mission at the Texas Medical Center, the term Rabbi seemed to be more appropriate. Their preference for Doctor over Rabbi may have reflected some uneasiness with clergy receiving an appointment on a medical faculty.

Defining Spirituality

Our working definition of spirit or spirituality was based on the premise that we humans are meaning-seeking creatures. Meaning is the sense that I have something to live for, there is still a purpose to my life even when I have been assaulted by radical economic losses, the loss of a loved one or serious, perhaps life transforming illness. All of these can precipitate a crisis in meaning.

What are some sources of meaning that may help us recover the sense that, in spite of its darker side, life is worth living? Certainly our power to love and the experience of being loved, or work that makes us feel needed and useful. A third source of meaning is to know that because of the way we have touched other lives, by the children we have parented, by our helpful, guiding presence in others' time of need, by the causes we have served—there will be persons who will remember and miss us after we have died.

Love, work and the sense that by the way we live we will be remembered and missed may all be part of a non-religious spirituality. For those of us who are avowedly religious, God's love for us empowers us to love, God calls us to make our work a sacred vocation—God is our ultimate source of meaning.

Practicing a Relational Medicine

As part of a state-sponsored medical school our program's default mode is a non-religious spirituality or the art of practicing a relational medicine. I have found that most future physicians feel more comfortable speaking with patients in purely clinical terms. Our goal is to help them appreciate the importance of relating to the patient as person. This can best be achieved generally, by not starting with the medical chart.

A woman made an appointment to see a new gynecologist. In the waiting room she filled out a lengthy questionnaire. When she was ushered into the doctor's office, he invited her to be seated, then scanned the questionnaire and exclaimed, "I see you are a post-menopausal woman who is not on hormone replacement therapy. That's not good." The woman reported feeling like a "hormone deficiency case" rather than a person seeing a new physician for the first time. When I asked her to describe an alternate scenario, she replied, "I came in with a book I was reading. He might have asked how I felt about the book." That would have connected the doctor to the patient as a person.

Third-year students see patients in the clinic who wait between one hour and two before getting to see them. Instead of beginning with the medical chart, I suggest, "How long did you have to wait before seeing me?" When they tell you, why not say, "I'm sorry. I wouldn't want to wait that long, and your time is as important to you as mine is to me. But there are more of you than of us, and we try to do the best we can. Now, how can I help you?" Those words took less than thirty seconds, but they dramatically altered the tenor of the doctor/patient relationship. The physician signaled that he doesn't take that long wait as his entitlement. He affirms his respect for his patient's time.

The Second Year Curriculum in the Medical School

At the center of the second-year curriculum is a method of teaching called PBL (Problem Based Learning). Students meet three mornings a week with a facilitator in groups of seven sitting around a table. They are assigned a clinical case and asked to make a diagnosis and prescribe treatment. They consult their medical texts and the Internet to prepare for the class. Much of the class consists of student reports with guidance from the facilitator.

As initially written, the case material and the questions students addressed were strictly biomedical. At first, at the invitation of a number of facilitators, I attended the last segment of the last session in a unit and was given forty-five minutes to focus on the non-biomedical dimension of the case. If they were considering a chronic condition like Crohn's Disease I would shift the conversation by asking, "What do you think is the most difficult thing for a patient with Crohn's Disease? What is the non-clinical healing role of a physician in such situations?" He or she might respond, "Knowing that it's chronic; the patient will have to live with it rather than be cured." That usually led to a discussion of the doctor's special ongoing role to manage the disease, to handle the crises, to empathize with the patient during moments of discouragement and, yes, to foster hope that she can still live a meaningful and even joy-filled life.

I would help future doctors realize the special bonding that can happen in such chronic situations. A doctor becomes even more a potential healer of the patient's spirit or morale than a curer of the body. The patient needs a physician's validation of his or her feelings. The physician must be perceived by the patient as one who really cares about a good outcome, who is not just a dispenser of biomedicine but an advocate and partner to help the patient live with the condition.

The Third Year Curriculum

In the third year, the students spend at least a month in the various medical specialties; surgery, internal medicine, pediatrics, etc. At the outset, I urged that the seven hours during that year assigned to the Health and Human Spirit program be required rather than elective. Otherwise, our program would be marginalized and devalued by the students. Fortunately, I was able to persuade the administration that this program should be integrated into the actual third-year clinical program, which would make me a partner in each instance with a faculty clinician.

When I first initiated this partnership I virtually monopolized the hour and relegated my clinical partner to the role of observer. After one or two clinical physicians excused themselves from the next session, I got the message. I reflected on the reason for my own conduct and their response. It seems that, unconsciously perhaps, I felt that since this time devoted to non-biomedical or relational issues was so new for these faculty members, I had to demonstrate to them my bona fides and the added value I as a non-clinician brought to the curriculum!

Fortunately, I realized in time what I was trying to do and how misguided it was. Thereafter I began to insist that the clinician and I sit up front together and I actively elicited his or her perspective based on the physician's clinical practice. Once the dynamics of the sessions changed, the clinicians not only gave biomedical credibility to our sessions, but they also enjoyed an opportunity to share their personal experience of the relational aspect of their medical practice.

The Role of the Physician in End of Life Care

The first genuine validation of the program by students themselves came with the second year class. One of the PBL cases dealt with an end of life situation. It was time for the physician to change from the interventional biomedicine to palliative care. One of the three sessions of that unit was my talk to the plenary. It was titled, "The Role of the Physician in End of Life Care."

I introduced my topic with a brief historical note. Before the recent reemergence of relational healing, physicians were known by their "fight or flight" syndrome. When their aggressive medical intervention proved inadequate and the patient was declared "terminal," the physician tended quickly to flee the scene. When you go into medicine to cure disease, you perceive an inability to cure as a personal failure. Rather than immerse yourself in a sense of impotence you may be naturally inclined to move on to situations where your biomedical prowess can be usefully deployed. Moreover, a deeper reason is suggested in studies that find persons who choose medicine as a vocation are more fearful of death than any other profession. Thus doctors go into medicine in part to conquer that monster, death and when they are not successful "it brings back all those primitive fears." Those words by Dr. Sherwin Nuland lead him to remind his colleagues, "When you cannot cure you can still care."[69]

I expressed that more positively. Virtually every human interaction is not neutral; it is either healing or harming. Even when a doctor cannot heal the body she is still capable of contributing to the healing of the patient's spirit. I shared with those students my own pastoral experience. Some of the most meaningful encounters of my life occurred in conversation with those who knew they were dying and I knew they were dying. If I had a long-standing relationship with them, I would share some of the attributes I valued in them. I would invite them to share what gave them joy and meaning in their lives. This life review previewed the eulogy they would not be able to hear. Those moments with the patient were often extraordinarily poignant to the one whose life was ending and to me.

I shared with students the important multiple healing acts they as physicians can perform during such end of life situations. Too often, members of the family will keep a silent vigil or, what is worse, engage in small talk as if they were oblivious to the reality of this moment. Thus, they miss an opportunity to share what was so nourishing in their relationship to the one who was dying, what they are grateful for and, where appropriate, to ask for forgiveness for past hurts. Sometimes the physician can encourage the family members to make use of this precious time when their loved one can still hear and understand their words. The physician may be in a position to help both the living and the dying realize they have the power to bless each other by the words of validation they speak to each other.

I would also suggest that if a physician has been with a patient through years of interventional chemotherapy and radiation—especially when members of the family would insist on continuing such measures after the physician and the patient agree there should be only palliative care—the physician may be able to help the family give their loved one permission to die.

On the other hand, if after six years of bonding closely with the patient during interventional therapy, the physician abruptly cuts off all presence during palliative care, the patient may feel a sense of betrayal and a great sense of disappointment. I often shared with the students my knowledge of physicians who continued such presence; who made a phone call and in some instances even made one brief visit to the hospice. When the death occurred, the family was so deeply moved at the physician's gesture that they invited him to be a pall-bearer at the funeral, and he accepted.

During this forty-five minute talk to the students, I sensed rapt tension and when I concluded they paused for a moment and then erupted into a standing ovation. Some came up to say, "Thanks; that was very helpful." I gave essentially the same talk for each second-year class, with some minor modifications, and in each of those twelve years there was the same rapt attention and the standing ovation. That kind of validation helped make those twelve years at the Medical Center a great personal blessing and convinced me that I had found a second vocation.

In all our classes we used the case approach. The clinical faculty partner often assured students that the cases we are considering are real and the sooner they consciously realize the need to make these judgments in real time the more useful our simulations would be for them. We wanted to help them simulate the most helpful ways of approaching these non-biomedical issues. We wanted them to actually practice the art of relational medicine. So, in each case they were asked to share what they would do or say in that situation.

In each third-year rotation we focused on a different issue. The internal medicine rotation focused on conveying potentially life-transforming news without prematurely snuffing out hope. The loss of hope can weaken the patient's healing potential and even dissuade the patient from submitting to chemotherapy which could give him a meaningful extension of life with family. Physicians are encouraged to be humble in their medical projections—to remember that statistics are averages. They do not necessarily predict the trajectory of the disease for this particular individual. Patients do sometimes outlive their physicians' projections.

Students were actually asked to simulate this challenging task in our "lab" by meeting with an actor who played the part of a patient and conveyed that this patient had a potentially life threatening illness. We the faculty could observe them "in the lab" on a video screen and then meet with the students to discuss how they fulfilled this difficult and important task.

How to Cope with Non-Compliance

We encouraged these future physicians to realize that the best biomedicine is worthless if the patient is non-compliant.

If the patient does not honor the diet prescribed or take the medication regularly or agree to be treated for a potentially life-threatening condition, the physician cannot fill the mandate to heal. I was personally shocked to discover that the problem of non-compliance in this country is somewhere between 20-50%! If a patient feels listened to and respected and if the physician effectively conveys that she truly cares about a good outcome, the probability of compliance may considerably increase.

Students discover that sometimes they must first be a healer of the patient's spirit in order to receive permission to treat the patient's body. One medical student accompanied a resident on rounds. When they were in Mrs. Matthew's room, the resident informed her that she had an abscess that was potentially life-threatening, and they came in to receive her permission to treat it. Mrs. Matthew responded curtly, "I don't want to be treated. Just leave me alone. I want to go home." After reiterating that the abscess was life-threatening, the patient responded, "I don't care. Just leave me alone." At that point, the resident told Mrs. Matthew that he regretted her decision; but, if she changed her mind, she should notify the nurse and they would return.

The student and resident then left the room. With more discretionary time than the resident, the medical student returned a few hours later, sat by the bed, held Mrs. Matthew's hand, and asked her, "Mrs. Matthew, please tell me, why don't you want to be treated?" The student physician must have asked the question as if he really cared about Mrs. Matthew and wanted her answer, because she began sobbing bitterly as she told him, "I don't want to be treated because I've been HIV positive for ten years. I don't deserve to be treated." The student replied, "Mrs. Matthew, you deserve to be treated as much as I, and you owe it to yourself and your family to be treated. Please, let us treat you." At that point, Mrs. Matthew agreed to have the abscess removed. The medical student realized that often we need to be healers of the patient's spirit and relate to the patient as person in order to be permitted to heal biomedically.

Confronting the Fear of Engagement

More than a few students expressed their need to be detached rather than emotionally engaged with patients in order not to compromise their clinical objectivity or to risk burn-out by allowing themselves to feel each patient's plight internally.

Rachel Naomi Remen is a renowned physician and psychotherapist who has specialized in treating physicians with burn-out. From her many years of clinical practice, Dr. Remen has challenged conventional wisdom. She has discovered that, contrary to popular expectation, the physicians most vulnerable to burn-out are not those who allow themselves to engage with the patient but those who have allowed their medical practice to be reduced to an emotionally detached exchange of medical skill and knowledge for compensation.

From my experience as rabbinic pastor, I suggested to my students that it is possible to be fully present emotionally to congregants even in tragic situations such as the death of a child. I have witnessed the agony of parents' grief; at times even cried with them. I would preside at the funeral service and try to find some words of comfort. I accompanied the family to the graveside and observed them as the coffin was lowered. Both at the synagogue and the grave, the traditional prayers expressed our faith that God is with us even here; that the soul of our beloved is with the source of all being.

When I left the cemetery and returned home, I told my students I would invariably hug my wife and children with a more passionate intensity and then sit down to eat a meal. My encounter with death had deepened and made even more precious the fragile gift of life and love. I suggested the same could be true for them.

When students asked, "Can doctors become too emotionally engaged, and how do you know?" I replied, "If you are so involved with the pain of a patient or family that you cannot enjoy your spouse and children, you are over-involved and need help." But in our time, the greater danger seems to be not over-engagement but under-engagement. Most complaints about physicians I have heard refer not to biomedical but to relational insensitivity. One of the primary thrusts of our program was to help future physicians realize that the practice of relational medicine is good not only for the patient; it is also good for the doctor.

The Sacred Vocation Program

The curriculum that I created and taught to future physicians brought me much joy and satisfaction. Hopefully it has had and will continue to have a salutary influence on how many of them strive to practice a genuinely relational medicine. If asked, however, to identify the program that was my personal favorite I would refer to SVP, The Sacred Vocation Program.

The idea for such a program came from my experience of the hospital environment. Even at best, hospitals are depersonalizing. Almost at once, you surrender your regular clothes for unisex gowns; you are likely to spend more time with a technician who exposes you to the cold steel of a diagnostic test than with your physician. Your sense of privacy is flagrantly compromised. Hospital personnel may barge into your room at all hours of the day or night. You are expected to do in the presence of perfect strangers what you normally do behind closed doors.

And yet, some hospitals are much better than others. The key determinants are the quality of clinical care and the manner in which the staff relates to the patients. Unexpectedly, when I entered a local hospital the afternoon before my surgery, I personally experienced the stark difference in an encounter with two nurses. The first nurse appeared shortly after I was taken to the hospital room. Nurse A was very brusque, officious and insensitive. I entered that hospital room with more than a little anxiety about the surgical procedure that awaited me the next day. At no time did I sense her effort to acknowledge my uneasiness, much less relieve it. She rattled off some rules to be observed, making it quite clear that in this domain she was boss. My wife, Joan, who accompanied me, clearly shared my reading of the scene. I was glad to see Nurse A leave.

My congregants were well-represented on the hospital medical staff, and the hospital CEO and I had served on a few of the same civic boards. By early evening before they called it a day, both the CEO and some of the physicians from my congregation came by my room for a brief visit. This led Nurse A to surmise that I might have some "important connections;" because, when she returned to my room, she became conspicuously and unctuously accommodating. She assured me that

CHAPTER 13 — RETIREMENT & MY SECOND VOCATION

her only goal was to make me as comfortable as possible for the surgery. I didn't know whether to laugh or cry.

How sharply contrasting was the manner of Nurse B who was on duty that night. She came in at least three times in the course of that night. She gently apologized each time for disturbing my sleep. As she took my vital signs her touch was tender and comforting. She knew not of any connections I might have with persons of authority. I have every reason to believe she acted and spoke with the same tenderness to every patient visited that night. Nurse A was a troubler of my spirit. Nurse B was a healer. I regard as one of the truest measures of a person's character how we treat those who are not in a position to help or hurt us. By this standard the two nurses differed as day from night.

To account for the difference between the manners of those nurses requires much more information than I possess, and in the end it may still be shrouded in mystery. I do understand, as does every successful retail merchandiser, that if you want your sales associates to nurture your customers you must nourish the spirit of your sales people. Caregiving is stressful. If hospital management wants the caregiver to nurture the patient they must find a way to nourish the caregiver. The Sacred Vocation Program for healthcare givers is based on this premise.

In my mind I had an outline of a program with six hour-and-a-half sessions. Each group would be small, between eight and twelve persons. They would meet with a trained facilitator in a comfortable ambience at the hospital. Confidentiality would be honored. Nothing said in that room would go beyond it without the express permission of the speaker. Each participant would pledge to listen to each person's comments or story non-judgmentally, and each pledged to trust the others enough to share honestly and openly their thoughts, feelings and experiences at work.

The second part of the program would invite a representative of each group to meet with the facilitator to focus not on the inner world of attitudes but on the quality of the work environment. I firmly believe that effective efforts of social change require not only an internal attitudinal change but also an alteration in the work environment.

When I proposed the program to Dr. Low, he liked the idea and suggested a local hospital as the perfect venue for a pilot. A meeting with the CEO and senior staff of that hospital resulted in an agreement to fund a pilot program with nurses' aides.

These patient care assistants, or PCAs, tend to have a very low morale. They have at best a high school education, are modestly paid and see their tasks as grunt work. Most do not even see themselves as part of the healing team. Yet, as the head of nurses declared, "They can make you or break you." The PCAs interact with patients more than any other staff, including doctors and nurses. They make and change the beds. They give baths. Some take vital signs. They will bring in the bedpan or portable commode when needed. They bring in the food trays and set them up and will take the post-surgery patients for walks down the hall. Generally they get very little recognition even though they are a prominent and significant part of the healing—or harming—team.

The Need of a Partner
At this point, I realized that I needed a partner. My comfort and knowledge level was best for the first phase, the

attitudinal phase of the nursing program. But I felt unprepared to structure and implement phase two which focused on the work environment. Fortunately, during my first few years, although most of my work was in the Medical School, my office was in the School of Public Health and virtually next door to Dr. Ben Amick, a professor of epidemiology (that specialty which focuses on the determinants of public health). Ben often served as a consultant to corporations on issues of worker morale. We complemented each other and worked well together. Ben was instrumental in helping to translate my structure into a detailed study guide that we could use to train facilitators and enable others beyond ourselves to conduct the program.

The pilot at the hospital was a great success. I led the sessions in the first phase and Ben Amick conducted the sessions in phase two. A wonderful, unintended consequence of working with PCAs is that it enabled me to work and bond with a socio-economic and ethnic racial group I did not get a chance to really know in a congregation that was Jewish and for the most part upper middle-class.

Fortunately, during my entire adult life I seemed able to communicate with persons very different from me in levels of education, standard of living and socio-cultural background. For instance, my two years as an Air Force chaplain, the SVP program enabled me to reaffirm my great respect and affection for persons with very little formal education who were often "street smart," who had to deal with economic and social adversity. I listened to the stories of PCAs who became mothers in adolescence and whose grandmothers took care of the baby while they worked toward and received their high school graduation certificate.

I had asked the chief of nurses to locate our sessions with PCAs not in the basement but in a place that signaled the administration's appreciation of their importance to the healing mission of the hospital. Their response to my request exceeded my expectations. We were situated in the executive boardroom where none of the PCAs had ever been.

After enabling the group members to identify themselves to each other, we would raise this question,

> We know that we live on this Earth for a limited time and that each of our lives will someday come to an end. I want you to imagine that you have lived a very long life and your life on Earth has ended. A funeral service is held in your church. [Virtually all the PCAs are religious]. Your pastor or priest will conduct the service. He or she will also give the eulogy which is intended to give a true portrait and hopefully enable all assembled to affirm that your life was a blessing, that you did not live in vain.
>
> At that service to celebrate your life and mourn your death are your grown children, grandchildren and hopefully great-grandchildren, your extended family, co-workers at the hospital and your friends. What do you hope your pastor or priest will say about you in that eulogy?

The facilitator would then ask each participant to take seven minutes to write his or her eulogy. We cautioned them that a portrait is truer to life and more interesting if you include items that make you sound human. They could write it in outline form or as a narrative. They would write and then most agreed to share their eulogies with the group. Some were so moved by the assignment that they teared up and asked the person next to them to read theirs. Incidentally, the facilitator was also expected to do the assignment and share.

From this activity the PCAs discovered that some items are more life-validating than others. It's okay to write, "He loved to go to baseball games, cuss out the umpire and have a few beers." Or, "She dyed her hair five times in high school." But you wouldn't want an entire eulogy of such items. Much more life-validating are items like, "He was kind to her patients and tried to give them a word of hope when they were discouraged." Or, "When she gave a bath, she did it tenderly and with love in her heart."

In the second session we discussed the PCAs' power to be a healer of the body by keeping the room clean, frequently washing her hands, etc. And also a healer of the patient's spirit by the way they listened to or talked to patients. When they were asked to share with the group a time when they were healers of the spirit, one of the PCAs told of a woman whose room she entered. Seeing that the patient was teary eyed, she sat by the patient's side, held her hand, and asked, "What's the matter?" The woman replied that she had never had surgery before except to undergo a Cesarean delivery of her children. The PCA said to the woman, "Oh, I know many persons who are on this floor and they've done very well with that surgery, and so will you. I'll be praying for you." Two days later, after surgery, the PCA described returning to the woman's room. As she entered, she was greeted by a fervent "I needed your words so much that day before surgery!" Teary eyed with a smile, the patient added, "I can't thank you enough. I'm so grateful."

As the PCA related this incident, she said she now knew her power to be a healer of the spirit. After the others had done their sharing, I asked the group not to forget their power to heal. Such acts make their work a sacred vocation, part of what gives meaning to their lives because we know we are here on Earth to heal and love rather than to harm and hate.

The third session invited PCAs to think of a patient encounter when they were not at their best—when they might have been more harmers than healers—and to share that experience with the group. We all have such moments when, because we are not feeling well or are worried about something in our personal life, we have not been the healers we are intended to be.

One PCA reported that after an argument with her boyfriend, she was so upset it affected her work that day at the hospital. She was giving a bath to a patient and did it quickly and even somewhat roughly, as if she wanted this chore to end as soon as possible. Later she realized the connection between being upset at her boyfriend and the harsh and superficial way she bathed her patient. The patient was discharged before she had an opportunity to ask forgiveness but she resolved to try harder not to allow what happens in her personal life to be taken out on her patients.

After others had an opportunity to share times at work when they were not at their best, I told the group, "To be human is to be less than perfect. Not even the greatest baseball players ever bat a thousand. The key is that I noticed that each of you described the errors with regret and with a determination to do better. Because of that, I have confidence in your capacity to be great healers. And I believe that you will."

The next session was based on the premise that no one can take away your power to heal. Even in a difficult work environment, when, for instance, a nurse or a co-worker doesn't treat you respectfully, or a patient or family is difficult, even then there are ways to continue to be a healer. I invited them as a group to discuss coping strategies that would enable them to be healers, even when the environment was not supportive. I also mentioned that, "Life does not give us perfect situations to be the best that we can be and do the best that we can do, but two persons facing the same situations will act differently; and that difference may be called character."

At the final session, the group is given the challenge to list five or six core principles or standards by which they would be willing to judge whether or not their work is a sacred vocation. These items were to be written in the form of an oath, each beginning with the words, "I will…" as in, "I will treat my patients as if they were members of the family that I love." Each participant offered suggestions for the oath and each member of the group has veto power. The final oath must be unanimously endorsed. The exercise involves a lot of conversation and sometimes controversy but every group, within that hour, comes up with an oath.

The oath is printed and laminated on a card that can be attached to their badges. At a graduation ceremony to which their supervisor is invited, they take the oath publicly and are given time to submit anonymous evaluations of the program. Generally, those evaluations have been overwhelmingly positive.

Some weeks later, a facilitator meets with representatives of the various phase one groups to focus on the environment.

"Imagine that you have a CEO who wants to know what changes you would recommend in your work environment that would make you feel even better about working here and better able to care for your patients?" The hospital administration pledges to consider each recommendation, endorse and implement it wherever possible and explain why any particular recommendation has been rejected or deferred. At a concluding session, members of the group actually present the recommendations to a CEO or a very senior official at the hospital who sees them in advance and explains to the group what can be done and what is not implementable at this time. The fact that some are generally accepted for implementation obviously affected the morale of the group in a very positive way.

The hospital administration was very pleased with the pilot but did not feel they could embark on such a program at that particular time. Fortunately, some months later the Sacred Vocation Program came to the attention of the chaplain and head nurse at Baylor University Medical Center in Dallas. They have eleven affiliated hospitals in the metropolitan area and engaged us to do a program on their flagship campus. They were so pleased by the pilot and by the evaluations by the participants and by the perceptible elevation of PCA morale that the CEO called the Sacred Vocation Program the most important programmatic investment the hospital made in ten years. They contracted with us to do the program in all affiliated hospitals. It was a five-year contract. My partner Ben Amick and I trained the initial facilitators, and the person they designated to direct the program and train the trainers and facilitators in the various hospitals. At this writing, the implementation is still ongoing. More than

2000 PCAs and nurses have gone through the program and the administration is very pleased with the results.

SVP for Residents

The most exciting breakthrough in the SVP was the extension from PCAs to actual physicians in our medical school residency program. Surely the young physicians in the internal medicine residency have even more vulnerability to burn-out because of their greater level of risk and responsibility. They are, perhaps, even more in need of nurture.

The residency years are exceedingly stressful. Residents put in eighty-hour weeks caring for patients. Virtually living in the hospital, those with families must juggle their heavy hospital burdens with the need to be present for their spouses and children. They must assume basic responsibility for the life and health of patients and are obliged to perform procedures with so little experience behind them. They must learn to tolerate a high level of sleep deprivation. Moreover, they are expected to nourish their patients without receiving nurture from some attending physicians, who generally believe that their years of training were so much more difficult and that the present generation of residents is being coddled!

Our initial approach to the residency directors was met with some skepticism, but they gave us permission to conduct a pilot program with internal medicine residents if we could enlist a core group. We did, and the ensuing confidential evaluations of the program were overwhelmingly positive. The most common comment was, "Everybody should be exposed to this program."

We continued for a year on a voluntary basis but realized

that it became harder and harder to recruit the minimum of volunteers. It seems that residents are so stressed out that they will not voluntarily add to their schedules anything they don't have to. Yet the evaluations of all who took the program were quite positive, so we persuaded the directors to make SVP a required program, on the condition that, if they did encounter a lot of resistance, we would understand the need to abandon it.

Fortunately, we did not have to abandon it. The program turned out to be user-friendly and quite nourishing. Sessions were held during the lunch period when other residents were gathered together for a lecture. On Tuesdays and Thursdays, when we met over a four-week period, we provided participants a superb choice of sandwiches and salads with the opportunity to choose their menu in advance of each session. Rather than stand in a long line to eat lunch, they could enjoy the lunch of their choice delivered to the table where we met. They willingly surrendered their pagers, which were monitored so they could be summoned in case of emergency and receive a message to call back after the session when appropriate.

Most found each session relevant, engaging and enjoyable. The evaluations continued to be exceedingly positive. At this writing, the program has been extended from internal medicine to include pediatrics, psychiatry, neurology and family medicine.

We discovered that the SVP program, adapted to a higher level of sophistication, could include the same elements that were present for the PCAs but in a different context. Thus, when we asked residents to describe a patient encounter that involved being a healer of body and spirit, one resident shared her experience in treating a patient with an obstructive lung episode. When asked how she responded medically, she told of applying a standard protocol that resulted within twenty-four hours in the restoration of the patient's capacity to breathe normally without struggling. When I asked her to describe the non-biomedical or relational component of the treatment the resident answered, "When the patient first came in, he could not finish a sentence without struggling for breath. He was close to a panic attack. I calmly explained to him what he had, that it was very treatable and that within a day or less he should be feeling fine. I also explained that I knew from experience how scary this could be and encouraged him to try to relax and entrust himself to my care. My comments resulted in a perceptible reduction in his stress level almost immediately." That physician could readily acknowledge that in this encounter she was a healer of body and spirit. She had been successful clinically and relationally.

User-Friendly for Believer and Non-Believer

Both those who are religious and non-religious find life's deepest meaning in our power to love and be loved, in work that makes us feel needed and useful and in so living that there will be those who remember us and miss us. For a non-religious physician, practicing a relational medicine that is characterized by love and empathy is an authentic non-religious spirituality. For the religious physician, his power to empathize and love, and to heal body and spirit, is rooted in God's love and God's commandment.

At times of serious illness, many patients do regard their religious faith as their ultimate comfort and support. As long as there is chronic and disabling illness, as long as we must confront our mortality, as long as there are persons who experience intimations of God's presence within and beyond them, many will seek in religious sacred texts and spiritual disciplines their ultimate source of meaning and hope.

Whether personally religious or not, the physician should support the patient's sentiment and respond to that need directly or indirectly. In my early years as a congregational pastor, when I made visits to the hospital and my visit was suddenly interrupted by the doctor's arrival at the hospital door, by tacit agreement, I would immediately excuse myself. When I presented this situation to my medical students or residents, they invariably responded, "I would excuse myself and see another patient before I returned." I believe programs such as ours have raised the medical community's consciousness that at times of serious illness or upcoming surgery, many patients want the best biomedicine and the best surgeon but many need and welcome a visit with the clergy of their congregation or a hospital chaplain. Obviously, there are situations that dictate an immediate meeting of patient and physician, but the students made clear that their default response would not assume their visit trumps the visit of the pastor.

The Transition from Director to Staff Member
About five years into my tenure, I realized I was essentially a one-person operation; that the program had great potential for development and expansion, and at this stage of my life I had no "fire in the belly" to grow a program and wanted to be relieved of all administrative responsibilities so I could simply work as part of the team.

Fortunately, I was able to entice my good friend, Tom Cole, then teaching medical humanities at our medical branch in

Galveston, to apply for the position of director. He was offered the job, and the rest is history. Under Tom's inspired leadership, "The Health and Human Spirit Program" morphed into "The John P. McGovern Center for Humanities and Ethics." I continued to teach the same sessions with medical students and residents for an additional seven years. When asked why I retired in 2011, I replied, somewhat facetiously, that on my eightieth birthday, it was time, finally, to discover what I would do when I grew up.

I left knowing that the programs I instituted would remain in place as a required part of the medical student and resident curriculum. Before retirement, I chaired the committee to select a new medical ethicist for our center. Concurrently, some friends in Houston established a named professorship at the McGovern center in my honor. Our new medical ethicist, Dr. Jeffrey Spike, holds the "Samuel E. Karff Chair" at the medical school.

Assessing the Connection Between My Two Life Vocations

During four decades as a congregational rabbi, I was a teacher and defender of the Jewish faith. During the past decade and more, I have taught primarily the non-religious spirituality of relational medicine. Martin Buber's thought, which was so much a part of my formative years, as a rabbi, provides a natural bridge between the two vocations. In his slender classic, *I and Thou,* Buber describes two modes of living in this world. He labels the first, I-It and the second, I-Thou. The I-It mode is impersonal and functional. It is the mode of problem solving and analysis. It views people and things as useful in our pursuit of some further goal. To develop the technology for space travel or to chop down a tree for firewood, the scientist and the lumberjack are primarily in the mode of I-It.

By contrast, when an American astronaut, awed by viewing our planet from a capsule in outer space, read a biblical quotation from the opening pages of the biblical creation story, or when a nature lover views a tree, not as potential firewood but as an awesome expression of the beauty and grandeur of the natural world, they have entered the I-Thou mode. Buber also taught that we come to know persons best not by studying them as objects but by being present to them in love as an I to a Thou.

Buber believes both modes are essential to human life. At their best, physicians alternate between the two modes. The surgeon in the operating room and the cardiologist studying a patient's electrocardiogram are appropriately in an I-It mode. However, when that surgeon emerges from the operating room to convey heartbreaking news to the anxious family, the surgeon's most important tools are not clinical knowledge and skill, but empathy and compassion. Her most healing gesture is a hug or its emotional equivalent.

Buber's two modes of being provide a way to view the relationship between treating the patient biomedically and relating to the patient as person. Buber also provides the best language to understand relational medicine as a non-religious spirituality. For Buber, to treat the patient as a person rather than as merely the embodiment of the disease is itself a sacred act of transcendent significance even if the physician is not "religious." In Buber's view, that sacred act becomes religious when the physician perceives the drive to relate to the patient in this way as a divine call ("Where are you?") and the act itself as a response to that call ("Here I am; send me."). To Buber, God is the Eternal Thou whom we may glimpse only in, through and beyond our I-Thou relationships to persons in God's world. In a religious perspective, we are called into the world to repair the brokenness in that tiny corner of God's world entrusted to our care. An ancient rabbi refers to us humans as, "partners of the Holy One." Martin Buber sought to reconcile the ultimacy of God's power with a God who is in need of our efforts in the statement cited in Chapter 12, "You need God in order to be—and God needs you for the very meaning of your life."

This links to ancient Rabbinic statements which speak of our partnership with God. A sample: every judge who judges justly even for a single hour is considered to be a partner with the Holy One blessed be He in the creation.[70]

It was not difficult for me to discern the connection between my rabbinic vocation and my teaching at the Medical Center. I became a rabbi to help persons wrestle with life's meaning. At the Medical School, I helped future physicians and residents to affirm the meaningfulness of their vocation and their power to heal the spirit of their patients.

"The Three Amigos" became a shorthand reference to two dear friends and me because of our collaboration on social justice issues in Houston. In this photo I am flanked by Archbishop Joseph Fiorenza, who for many years led the Catholic Archdiocese of Galveston-Houston, and Reverend William Lawson, Founding Pastor of the Wheeler Avenue Baptist Church in Houston.

Chapter 14
THE THREE AMIGOS

AFTER TWELVE YEARS AT THE TEXAS Medical Center, I decided it was time to experience a second retirement. The programs I created and taught at the Medical School were firmly established and virtually assured of outliving my own tenure—and, I was close to observing my eightieth birthday.

I did manage to retire and had no plans for the future beyond doing some additional writing and spending as much time as possible with my family. Then came that fateful phone call from longtime friend and colleague in the ministry, Reverend Bill Lawson. After a brief exchange of pleasantries, Reverend Lawson explained the mission of his call, "I know you are retired and I'm retired and so is Joe Fiorenza, but I need you."

He went on to explain what he had already explained to Archbishop Fiorenza in an earlier call: our county was the largest in the nation without a Public Defender Office. That means indigent citizens accused of a crime are represented by an attorney who is selected, appointed and potentially reappointed or dismissed by the presiding judge. That being the case, the attorney is, in fact, more accountable to the judge than to the poor client. Judges tend to want to diminish their docket as rapidly as possible, which means that they may urge the attorney to persuade the client to plea bargain the case rather than try it. This can all too easily result in a miscarriage of justice by denying the accused a fair trial.

Before exploring the developments from that fateful call, let me explain that I have known Reverend Lawson and Archbishop Fiorenza for at least thirty years. Bill Lawson is the founding pastor of Wheeler Avenue Baptist Church. During the Civil Rights struggle in the sixties, Lawson was part of the Coalition of Black Leaders, members of the "white power structure" and the press which managed to integrate Houston's public facilities overnight without incident.

Joseph Fiorenza is now the Archbishop Emeritus of the Galveston-Houston Archdiocese and is a past president of the United States Council of Catholic Bishops, which is the highest honor his peers could bestow upon him. Incidentally, during his occupancy of that high office, he made it a point to fly economy class.

Through collaboration on issues of social justice, the three of us have bonded and become soulmates. One of the earliest instances was our community's campaign for the homeless thirty years ago. We are close enough to call on each other with our concerns and we care for each other's welfare.

CHAPTER 14 ❖ THE THREE AMIGOS

When my home was struck by lightning and burned to the ground, the following day I received a call at the temple from Reverend Lawson in which he declared that his church wanted to replace the books I had lost in the fire. The fire occurred in January. Joan and I moved into a small, furnished apartment and were not re-nested until shortly before Passover.

One day, at our new home, a woman from Reverend Lawson's church showed up at our doorstep with a basket of Passover goodies and a note: "This is being sent to you by an angry Baptist preacher who is still waiting to hear from you about your books." A few weeks later at a Sabbath Eve service, Reverend Lawson formally presented me with one of the most precious books I had lost, which was a collection of Agada.

So much for the context of Bill Lawson's phone request to the Archbishop and me. He told us that on a few occasions he had invited the county judge to attend and speak at a meeting of black ministers about the need for an independent public defender's office. Each time, the judge spoke positively, but nothing happened.

Reverend Lawson was calling to tell us that the county judge had agreed to come to the next meeting of the Clergy Association and speak. This time he wanted Archbishop Fiorenza and me to speak and to bring some clergy from established white churches so the judge would see that this issue is of concern not only to members of the black community but also to all of us. We did attend and speak, and apparently this made a difference because shortly thereafter, a Public Defender's office was created. As a result, my intention to really retire and focus on more writing was transformed into a new vocation: to join with my friends and others in addressing other issues of criminal justice in our community.

We had become aware that for too many of our city's children, school had indirectly provided a "pipeline to prison." When students are either unmotivated or feel incapable of learning, they act out their frustration behaviorally and are expelled from class and/or suspended from school. We learned that six out of ten Texas public school students were suspended or expelled at least once between the seventh and twelfth grades. In our region, 218,000 students were removed from class for behavioral issues during the last year. Often, once the students leave the campus, they never return to make up the time and graduate. In too many cases this becomes a pipeline to involvement with the juvenile justice system.

Our meeting on this problem with leaders of the Greater Houston Partnership, a powerful group of civic and business leaders, and with the CEO of The United Way, resulted in a meeting of about one hundred community leaders ranging from the county sheriff, to superintendents of independent school districts in the greater Houston area.

Anna Babin, the amazing CEO of The United Way in the Gulf Coast region, arranged for the call to the meeting at United Way headquarters. We "Three Amigos" were listed among the conveners. We asked the invitees not only to agonize about a serious problem but also to help launch a pilot program that could be the first step in addressing the problem.

Through our meeting with Anna Babin and a small group she convened, we learned that a juvenile court judge in Clayton County, Georgia, sought to decriminalize low level delinquency and simple misbehavior, and to provide a support system outside the home that involved education, mentoring by volunteers and social service agencies.

As part of the call to the meeting, we announced that Judge Stephen Teske would be our speaker and that his initiatives have resulted in 72% fewer criminal charges, 59% fewer juvenile complaints and a 24% increase in graduation rates. We announced that our aim was to bring Judge Teske's program to Houston.

Anna Babin asked me to frame the morning with some brief remarks. Although "brief rabbi" may be an oxymoron, I managed to hold my remarks to ten minutes. I was assigned to pave the way for the introduction of Judge Teske.

At the outset, I explained to those in attendance that while Archbishop Fiorenza, Reverend Lawson and I respond to our distinctive individual religious stories, we passionately share this one overarching truth: God loves us, and we best show our love for God by caring for God's children, especially the most vulnerable among them.

One of the great ideals that make this country special is what we call "the American Dream." We are taught to believe that if we work hard and play by the rules we can aspire to great heights. We are not frozen in a caste system. Social mobility is our trademark—or was. I then cited those statistics on high suspension or expulsion rates coupled with low rates of graduation from high school and admonished those of us in attendance that "unless we do something constructive to alter this pattern, we are in danger of creating and perpetuating an ever growing underclass who lack the basic skills to participate constructively in the increasingly high-tech global economy."

What does it take for a child who is economically and socially at risk to stay in school, observe proper norms of behavior and feel some ambition to make someone honorable of himself or herself? I suggested that normally it takes at least one parent who is a precious combination of unconditional and tough love; a combination of "I love you, believe in you and will root for you—and I'll set boundaries and hold you accountable."

What if there is no such parent in the home? That child is much more likely to end up in the criminal justice system unless there is a safety net: unless there are persons outside the home who show they care, who mentor the child, provide social and emotional support and an alternate path for these at risk children.

My remarks helped to contextualize the appearance and presentation by Judge Teske. His talk was informative and inspirational. Later, Anna Babin introduced the superintendent of schools in the Spring Branch section of Houston. His district included the demographic described in our statistics. He and his Board had agreed to launch a pilot.

Eleven students who were chronically truant and/or misbehaving were enrolled in a one-on-one mentoring program conducted by Houston Revision, a non-profit group of volunteers from several local churches. Although they were motivated by their faith to participate in this program, they avoided any proselytizing agenda.

A year after our initial meeting at United Way Headquarters, we reconvened a similar group to hear a report on the results of the pilot. The news was favorable. All eleven participants were back in school and more empowered to aim for graduation from high school.

CHAPTER 14 ❖ THE THREE AMIGOS

Director of Revision, Charles Rotramel, told the assemblage about one of the participants, a six-foot-tall, angry, intimidating, black teenager who was assigned to a seventy-five-year-old volunteer from a local church. What initially connected them was their shared passion for basketball and the teen's seemingly futile obsession to play on a high school team. As a result of their bonding over the year, that student is now back in school, attending class regularly and is playing on the school's basketball team.

We reconvened that day to disclose these inspiring results and commit to sharing the program with more troubled youngsters during the coming year. Our overall goal was to expand the core of mentors and to greatly increase the number of young persons enrolled.

The Three Amigos were present and shared our thoughts with those assembled. In my remarks, I focused on the probable impact of the program on the mentors. I cited an ancient rabbi who taught that if one saves a single life, it is as if he or she saved an entire world. To the extent they motivated these teens to further their education, those mentors were contributing mightily to saving a human life! By the very nature of their relationship to these at-risk persons, the mentors deepened the sources of meaning in their life. They enlarged their power to love, increased their sense of being needed and useful and had reason to believe that they would be remembered for blessing by those whose lives they touched.

Generally, we Three Amigos try to link social issues to the teaching of our religious traditions. We aim to appeal to our listener's better angels. But our traditions themselves, grounded in an understanding of the human condition, also appeal to our enlightened self-interest. That day, I also cited the words of the prophet Isaiah who asked his people a rhetorical question: "Do you want rest," meaning do you want to live in security and peace? Isaiah's response, "Then give rest to the weary" (Isaiah 28:12).

The leaders involved in the pilot are now exploring ways to increase the number of mentors and the number of needy students addressed by the program. As of this writing, we are considering another program of a similar nature. This program, currently being used in Seattle, seeks to provide selected low-level drug offenders with an opportunity to avoid prosecution and imprisonment by participating in a diversionary program of support services that address some of the underlying causes, with the hope of averting future criminal behavior and a cycle of imprisonment, release and recidivism.

With the encouragement and support of the Texas Criminal Justice Coalition (TCJC), we were able to persuade the county sheriff, the Houston police Chief and the district attorney to join Reverend Lawson and me, and some members of the Commission, on a fact-finding mission to Seattle. Over two and a half days, we were able to directly observe that city's "Law Enforcement Assisted Diversion (LEAD) program. It is so named because selected, carefully trained police officers are empowered to divert persons who are deemed viable candidates from arrest and imprisonment to a mentoring relationship with "case managers." Results of the pilot have moved Seattle to a full-scale endorsement and adoption of the program. Our Houston law enforcement leaders returned from the trip with the view that some form of LEAD might be adopted locally. As of this writing, that has not happened.

CHAPTER 14 ❖ THE THREE AMIGOS

Let me now simply indicate what should have been obvious: my full retirement has been deferred for now, and my life continues to be immeasurably blessed by my continuing friendship and collaboration with a Catholic priest and a Baptist minister.

These are my lovely daughters in whom I take immense pride and who are the source of many of my life's precious memories. From left to right they are Amy Halevy, Rachel Weissenstein and Liz Seitz.

Chapter 15
WHY I AM A WEALTHY MAN

W HENEVER I WOULD MEET WITH EN-gaged couples well in advance of presiding at their marriage ceremony, I invariably said to them, "The two most important decisions we make in our lives are who will share our life as lover and friend and what will be our life's vocation?" After forty years as a congregational rabbi and fifty-five years of marriage to the same woman, I am grateful that for me, both of these decisions have proved to be a blessing

After completing two years as an Air Force chaplain, I was invited to serve as assistant rabbi at Congregation Beth Israel in Hartford, Connecticut. In the summer of 1958, at age twenty-six, I had still not found my life partner. That October, as I indicated earlier, Joan Gabrielle Mag attended the Shabbat Eve service with her parents and grandmother. She had come home for the weekend to observe the *yahrzeit* (anniversary) of her grandfather's death. As customary, the name was read preceding the congregational recitation of the Kaddish memorial prayer. That night I gave the sermon. When we were introduced following the service Joan responded to my initial greeting with a, "Good Shabbas, sir." That Sunday she returned to New York to resume her teaching of modern dance at Hofstra College.

We did not have our first date until she returned to Hartford for winter break in December. After four more dates scattered over the following four months, we were engaged in April and married at the end of June. By nature I am a cautious person, not given to quick decisions, especially in serious matters—but this was to prove the exception. I later learned that during much of the preceding year Joan had dated my immediate predecessor. He was a wonderful dancer and a fine person but the "chemistry" was missing, and Joan gracefully exited by telling him that she "could never marry a rabbi." In truth, having grown up with a very limited exposure to religious Jewish life, our decision to marry may well have seemed like a vast improbability.

Joan's father, a very warm-hearted person and an able business man, deferred in matters of religious observance to Joan's mother, Fanny Mag, whom he adored. Fanny, a woman who I came to admire and love, was a person of great moral sensibility, a social activist, a self-defined Universalist and a voracious reader who, without the benefit of college, was one of the most well-educated and most well-read persons I had ever met. However, not unlike more than a few in her generation, Fanny experienced her Jewishness more as a burdensome fate than a privilege. Joan never celebrated a Passover Seder until she was engaged to me. As I have mentioned, she spent her high school years at a Christian boarding school. (In the years to come, when Joan would accompany me to a church where I gave the sermon, she would usually sit with the Pastor's wife, and she showed a great familiarity with the Christian hymns.) At Mount Holyoke, Joan majored in economics (there was no dance major) and wrote her honors thesis on the kibbutz movement in Israel. This in turn led to her first intense exposure to a positive Jewish experience by joining a group of Orthodox Jewish collegians on a summer trip to Israel.

Joan returned from that summer in Israel fascinated by the country and positively affected by getting to know a group of young, highly intelligent Jewish adults who were imbued with great pride in their heritage. Perhaps that summer's intensely positive Jewish experience made somewhat less inconceivable the prospect of being the helpmate of a rabbi.

After the first date we each knew that this could be the beginning of a long-term commitment. We seemed so comfortable with each other. We respected and were physically attracted to the other. Each of us valued the life of the mind and had been serious students during our college years. After one or two evenings together I was able to set aside a deeply rooted concern that could have prevented any serious commitment on my part. I needed to feel that there was no danger in such a marriage of my reliving the stressful lack of tranquility or deep respect in my parents' marriage. Fortunately, I was reassured on that score.

As for Joan's capacity and inclination to support and share in my deeply Jewish life, I never doubted that she could and would. As I expected, Joan was a quick learner and created a home in which Sabbath candles were kindled and blessed, Passover Seders were decorously created with all the symbolic foods, and she comfortably partnered with me in creating a home that lived in Jewish sacred time. She in turn felt personally nourished by the richer Jewish life to which our marriage introduced her.

Generally, becoming a regular synagogue attender was not a hardship for her. Joan especially loved when the sacred music was singable. Fortunately, she appreciated most of my sermons. Over the years, I never prepared a serious sermon or lecture that she did not hear or read in advance. Joan was undoubtedly my most honest critic and my most loyal supporter.

The delicacy and importance of that role cannot be overestimated. Joan performed it with great discernment and sensitivity. More often than not, she had no suggestions or her proposed revision was minor. Even when she felt strong reservations about a section, she usually prefaced her critique with a genuine endorsement of the sermon as a whole. Much of the time her suggestions were valid. She helped make a potentially bad sermon good and a good sermon better.

Occasionally I would reject her suggested revision and defend the original text. At other times I would initially reject her suggestion only to embrace it as I was making last minute edits. In spite of an occasional pang of ego-defensiveness, I genuinely appreciated her helpfulness and would not have accepted being married to a woman whose judgment I could not respect. Joan in turn came to regard her editing role as in integral part of her job description.

We were different in temperament. Joan leavened my

CHAPTER 15 ❖ WHY I AM A WEALTHY MAN

excessive seriousness with her playfulness and her penchant for unbridled giggling. We had very different food preferences. In desserts I gravitated to a baked apple while Joan never met a gooey, rich chocolate dessert she did not love.

Joan was part of the "in-between generation". Her generation could no longer view a college education as simply a prerequisite for carrying on an intelligent conversation with one's husband, but she was not encouraged to pursue a full time profession. When our children were young, Joan was fully present for them and in their primary, middle and senior high years she made sure to be there for them when they returned from school.

For Joan's emotional and spiritual well-being, she needed to carve out some independent space to be creative and appreciated. As one who from childhood on embraced her mother's love of the dance, Joan naturally gravitated to that world by taking instruction from such luminaries as Martha Graham and Eric Hawkins, by teaching dance and later by choreographing and arranging concerts for her own dance company. During our years in Houston she created "The New Dance Group," which she sustained for twenty-five years despite the stress of fund-raisers, losing dancers to the New York dance scene and more than a few unfair reviews. The photo gallery in our home beautifully preserves some of her best choreography.

After one of Joan's concerts I was moved to write a column in our congregational newsletter on "The Meaning of Love," which I excerpt here:

> The other night The New Dance Group whose director and principal choreographer is Joan Karff completed a

highly successful concert. I realized how anxious I had been before the concert and how exuberantly joyous I felt when the audience (and later the critics) rendered hearty appreciation. I knew how important this concert was to Joan—how much of her energy, creativity and worry had been invested in it.

As I sorted out my post-concert exhilaration (while carrying a suitcase of costumes to the trunk of the car) I realized that my love for Joan has been expressed by encouraging, supporting, and in part sharing in a career which was an integral part of her growth and fulfillment as a person. Her love for me has been expressed by encouraging and supporting my Rabbinic vocation.

This act of love is not always spontaneous. It must be willed. It must contend with the narcissistic impulse to be concerned with our own agenda and not with our partner. Yet by that extension of self each partner to a marriage can be enriched.

Not every couple will maintain the two career household but the partners to every loving marriage must stand prepared to extend themselves, to nurture each other's growth as each defines it…

There are strains in the new marriage contract as there were in the old, but our lives are truly enhanced when we extend ourselves to foster the growth of the person with whom we share a life, I can personally attest.

In later years, Joan needed another way of feeling needed and useful. She created a mentoring program for high school senior women in an inner-city high school. With the cooperation of the principal, Joan picked ten students and met with them for an hour and a half each week for a year. The curriculum was a combination of life skills and cultural enrichment. Her participants learned the art of making an effective oral presentation, how to read and review a serious book and parenting skills. Joan's women were also introduced to the history of art, the theater, the world of dance and classical music. Field trips included attending a play presented by our repertory theater, a guided tour of the Museum of Fine Arts, a concert by the Houston Symphony and a modern dance concert.

Each faithful attendee was presented with a $1,000 scholarship toward tuition to a college to which she had been accepted. The program is called, "Women on the Way Up" and includes guest talks by minority women who have become successful in a variety of fields, including medicine and architecture. The message of the course is: believe you can become almost anything you are determined to become. By now there are over a hundred alumnae. Joan keeps in regular email contact and she arranges annual reunions.

My Confidante

One of the precious hallmarks of the rabbinate is the privilege of entering so many other persons' lives at moments of peak joy and great distress. In this latter role, I inevitably became a trusted listener, confidante and under the best circumstances, a healing presence. This role is both a privilege and a burden. To be the keeper of many persons' painful secrets can be a lonely and stressful task.

Being married to a helpmate who can be trusted to honor the confidences I might share was important to my own spiritual and emotional well-being. Still there were confidences that should not be shared even with my wife. Sometimes a person would actually tell me they assumed all they had revealed would be shared with no one, not even my spouse. Even absent that explicit request, there are confidences I must keep even from Joan. I have no algorithmic formula for distinguishing one kind of confidence from another but my "gut feelings" prove a helpful guide. Fortunately, in many other instances I can have the emotional release of unburdening myself to Joan with perfect trust that she will keep it to herself. She's given me many blessings. None has been more essential to my personal well-being than her presence as a trusted keeper of my confidences.

Thanks to Joan, our home has been a welcome refuge from the turmoil and stresses of the world out there. My concept of multi-tasking includes sitting in my back-friendly chair reading a book or an article from one of the many periodicals we receive while listening to the music of Mahler or Bartok. Joan is simultaneously feasting on the home decorating TV shows.

We are news junkies, we relish going to the movie theater and we are passionately hooked on baseball—but thanks to the performance of the Houston Astros, we must constantly allow faith to triumph over experience.

Joan is a speed-reader who never abandons a book before she has completed it and has written her personal critical review. I do serious reading during the day and reserve the night for fiction or memoir. I read more slowly and have no compunction about abandoning a book that has failed to grip me, and I generally annotate the margins and record pages on the inside cover with paragraphs on subjects I want to revisit and possibly add to my files. (Yes, I continue to place items in my preaching files although I have not had regular sermon preparation since my retirement now almost fifteen years ago.)

Joan loves to be our comptroller. With my eager consent, she handles incoming funds, pays bills and gives me a regular allowance. All major decisions concerning allocation of monetary resources are made jointly. When there is disagreement on what we can afford to do, since I am the spendthrift and she the overly-cautious conserver we rely on our wonderful accountant and friend to mediate and resolve the issue.

Our marriage has worked exceedingly well. For sure there have been moments when we were intensely annoyed with the other, but we have not allowed such periods of pique to carry over to the next day. In fact, our children witnessed so few contentious moments in our relationship that they could not tolerate even a mild argument, fearing that it must mean our marriage was collapsing. When they faced any serious tension in their own marriages they told us, "You made it look so easy!"

That said, there was a fundamental challenge to our marital happiness that periodically needed to be renegotiated. Because the clergy role is potentially all-consuming, as I have alluded, there were times when I needed to do a better job at setting limits to congregational expectations. Even those congregants who encourage you to set those limits and say, "Rabbi, take care of yourself and your family," did not generally apply it to their own expectations. At times I needed to do a better job of setting those limits.

I must confess that the problem arose not only from expectations imposed by the congregation; some were self-imposed, driven by my inner-pressure to prepare and sometimes over-prepare a sermon or other writing project. I had a passion for excellence that was driven in part by the highest motives—but at times by that lingering neurotic fear of lapsing into the under-achievement patterns I discerned in my father.

This dynamic was certainly a significant cause of whatever tensions and dissatisfactions would arise from time to time in our marriage. But fortunately they were addressed and continually resolved so that our marriage has been overwhelmingly successful.

One of the many great blessings of a good and abiding marriage is the reservoir of shared experiences that become precious memories to be recalled and savored and the ability to intuit what the other is thinking or is about to say.

Neither of us has been spared life's darker side. We have known disappointment and loss. We know what it is to have your home struck by lightning, completely destroyed by the raging flames. Joan has dealt with both lung and ovarian cancer and I with prostate cancer but each of us knows and feels that our life has been richly blessed. At those difficult times we have been there for each other as a supporting, loving presence.

Before a major struggle with illness and the confining, isolating effect of an extended recovery period, Joan was inclined to leave the pastoral ministry almost entirely to me, except for that small circle of family and very close friends. Ever since her own serious illness, however, and her own sense of isolation and deep appreciation of any genuine gesture of caring, she has considerably widened the circle of her acts of loving kindness. Whenever Joan hears of persons who are dealing with the collateral effects of serious illness, she is moved to prepare and deliver her inimitably healing chicken soup or to call or write them as an expression of her deepened understanding and empathy.

When I retired from the congregational rabbinate, people asked me if I missed being in the pulpit rather than in the pew. I would respond that my pulpit years were enormously satisfying, but I feel more than adequately compensated for their loss by being able to sit and even hold hands with Joan at each service we attend. Also cherished are the times when our children and grandchildren with us.

Our Children and Grandchildren

In our generation of parenting, the mother was cast as principal caregiver. This meshed well with the stringent demands of the congregational rabbinate. In retrospect, I wish I had been more of a major sharer in that parental role. The current generation of my colleagues is culturally cast more as equal partners in parenting. I regret not being more extensively involved in caregiving to my three daughters in their infancy and early childhood.

Our three daughters have each brought us enormous blessings. From birth to the present, their mother has been a great nurturing and guiding presence. The memories they have shared of childhood in our home are overwhelmingly positive. Thankfully, in spite of my rabbinic preoccupations, I also emerge in their consciousness as a parent who was there when needed for affection, comfort and counsel. I would schedule individual dates with each on a rotating basis when they could choose our agenda, which embraced such possible options as going to a movie, seeing a play, visiting the zoo or one of the great museums accessible to us in

Chicago and Houston. One of the reasons they each loved the summers in Charlevoix is because I was so much more present for them and much more relaxed and playful. I have previously noted that Joan and I made a fateful decision at the very beginning of our Charlevoix summers; we did not become part of the social cocktail and dinner party world. Most of our time in the afternoons and evenings revolved around our children.

Much has been written about PKs (Preachers' Kids) who felt adversely affected by their fathers' symbolic role (now we can say father or mother). Far from feeling disadvantaged by being an RK (Rabbi's Kid) our children fondly remember the perks. Whenever they entered the temple gift shop the ladies would dote on them and shower them with free candy and other goodies.

I sometimes feel I overplayed my attempts to shield them from the special burdens of being RKs. Once they reached an age where they did not want to attend a worship service with us, we did not make them feel guilty for choosing to be at a friend's home rather than at the synagogue. I helped prepare each of them for their bat mitzvah but did not impose a greater expectation of Jewish study with me. (I sometimes regret that I did not study with them the collection of classic Rabbinic stories which my private tutor studied with me.)

Fortunately, each has great memories of our Jewish holiday observances; from Passover Seders to the eight nights of Chanukah to visiting an apple orchard to collect fruit to adorn our Sukkah during the Feast of Tabernacles.

In our Chicago years, the Sabbath Eve service on Friday preceded dinner, so we had leisurely Shabbat dinners where each received a blessing as mother kindled the Sabbath lights and we sang the joyous prayers over the wine (or grape juice). We accepted no social engagements on Friday nights. Instead, about an hour or so before bedtime, we would all converge on the king-sized bed in our room to watch appropriate sitcoms on television.

When the girls were of an age when they wanted to be with friends on Friday night, we did not discourage them, but we did insist that they share the Shabbat meal or at least be with us until after the traditional Sabbath prayers and blessings had been shared.

Sibling rivalry did not skip over our family home. At different times each daughter felt she was favored or disfavored by us relative to her sisters. Happily, those feelings diminished in later years, which is especially welcome because they each live with their families no farther than a ten-minute drive from our home. When asked how we managed to beat the centrifugal force that typically disperses American families, we recite a number of factors.

Growing up, the girls were required to choose their clothes within a strictly enforced budget, and thanks to their mother's modest spending habits, we managed to invest enough in a mutual fund to allow each daughter to attend any college which accepted her. They each chose expensive Eastern schools, which meant that by the last graduation the education fund would be exhausted. So we explained to our daughters that if any expected to attend graduate school she must either receive a fellowship or come back to attend a graduate school in Texas. Each returned to Houston and thereby increased the probability that they would meet and marry a Houstonian.

Also in our favor, many young people view Houston as a great city for members of their generation. Certainly our daughters did not regard returning home or living at home as a hardship.

Last but hardly least is the factor of daughter/parent bonding. All three daughters chose living near us. We know we are blessed. We can observe holidays together without the hassle of travel. We are able to be available to each other in time of need without being intrusive or seeking in any way to limit each other's privacy.

In their marriages two of the three were not able to follow the model of one partner for lifetime. The two who left their first marriages did so for reasons we could understand and endorse. One was blessed with a second marriage that shows promise of being sustained for a lifetime. Happily, we learned that our remaining single daughter has found her intended, is engaged and is planning to be married next spring.

Each of our daughters is a strong, lovely and highly gifted woman. Rachel Weissenstein is a much-admired teacher of English at our city's most academically rigorous private high school. Amy Halevy is a highly respected senior law partner who specializes in employment issues at one of our city's large and venerable firms. Liz Kampf Seitz is a very successful family therapist in private practice.

My heart has been filled with the deepest satisfaction when I have been told by others of their professional accomplishments. Daughter Rachel, who was born on my birthday, receives rave reviews from students and their parents. More than a few parents have told me how much their son or daughter learned from and loved Rachel's high school English classes.

CHAPTER 15 ⬥ WHY I AM A WEALTHY MAN

When Rachel was invited to address the upper school chapel group she chose to speak about change in human life, with special reference to her own divorce and single motherhood. Without skipping over its difficulties, she also testified that the change had strengthened and renewed her life. When someone (not Rachel) reported to me that her "cool" audience of high school adolescents responded to her talk with a standing ovation, I teared up. Rachel has also emerged as the preeminent gourmet chef in our family.

Daughter Amy Halevy has experienced comparable validation. More than once I have heard a client tell me how she has handled their employment issues with great competence and enormous sensitivity. The managing partner of her firm once told me that the "only thing wrong with Amy is that we can't clone her!" In her family life, Amy somehow manages to attend all the significant occasions in her sons' lives and she has been a great sister to her two siblings.

Daughter Liz Seitz never reveals her clients to us but some of them have identified themselves before expressing enormous respect and gratitude for the way Liz combines keen therapeutic insight with spirituality and humor. Because of her own successful struggle with life-threatening illness at age thirty-three, Liz was invited to give a talk at the Yom Kippur Symposium. Her remarks included the following paragraph:

> My faith sustained and comforted me. Before each operation, often at the crack of dawn, my father stood by my bedside with his hands gently cradling my head as we recited the Sh'ma together. It had never felt as powerful and meaningful as it did at those times...my cancer

history does not define me but it has helped define my life and serves as a reminder of how fragile life is and how lucky I am to be here.

During Liz's poignant and beautiful presentation, Joan and I were not the only ones who retrieved our hankies to catch our tears.

Each daughter is spiritually sensitive. Each takes pride in her Jewish heritage and each has given birth to and parented children in whom they and we delight. I had the enormous joy and privilege to name and bless each grandchild at birth; to speak to and bless each at their bar or bat mitzvahs. Our grandchildren, five boys and two girls range in age from nineteen to twenty-nine at this writing. From oldest to youngest they are Josh, Ben, Jacob, Emily, Zack, Daniel and Zoe.

I have long told others that grandparenthood is the most compelling consolation for growing old. Ever since our first grandchild was born, I incorporated into my daily prayer discipline this petition, "Incline my grandchildren to lives of dignity, love, honor, faithfulness and menschlichkeit (the Yiddish word that is inadequately translated as possessing the qualities of a decent person)." I've lived to witness enough years in their life trajectory to feel confident that prayer is being fulfilled. My sister Elana, who was entrusted to my care so frequently in her childhood, has remained a precious member of my family, as has her husband, Lou Kohn.

Whenever I love life so much that its brevity and death's inevitability threaten to distress me, I need only recall the beautiful prayer we recite at every Yom Kippur Memorial Service.

CHAPTER 15 ❖ WHY I AM A WEALTHY MAN

If some messenger were to come to us with the offer that death should be overthrown, but with the one inseparable condition that birth should also cease; if the existing generation were given the chance to live forever, but on the clear understanding that never again would there be a child, or a youth, or first love, never again new persons with new hopes, new ideas, new achievements; ourselves for always and never any others—could the answer be in doubt?[71]

My wife, Joan, and our grandchildren. Back row from left to right: Jacob Halevy, Emily Weissenstein, Ben Wiessenstein; middle row: Daniel Halevy, Zoe Kampf, Zack Kampf; front row with us: Josh Weissenstein.

Photo Credit: Gay Block

EPILOGUE

Two years ago, when I began this life review, I had reached "four-score" years. I conclude this effort with a grateful heart. While my health is good, I know this is the dusk of my life. So, with each passing day, the first prayer we are called upon to recite each day attains greater poignancy: "I thank You living God that you have restored my soul within me, how great is Your faithfulness."

Yes, I want more years to experience within my family circle and in the larger world, but I can affirm robustly that my life has been "very good" indeed. If it were ever appropriate to live one day at a time, now is that time.

Our years on earth are a continuous alternation of separation and reconnection. The newborn infant's emergence from the womb is a dramatic separation which is followed, in the best of circumstances, by reconnection to the mother's nursing breast.

Some years later, when we leave home for the first day at school, that potentially dramatic separation leads to a teacher who is a surrogate mother and to our first peer group.

Years later, as scripture suggests, "A man leaves his father and mother and clings to his wife" (Genesis 2:24). Alas, occasionally, this may require the help of a therapist before a true separation can occur!

Then, after what we hope has been a long and fruitful life, we face that separation from this earth called death. In the best of circumstances, we may expect to be reconnected to this world through those who will remember and miss us.

In faith, I dare to hope for more. Our separation from this world may also be regarded as a return to the Source of our being. During a memorial service for deceased classmates at my sixtieth college reunion, I concluded my homily with these words,

> For persons of religious faith, our ultimate source of meaning is that we live in the presence of our Creator, who has made known to us the way we should live, who is active in our lives and in the world, to fulfill the divine dream for creation, and who will be with us and embrace us when we have crossed the threshold from life on earth to Eternity.

ENDNOTES

1. Babylonian Talmud (henceforth BT) Shabbat 32a
2. All citations from this address are taken from "A Jew at Harvard", part of a collection of essays entitled *The Soul of the Rav*, Eakin Press, Austin, TX 1999, pp. 3-7
3. Ibid pp. 279-290
4. *The Philosophy of Martin Buber*, edited by Paul Arthur Schlipp and Maruice Friedman, Open Court Press, Lasalle, IL, 1967, p. 26, "A Conversation"
5. Ibid
6. Meyer, M.A. *Response to Modernity, A History of the Reform Movement in Judaism*, Wayne State University Press, Detroit, 1995, p. 24
7. *The Soul of the Rav* op.cit. pp. 282, 284
8. BT Pesachim 56a
9. BT Berachot 5b
10. Bellow, S., *Herzog*, Viking Press, NY, 1961, p. 75
11. Ibid p.314
12. Bellow, S., *Mr. Sammler's Planet*, Viking, N.Y., 1969, p. 316
13. P. 78 Nobel Academy statement quoted in the New York Times, October 22, 1976
14. Mishneh Avot 3:2
15. Ibid 5:11
16. BT Avodah Zarah 54b
17. Avot d'Rabbi Natan 10:7
18. BT Baba Metziah 87a
19. Karff, S., *Agada: The Language of Jewish Faith*, Hebrew Union College Press, Cincinnati, 1979 inside cover
20. Karff, S., *Permission to Believe*, Abingdon, Nashville, 205, IX-X
21. Cited in Isaac Barzilay, The Jewish Quarterly Review, vol. 52, 1961, p. 92
22. *The Jewish Week*, November 15, 2011
23. Jerusalem Talmud, Hagigah chapter 1:12
24. Clifford Geertz in *The Religious Situation*, edited by Donald R. Cutler, Boston, Beacon Press, 1968
25. Gollub, H., *Me and Shakespeare*, NY., Doubleday, 2002, p. 20
26. Gollub, ibid p. 23
27. "The Legacy of Classical Reform" in *The Soul of the Rav*, op cit. p. 148
28. Ibid p. 155
29. *At One Hundred Years*, edited with an introduction by Samuel E. Karff, Hebrew Union College Press, Cincinnati, 1976. Excerpts from pages XVI and XVII
30. Gelernter, D., *Judaism: A Way of Being*, Yale University Press, New Haven, 2009, p. 106
31. Ibid p. 109
32. These citations and complete text in *CCAR Yearbook*, Phoenix Conference, 1979, edited by Elliot Stevens, CCAR, NY, 1980. See pp 148-155 for Dow Marmur presentation and pp. 155-160 for my response.
33. Ibid p. 160
34. "Demography Before Halacha," *Canadian Jewish News*, October 26, 2006
35. Mishneh Sanhedrin, Chapter 8
36. The Report, the debate, and the outcome are recorded in CCAR Yearbook (Seattle Convention 1990), edited by Elliot Stevens, CCAR, NY, 1991, pp. 98-112
37. Ibid p. 109
38. Tosephta Sotah 15:10
39. BT Menachot 37b
40. Kazin, A., *The Atlantic Monthly*, "What Do We Do Now?" April 1974, p. 77
41. Maslow, A., *Toward a Psychology of Being*, 2nd edition, Princeton: Von Nostrand, 1962, p. 71
42. Ibid
43. Berger, P., *A Rumor of Angels*, Doubleday & Co., Garden City, NY, 1969, p. 67
44. Pargament, K., *Spiritually Integrated Psychotherapy*, The Guilford Press, NY, 2007, p. 39
45. Ibid p. 345
46. Phillips, W., part of the third in a series of conversations among leading scientists and scholars about the "Big Questions" by the John Templeton Foundation at www.templeton.org

47 Karff, S., *Agada: The Language of Jewish Faith*, Hebrew Union College Press, Cincinnati, 1979, p. 127
48 Ibid pp. 130-131
49 Ben Horin (Borowitz), "The Reform Rabbis Debate Theology: a Report on the 1663 Meeting of the CCAR," *Judaism Quarterly* 12, Fall 1963 p. 480
50 Ibid pp 481-482
51 CCAR Conference, Philadelphia 1963, CCAR Yearbook, edited by Sidney Regner, CCAR NY, 1964, p. 193
52 Ibid p. 196
53 Genesis Rabbah 12:15
54 Steinberg, Milton, *Basic Judaism*, Harcourt, Brace & Co., NY, 1947, p. 155
55 BT Sukkah 52a
56 BT Nedarim 39b
57 Mishneh Abot 1:14
58 Adapted from Midrash on Proverbs 31:10
59 BT Shabbat 10a
60 BT Avodah Zarah 54b
61 Maimonides, M. *The Guide for the Perplexed*, translated by Shlomo Pines, Chicago University Press, Chicago, 1963, pp. 443-444
62 BT Berachot 33b
63 Genesis Rabbah 22:22
64 Buber, M., *I and Thou*, 2nd Edition, Charles Scribner's Sons, NY, 1958, p. 82
65 BT Avodah Zarah 17a
66 Hippocrates Precepts VI, cited in S.J. Reiser, A.J. Dyck, and W. J. Curran, eds., *Ethics in Medicine: Historical Perspectives and Contemporary Concerns*, Cambridge, MA, MIT Press, 1977, p. 203
67 G.L. Engel, "The Need for a New Medical Model: A Challenge for Biomedicine," *Science*, April 8, 1977, pp. 129-130
68 The American Association of Medical Colleges, "Guidelines for Accreditation," 1999
69 S. Nuland, quoted in the New York Times, "A Doctor's Look at Life and Death," November 16, 1997
70 BT Shabbat 10a
71 *Belief and Action, An Everyday Philosophy*, by Viscount (Hebert Louis) Samuel (1870-1963), Pan Books, 1953, pp. 67f

ACKNOWLEDGMENTS

Tom Cole, friend and leader in the field of medical humanities, read the first draft of the manuscript critically and significantly improved its subsequent versions. Ken Pargament, friend and eloquent advocate for the spiritual dimension in healing, was among the first to encourage the manuscript's publication.

Heidi Miller typed the various versions and made some helpful suggestions. Judy Weidman, our synagogue's librarian, helped me to locate elusive sources.

From first reading to editing to layout and publication, Lucy Chambers, Lauren Adams, Eva J. Freeburn and the entire staff at Bright Sky Press have been indispensable and pleasant colleagues on this journey.

In this, as in all my past projects, Joan, my life partner, has been a vitally supportive presence.

To all of them, I offer my deep gratitude.

The last word is embodied in a traditional rabbinic prayer: "Praised are You Eternal God, Sovereign of the Universe, who has kept us in life, sustained us, and enabled us to reach this moment."